The Western
Construction
of Religion

THE JOHNS HOPKINS UNIVERSITY PRESS

The Western Construction of Religion

Myths, Knowledge, and Ideology

Daniel Dubuisson

Translated by
William Sayers

The Johns Hopkins University Press
Baltimore and London

Originally published as *L'Occident et la religion: Mythes, science et idéologie*,
© Éditions Complexe, 1998
English translation © 2003 The Johns Hopkins University Press

The Johns Hopkins University Press
2715 North Charles Street
Baltimore, Maryland 21218-4363
www.press.jhu.edu

Library of Congress Cataloging-in-Publication Data
Dubuisson, Daniel, 1950–
    [Occident et la religion. English]
    The western construction of religion : myths, knowledge, and ideology /
Daniel Dubuisson ; translated by William Sayers.
        p. cm.
    Includes bibliographical references and index.
    ISBN 0-8018-7320-7 (hardcover : alk. paper)
    1. Religion—Study and teaching—History.   2. Religion—Philosophy—History.
I. Title.
BL41.D8313   2003
200′.71—dc21
2002011062

A catalog record for this book is available from the British Library.

For Cécile

"Why," I said, "are there others in the whale too? "A great many," said the old man, "and they are unfriendly and monstrous in shape."

—Lucian of Samosata

If men were able to exercise complete control over all their circumstances, or if continuous good fortune were always their lot, they would never be prey to superstition. But since they are often reduced to such straits as to be without any resource, and their immoderate greed for fortune's fickle favors often makes them the wretched victims of alternating hopes and fears, the result is that, for the most part, their credulity knows no bounds.

—Spinoza

Contents

The Western
Construction
of Religion

Introduction
Religion, the West, and the History of Religions

"The West." "Religion." It is enough to pronounce these two words one after the other, even if only cautiously, or to yoke them together in a phrase such as "the West and Religion" for us to feel, albeit with some confusion, that we are facing one of the most substantial and challenging problems imaginable—one that seems situated beyond all our learning and science, in that poorly known, shadowy zone where our still rudimentary knowledge discovers and constructs its first associations. One of those problems, too, where we rightly sense that what hangs in the balance is, in reality, the signification of a world, a culture. Our world and culture. It is also we ourselves who are at issue.

The evocative power of certain words is perhaps only the reverse of their capacity to summarize a prodigious quantity of information, to symbolize countless connections, to recapitulate centuries and centuries of history in a few sounds. What word condenses the fate and face of the West into three syllables better than "religion"? Can all our rational speculation, all our intellectual analysis, ever claim to understand its genesis and tally the sum of its elements?

This is why, whatever its pretensions and the quality of its learning, the history of religions cannot and never will designate a kind of knowledge or discipline like others. It can still less do so in that it has too often remained something of an antechamber, more dark than lit, the meeting ground of presuppositions, insoluble paradoxes, and the bulk of the contradictions specific to those most typically Western disciplines, the human sciences.

However conventional and familiar it may become, the name of an academic discipline is never a simple, everyday designation, irrespective of whether it claims in all good faith to be scientific or to be moving in that direction. What this name designates in synthetic fashion always sums up a complex of institutional choices, the results of multiple historical processes, a multiform intellectual tradition, a field of theoretical controversy, a more or less heterogeneous system of opposing theses, a repertory of intel-

1

lectual practices and methodological claims and—to put a temporary end to this stock-taking—an inextricable tangle of interdisciplinary relations, the definitions and orientation of which, far from concerning only an isolated (and consequently harmless) sector of the human sciences, indirectly affect a great number of individuals through the partial and approximate knowledge they draw from this particular field.

In its immediate, almost obvious sense, the term "history of religions" seems to designate either the specific history of each religion or of an aspect of all of them—ritual, theology, cosmogonic myth, and so on. In reality, no such inquiry will ever achieve a truly historical character in either respect, whether because there is no documentary record for the religion in question capable of introducing historical perspective (as, for example, in the case of the religion of the Indo-Europeans or of an Amazonian tribe) or because the chosen approach calls for some other kind of analysis: the interpretation of symbols, the meaning of texts, the description of facts, the comparison of similar data. This also contributes to the relative imprecision of the term "history of religions," already evident in its simple referential function.

As a field of knowledge, academic discipline, or branch of science, the history of religions is itself a historical phenomenon. This signifies, commonsensically, that it appeared at a precise time—the second half of the nineteenth century—and a precise place—western Europe—that is, at the center of a world marked by largely irreducible characteristics, whose most salient features it behooves us to recover and describe.

But having a history really means being historical (and not just being "in history"). Consequently, in speaking of the history of religions, we would surely not think of the difficulties attendant on one unchanging attitude or other, but rather the modifications of something that can never be other than a singular configuration of hypotheses and bits of knowledge, more or less provisional (even if they were to survive for centuries) and more or less well distributed.

On the other hand, writing or tracing the history of disciplines or fields of knowledge does not take them beyond history nor shelter them from it. Nothing stops being historical simply because its history is thereafter written or better known. For this history (the history or, better, the historiography of the history of religions) is just as historical. That our science, to the first, second, or third degree, is reluctant to admit that it is condemned to this endless encapsulation (each point of view, because it is historical and can only be historical, will in turn become the object of a history that is itself historical, etc.) in no way modifies its fundamentally historical nature: the facts that are called religious, their analysis, the critique of this analysis, and the various metadegrees that will be extrapolated from them, all these are just as historical.

Yet are they all historical in the same fashion and to the same degree? That is, is the coefficient of historicity identical for each of them? Would not their periods, as we say of radioactive elements, be very different one from another? This is why, among all these facts, we should distinguish those endowed with a simpler, sturdier structure (which makes them suitable for sustaining phenomena of very long duration) from those, more ephemeral, that local microhistories reveal at every step. Among the former, we would unhesitatingly classify the great paradigms, the major themata and general schemas that, despite evolution and ceaseless change, seem to have served as a framework for the history of Western thought. It is to them that this history owes the reassuring impression that, despite everything, it imparts. Through the constant effort and the institutions that it presupposes, through new linkages that it introduces with each generation, the living intellectual tradition, even if multiform and filled with controversy, erects an almost indestructible rampart in the face of time.

While not losing sight of these perspectives and constructs, which seem equally likely to become lost in time or to defy it, we are fortunately able to modify the disquieting effect by henceforth making an indispensable, vigorous correction. The fact that humanity's creations, such as cultures and their various productions, down to their ultimate, most tenuous expressions, are historical phenomena is an obvious fact that is contradicted by another, no less massive and indisputable one, without which the very project of establishing the human sciences would lose all its meaning and collapse in upon itself. Because although historical, cultures are also, and just as fundamentally, human creations. Their diversity, so great that it often seems to discourage reflection and invite us, defeated, to adopt a relativist point of view, conflicts with another body of evidence, intuitively sensed by each of us, that suggests that all these differences, extreme as they are, are only the superficial expressions of certain unvarying, universally attested constants. They are the indisputable signs of human genius and of the unity of humankind.

But no sooner is it advanced than this hypothesis immediately raises other, very sensitive questions. Just where are these immutable properties situated and in what are they rooted?

Is it in the individual, seen as a relatively stable entity? But then on the basis of distinctions inherited from our own intellectual tradition (another specific historical creation!) and advanced by our most up-to-date science, we would have to distinguish everything that lies within the sphere of individual biological existence, our instincts, intellectual faculties, minds, our neurological and mental equipment, different levels of psychic being, and—why not?—our souls.

Are they situated in the socialized human being and in human societies? But do we not dispose of several mutually exclusive sociological models? Competing conceptions of religion issuing from the theoretical perspectives of Karl Marx, Émile Durkheim, Max Weber, Georges Bataille, and Pierre Bourdieu reveal no simple, rigorous definition, none endowed with undeniable heuristic value and thereby readily transposable to the collectivity of known human cultures. On the other hand, this network of competing conceptions does seem to lend credence to the idea, or the thesis (otherwise difficult to prove) that religion has a kind of sociological being. In the same way, theological controversies seem to lend some substance to the idea of divinity simply because they agree only on this one point. In both cases, the vigor of the debate tends to make us forget that the status of the initial premise (the existence of God or of religion itself as a fundamental anthropological datum) in no way depends on the outcome of these controversies, even if they were to go on for centuries.

Is it in some indescribable transcendence? The hypothesis, however far-fetched, should not be discarded, since among the contemporary human sciences, the history of religions offers the new and astonishing characteristic of harboring currents of thought (and some powerful lobbies) defending explanations that lay claim to such supernatural filiation.

As concerns the invariable properties, should we consider that they are more (or exclusively) functional, structural, transcendental, innate, revealed, and so on? Each of these references just as many, or at least some, competing philosophical explanations. In addition, there again immediately arises the question of the immersion of these properties in history and in the differences that each culture maintains as the unquestionable sign of its originality. How, in fact, are we to reconcile these two, to all appearances incommensurable, phenomena: the supposed permanence of the intrinsic and thereby immutable property, and the exuberant diversity of the unique configurations generated by history? Yet, by virtue of the very particular nature of the subject of the history of religions and of what that signifies for Western culture, the intellectual debate stimulated by the competing claims of history and anthropology seems almost always to be sidetracked by the untimely arrival of metaphysical arguments. Indeed, these often end up completely monopolizing the debate.

We need only briefly name these few options, from among those most in evidence, to conclude at once that the combinatory principle that integrates them is not of the most usual logical type, and that these same anthropological invariables or constants are in any case situated on a level completely inaccessible to direct observation.

At any event, the fact remains that it is in the domain of the history of religions that the existence of these invariables seems the most predictable, even admitting that a good many ulterior motives sustain such an anticipation. Don't we often say, in ordinary conversation as in learned treatises, that the "religious function" is a fundamental characteristic of the human phenomenon—unless the even more categorical claim is made that this function alone represents its most respectable and noble part? But do we even know what this "religious function" refers to and what this basic humanity consists of? And is the history of religions, such as it is and has constructed itself for more than a century, in a position (and on what grounds, with what instruments and what chances of success?) to calmly address the search for, and definition of, these invariables?

In this allusive evocation of the Western and very datable origins of the history of religions, we are already outlining the terms of the crucial choice with which the existence of this academic discipline confronts us. Despite its initial historical and cultural anchoring, has the history of religions succeeded in freeing itself from such roots and defined a body of concepts, methods, and analytical procedures that, transcending its origins, offers anthropological inquiry a set of heuristic means and tools that are relatively trustworthy and above all productive? Or, on the contrary, a prisoner of these same origins, has it not instead remained a *Western* creation, intimately tied to its own ways of thinking and being in the world? In which case, only an incredible ethnocentric illusion would authorize us to recognize it as still having a true scientific vocation today.

If, instead of viewing the history of religions in its totality, we set ourselves the question of the simple notion of religion, the alternatives would be at least as clear-cut and similarly oriented. Let us summarize: although born in the West of a culture for which it has been the unceasing symbol over these past two millennia, has this notion nevertheless acquired, thanks to critical studies conducted by the history of religions for more than a century, an indisputable and rigorous definition, capable of aiding us in discovering and understanding the much discussed anthropological invariables evoked above—or, on the contrary, captive to its origins and history, has it instead remained a kind of *native* concept, typically European, gathering and summarizing under its aegis the struggles of a Western consciousness grappling with itself?

By setting out the terms of these two alternatives, the central issue of this book has at least been clearly defined. With the history of religions and its central notion, religion, what is in question is, in fact, nothing more or less than certain pretensions of modern Western science to conceive of humankind and the world according to codes that *it* has elaborated and to points of reference that *it* has fixed. Or, if we prefer to turn this observation into a blunter question, is Western anthropology, religious anthropology in particular, in its quest for the Other and for our very humanity, capable of discovering anything but itself—that is, anything other than its own categories and its own ways of conceiving the world?

1 | The West and Religion

On the other hand, to despise this sphere, and the gods within it
or anything else that is lovely, is not the way to goodness. . . . For
how can this Kosmos be a thing cut off from That and how imagine
the gods in it to stand apart?

—Plotinus *Enneads* 2.9.1

Even if I knew nothing of the atoms, I would venture to assert on the
evidence of the celestial phenomena themselves, supported by
many other arguments, that the universe was certainly not created
for us by divine power; it is so full of imperfections.

—Lucretius *De rerum natura* 2

1 | A Central Concept

The Mirror of the West

Just like the notion itself, the most general questions concerning religion, its nature and definition, its origins or expressions, were born in the West.[1] From there, they were transferred, much later and at the cost of daring generalizations, to all other cultures, however remotely prehistoric or exotic.

The exclusively Western history of questions relative to religion is, of course, inseparable from the intellectual history of the West, since it is from its own history that the West drew a complex of systematic reflections (from philosophy to theology, from anthropology to sociology or psychology) that were to lead to the universalization of a concept born of Christian apologetics dating from the first centuries of our era. Before retracing these historical steps, it is crucial to pause for a moment to address three questions that should normally open any debate devoted to this subject:

- Is Christianity the special form taken in the West by something that has always existed and that similarly exists elsewhere, if not everywhere, namely, religion or the religious phenomenon?
- As the legitimate daughter of Christianity, is religion not rather an element wholly unique to Western civilization, one of its most original creations?
- Should we not, moreover, go somewhat farther and ask whether religion is not effectively the West's most characteristic concept, around which it has established and developed its identity, while at the same time defining its way of conceiving humankind and the world?

If the answer to the first question is in the affirmative, Christianity, in its capacity as *the* religion of the West, is the homologue or equivalent of Chinese Taoism, Siberian shamanism, or Indian Buddhism.[2] The second question suggests that Christianity, always in its capacity as a religion, and especially the very idea of religion, is a specifically Western invention, although we only perceive it as such with great difficulty, since we ourselves belong to the culture that fashioned this notion. It is through its categories that we conceive of others, and that these others, who are most often subject to our influence, conceive of themselves. Finally, the third question implies that it was on the basis of this primary notion, which has no equivalent in other cultures, that the most original features of the West's history and character arose.

A preference given to one or another of these three propositions conditions numerous other options and investigations. For now, I call attention only to the most obvious. At first sight, and this also reflects common opinion, it would be tempting to select the first hypothesis. Are there not religions everywhere, and is not the dominant Western religion Christianity, as it has been through that faith's long history and innumerable vicissitudes? But what do we know of the timeless, disincarnate, quintessential, abstract religion of which every culture, starting with our own, offers a specific hypostasis (ours simply being the most perfect, a little closer to the ideal)? What makes up its substratum? In the name of what authority would it be possible to say that "a religion is unconditionally and necessarily" this or that, or that "in essence a religion is this collection of features or permanent characteristics"? And to what registers of human experience are we to refer the "common features" of personal intuition, subjective feeling, and collective mechanisms? Or the instincts for self-preservation, poetic imagination, and metaphysical speculation?

Leaving in abeyance closer critical examination of these questions (always presupposing that we are able to escape the vast implicit tautology that the religious is what the West considers to be religious on the basis of its own religious experience), there is nothing to prevent us from viewing the second proposition with some favor. Conscious of the impasse to which the first hypothesis leads us, this option asks whether it is not first necessary to disabuse ourselves of a primary illusion in order to avoid a dead end: on the basis of its own experience and its own vision of things (and of them alone), has not the Christian West (and it alone), being secure in its hegemonic intellectual position, conferred, in quite arbitrary and artificial fashion, an anthropological—scientific—status and destiny on its own most valued creation, religion? Which then itself became the object of a specific discipline, the history of religions, universally valid because its object was thought and conceived of a priori as universal? Thus the West would in a sense have drawn around itself a magic—and narcissistic—circle that both limits its reflections and flatters its epistemological talents. And, with the inevitable reassuring effect that such a mechanism produces, the West believes all the more willingly in the relevance of this concept, since other civilizations merely faithfully reflect its own chimeras. And this will be the state of things as long as the debate is conducted exclusively on the conceptual field chosen and defined by the West alone.

The third proposition simply radicalizes the preceding point of view and draws from it only the most immediate and least controversial consequences. In this perspective, religion not only appears as one of the typical creations of the West, among the most prestigious of them, but also becomes the West's fundamental creation and central reference point, the reference point around which it constructed, organized, and developed itself by erecting its own system of beliefs and representations. In short, it is that point of reference by which it has become, in and of itself, its own world—the referential center from which it has conceptualized the others—all the others, both those that it has dominated or conquered and those it has influenced.

Several points, generally accepted but not always mentioned in this context or brought to bear on such concerns, may be made in support of the last two propositions.

To begin with, let us consider the banal but quite significant fact that religious phenomena seem ubiquitous in Western civilization. Do they not inform the majority of its constituent—or even simply decorative—elements? If we indulged ourselves by listing those chief works, literary or artistic, as well as the most general moral, political, scientific, or philosophical conceptions that escape the grasp of religion or its influence (if only to distance themselves from or oppose this influence), we would probably end up with very meager results. Around this privileged notion, the Christian West, spiderlike, has continued to spin its web of concepts, to wind the successive variations of its learned discourse, to superimpose its palimpsests of speculations, in brief, to affirm its own identity. Its reflections on the organization of the world, on the nature of reality, its conceptions of humanity, of life, its political theories, its most admirable or most derisory artistic triumphs, its loftiest spiritual accomplishments, as well as its most sordid crimes—all have been conceived or committed one way or another with reference to this dominant concern. From the domain of the most luminous rationality to the most constraining of superstitions, from insignificant detail to the most grandiose monuments, from the most extreme individual interiority to the vastest collective movements, no register of human experience, no order of things has ever escaped its diffuse, constant influence.

Atheism, skepticism, and the modern scientific spirit have scarcely enjoyed greater autonomy, for they define themselves only by reference to religion and its claims. An atheist who denies the existence of the soul and of God, and who believes in so doing that he or she possesses sovereign independence of judgment, accepts, often unknowingly, the spirit and terms of a debate (the soul/body dichotomy; a universe governed, or not, by divine providence) that religion has chosen. The positive aspect of Western atheism thus often comes down to an evaluation of the negation embodied in the privative prefix *a-* with which the word commences.

Religion, that is to say, the entire universe that the word summarizes (theological subtleties, conceptions of the human being and human destiny, the role of providence, moral choice, retribution in the beyond, the immortality of the soul, the discipline of the body), has never ceased to nourish our major controversies and ever appears as *the* essential locus, that on which all others with very rare exception depend.

In many respects this Christian conception of religion is also inscribed in a great debate that began well before the birth of Christianity, which would later engage all the latter's powers. From Critias, Plato's uncle, to Jean-Paul Sartre, and from Parmenides to Martin Heidegger, responses to the central cosmological issue of whether to admit or not admit the existence of gods and their wise providence revealed a major division in the West, one that stimulated most of the others and explains them, in the same way that in the Western individual, an imaginary caesura symbolically separates a mortal body from a disincarnate soul.

In asserting that the West invented religion and has continuously lived under its influence, we must, of course, understand that the West was not the only civilization to ask metaphysical questions, to try to understand the world in which it lived, to conceive of imaginary beings (gods, spirits, demons, ghosts), develop theologies, organize worship, invent cosmologies and mythologies, support beliefs, defend morals and ideals, and imagine other worlds—but that it made from this collection of attitudes and ideas an autonomous, singular complex, profoundly different from everything surrounding it. And it conferred on this distinct complex a kind of destiny or essential anthropological vocation: humans are held to be religious in the same way as they are omnivorous, that is, by nature, through the effects of a specific inborn disposition.

However, we are dealing here with a unique historical construction that could have been different or might not have been at all, which makes vain any debate whose subject is the search for its immutable essence. Yet while unique, it is only, in the words of Claude Lévi-Strauss,

> a point in space and a moment in time, relative to each other, and in which there have occurred, are occurring or will occur events whose density (itself in turn relative to other events, no less real but more widely dispersed) makes possible its approximate definition, always remembering of course that this nodal point of past, present, and probable events does not exist as a substratum, but only in the sense that these phenomena, of which it is the place of intersection, originate from countless other sources, for the most part unknown.[3]

Nevertheless, this unique historical construction also possesses all the properties of a *structure,* that is, it conforms to the ordinary definition of the word as a complex set of distinct elements and conceivable relationships. The fact that it may be possible to find elsewhere, in other cultures and in an isolated state, one or other element that is comparable to one of those contained in the Western system in no way authorizes us to infer the existence of the structure itself. In the sense of a structured whole, of a unique configuration—and formally it is only that—what the West calls "religion" exists only there, at its very heart.

Let us pause for a moment over a specific example, one of the most awkward for our thesis. Does the fact that a human being—a Benedictine monk, Roman augur, or Tungus shaman—addresses a supernatural suffice to authorize us to speak of a common religious phenomenon? In the minds of many for whom religion in the final instance means communication with superhuman interlocutors, there can be no doubt about it, so seemingly similar are these various situations. In reality, matters are neither so simple nor so obvious. What is scientifically comparable in this instance is solely the fact that these people address themselves to an imaginary being that their own pronouncements in some fashion transform into a real interlocutor, and a close analysis of the varying cultural and pragmatic contexts would quickly reveal important, irreconcilable differences.[4]

Would those who declare themselves partisans of the universality of religion wish to reduce religion to a linguistic, pragmatic situation that evoked imaginary beings, knowing that such exchanges appear in the most diverse contexts (magic rituals, sorcery, alchemy, superstitions, spiritism, demonic possession, childish beliefs, fetishistic practices, hallucinatory neuroses, paranoid or amorous delirium, and so on)? In addition, these three human situations occur within three distinct cultural formations (Siberian shamanism, Roman augury, and Christian monasticism) that are not homologous and doubtless not even comparable: the socio-pragmatic contexts, institutional frameworks, linguistic procedures, mental universes, objectives or outcomes that are sought, all these are each and always quite unique. Only a cavalier, superficial vision would be capable of ignoring these radical differences in order to recognize, despite everything, the ghost of one and the same anthropological fact. On this we would probably all agree. It is consequently obvious that the essence of religion, however tacitly invoked at the outset, is to be found neither in restricted, delimited experience (the linguistic and pragmatic situation) nor in totalized complexes, too differentiated one from another.

Similarly, on what grounds could we assert that the functions of shaman, augur, astrologer, initiate into Orphic mysteries, Cybeline subpriest, Breton curate, yogin, and *mambo* display an undeniable, identical religious character?

On the other hand, these examples allow us better to understand the workings of a very common process, which we might call recourse to naïve comparison.[5] It is because such a comparative methodology considers only localized situations, envisaged in superficial fashion and isolated from their respective contexts, that it so easily succeeds in creating a deceptive illusion. It dupes us into believing that we are in the presence of phenomena effectively comparable to those that we meet in the Christian tradition, which, thanks to this methodological subterfuge, is raised to the dignity of model or ideal point of reference.

While religion remains largely the incarnation of an atemporal notion or indestructible essence, it is, more prosaically put, only the result of a discriminatory act performed in the West and there alone. If it ended up occupying such a central, dominant position, it is first because it defined itself from the very outset in opposition to everything it judged not to *be* itself. Our idea of religion derives from this unprecedented division of the real and its ideological valorization (which it prefers to call "sacralization"). This is something that no other civilization had ever done nor would ever do on its own. Even if the Greeks as theologians often spoke of the gods, as we know, they had no special word to designate (and thus to think of) what the West would later gather under the word "religion." As for the Romans, if they knew and defined the word *religio,* it was with a very different significance, one that Saint Augustine would still remember with regret and discomfort at the beginning of the fourth century.[6] They would never have been capable of foreseeing its subsequent evolution, so contrary was it to their civic conception of cult and their specific techniques for communicating with the unknown. According to Cicero (*De natura deorum* 2.3–4), a religious mind is one that scrupulously follows traditional rules (for example, on the occasion of consular elections), in particular by submitting to the science of augurs and soothsayers, because, he says, if there are interpreters of omens, it is sure proof that the gods exist.

Facts, of whatever kind, are not in themselves religious in the sense that they are endowed with some kind of specific, sui generis quality, come from who knows where. They only become religious at the point where individuals isolate them by invoking a certain number of criteria and then apply this distinct designation. Yet this selection, specification, and attribution are intellectual operations that the West alone performed, from the moment it became Christian. Religion, however we may or may wish to understand it, did not preexist these subtle intellectual operations. It was rather they that created it.

This is why, instead of speaking of the religious consciousness of the West, it would surely be more judicious to say that the West is religious only in the very exact and strict sense that religion, as a notion intended to isolate a set of phenomena thenceforth considered homogeneous, is the exclusive creation of the West, and is thus what may constitute its innermost nature.

From this division is born a celebrated opposition: religious/nonreligious (and within the nonreligious we find, variously, the profane world, science, and atheism). This opposition runs through the intellectual history of the Christian West and, synchronically, if we so wish to view it, most of its domains of knowledge. It engenders and fuses with an immense paradigm, composed of two symmetrical but opposed currents. At the beginning of the fourth century of the Christian era, they are already apparent, for example, in the work of Eusebius of Caesarea, who in his *Praeparatio Evangelica* 15 opposes Aristotle and Epicurus (paired for this very purpose), Plato and the Hebrews. Assembled on one side are all those who associate the word "religion" with the recognition of a transcendence, whatever its exact nature and attributes. And in the opposite camp are the countless heirs of Epicurus and Lucretius (freethinkers, materialists, atheists, rationalists, scientists) who recognize in religion nothing more than a human creation, whether generated by atavistic fears, the cynical self-interest of the powerful, or the symbolic, identity-constructing mechanisms that are always at work in human groups.

Under these conditions, the principal dilemma lying in wait for the history of religions—from its very birth—was only too predictable. Was it to act as the heir of a tradition for which the Christian conception was compulsory and beyond discussion? Such an attitude could only lead it to make certain choices (theology rather than rite, individual faith rather than public ceremony, prayer and not dance, sacrament in preference to trance) and to deal with certain questions (the origin, nature, or classification of religions, for example), the formulation of which mirrored and, in their own way, gave expression to the persistence of the structures of a typically Christian theodicity. Or, on the contrary, having made the theoretical choices that would have led it to liberate itself from all that Christianity had bequeathed to the West, could it break with the past and succeed in defining an epistemological and anthropological field that was relatively new? We need only evoke these two options to feel excused from adding many more, so obvious does it seem that the history of religions was initially, fully, and in almost caricatural fashion a discipline that was heir to this legacy and burdened by all the ethnocentric, pseudo-scientific prejudices of its era.

Besides, if we confine ourselves to the general orientation, the grand paradigm whose existence has been briefly evoked, and to which I shall soon return, has it not maintained itself intact in the modern discipline of the history of religions? Are not the major contending theses unambiguously divided between these two currents? According to the terms of a nomenclature that has become traditional but especially in order to reestablish the true dimensions (ancient although not original) of the debates and theoretical discussions, let us distinguish the "phenomenological" current and a contrary current that, for the sake of convenience and simplicity, we may call "historical."[7]

The former posits the existence of the religious as an atemporal essence whose ultimate source lies in an experience of the transcendent or the sacred. In this capacity (and this is laxly tautological), its proponents too often reduce the object of religions to this suppositious (and mysterious) essence. In the opposing current are, willy-nilly, all those (sociologists, psychologists, historians, and anthropologists) who, while in the main accepting the idea or universal category of religion (though with considerable awkwardness), nonetheless categorically deny the existence or intervention of any kind of transcendence, and who, as a consequence, can conceive only of immanent explanations for the corresponding religious phenomena.

Singular Universes

Before returning in much more detailed fashion to the immense question of the relevance (scientific relevance, of course) or irrelevance of the idea of religion, we would do well to recall here that human cultures, from the great multimillennial civilizations to modest tribes clinging to the tropical forest, possess common constituent features, inherent in their existence no less than in their destiny. But these characteristics are no less relevant to the universes, practices, and beliefs that we habitually call "religious"— this habit offering the particular advantage of excusing us from trying to give these terms ("religion" and "religious") a rigorous, universal definition. Without these unexamined habits, it is also true that science would be just as impossible as mere existence would be.

It is for this reason (and for a number of others set out below) that it is preferable to here to assemble all those facts we call "religious" along with some others (collective conceptions and practices, symbolic constructions, corporeal and mental techniques, discursive and semiotic systems, imaginary worlds or beings, etc.) in the all-encompassing category of cosmographic formations.[8] This, to my mind, seems the only category today that allows us to overcome the sterile old antagonisms that culminate in the idea of religion and to relativize the importance of all the debates that are defined only with reference to its intrinsic criteria—precisely because this category is capable of subsuming the totality of the global, comprehensive conceptions of the world, whatever their philosophical orientation (atheist, theist, materialist, fatalist, cynical, indifferent, or agnostic),[9] the diversity of the elements whose existence they recognize (supernatural beings, cosmic, natural and historical laws, universal principles, vital forces or energies, transcendental concepts, ethical or political ideals, etc.), and the nature of the practices, the rules for living, and prescriptions that they imply.

With this comprehensive notion, Lucretius's *De rerum natura,* the Buddha's teachings, the Upanishads, the Confucianist conception of the universe, Taoism, the cosmogony of Plato's *Timaeus,* Stoic ethics, the discipline of yoga, the *Universal Declaration of the Rights of Man,* the *Communist Manifesto* of Marx and Engels, the *Celestial Hierarchy* of Pseudo-Dionysius, or even some totalitarian political program all reveal their common anthropological and cosmographic purpose: to describe the world and tell this or that group of humans, or even all of humanity, how to live in it. The step from cosmographic description to injunction, from speaking-the-truth to ought-to-be-the-truth, is often very short.[10]

The most puzzling features (even if they are not habitually the most frequently cited) that human cultures offer when we consider only their cosmographic functions are at least three. Each of these merits brief discussion.

Every culture is as tangible, as real as it is arbitrary, whether through its visible manifestations (institutions, practices, technical creations, etc.) or by the objectivity of the different structural relations that govern the cooperation among its diverse elements. Each culture is actually a contingent creation, which might not have existed or might have been different, even though it never appears as such to the individuals who comprise it, since, for them, it represents Reality, the reality to which their existence is attached by thousands of different threads, narrow or wide, commonplace or exceptional, prosaic or ceremonious.

Each of these cultures is the result of an incalculable number of choices, accidents, conditions, and successive adaptations, just as much as it is made up of distinct human acts of volition. If we consider their individual cultural physiognomy, that is, their status at any given moment, it is obvious that none of them ought to lay claim to having derived from some kind of absolute, preexistent necessity—whether we call it destiny, providence, history or, even worse, essence—that is exterior to the changing world in which each culture finds itself entirely immersed. The obligation to survive, which we might view as their most general property (but also the most trivial) concerns only their simple factual existence (the simple fact of *being there*) and not the unique complex formed by the totality of their special features, which were unforeseeable. And it is precisely this gap, the one that separates simple factual existence, amorphous in its very principle, from the unique cultural physiognomy, that the notion of the cosmographic formation fills. Into the reality that is moving and, like everything that exists, is exposed to destruction through entropy, it introduces a certain organizing power and, it is true, a certain teleology. But, to the extent that it is seen as a capacity inherent in cultures and human aspirations, this teleology does not show the intervention of any mysterious or ineffable power. To understand it, it suffices to observe different human cultures in all that makes them more than simple aggregations of disparate elements. On the other hand, this teleology basically obeys a simple principle, even if it is capable of shaping multiform processes. When all is said and done, it is just a simple principle of order, of which Lévi-Strauss quite rightly said: "This necessity for order is at the foundation of the thought that we call primitive, but only inasmuch as it is at the foundation of all thought."[11]

The second characteristic, also paradoxical, attracted Marcel Mauss's attention from the early 1930s on.[12] How, he asked, could entities composed of disparate elements (practices, beliefs, representations, rules, simultaneous interests in domains as diverse as economic production, pleasure, the multiple ties of dependency, the administration of the collectivity, or domestic life) end up as coherent complexes? Mauss replied that it was precisely these polyfunctional, multiform interminglings, reactivated and sustained from day to day, that assured and sustained this cohesion, this resistance of the social tissue to the destructive effects of time. To quote Jorge Luis Borges, it was to be found "in the same disorder that, repeated, would become an order: the Order."

The complexity and richness of these intertwinings guarantees the permanence and assures the preservation of this order, which can be thought of, symbolized, and substituted for mute reality. It is also these interlacings and interminglings that keep fluid the relations, they too plural and reciprocal, that are maintained both in the individual sphere and in collective life. There is probably not a great deal to be added to these remarks unless it is the following. Habit and a strong repugnance, very Platonic in spirit, for all that concerns the perceptible quotidian world often leads academic research not to address and even not to retain (from the civilizations they study) anything but their systems of ideas and beliefs (ideology, mindsets, value systems, intellectual representations and frameworks, artistic productions, etc.), which denies their physical incarnation, the day-to-day existence of individuals. However, and this to a great extent explains their strength and influence, these systems never belong to the realm of pure noetic construction. On the contrary, it is because people have literally incorporated them (and here, again, we should recall Mauss) into their most ordinary existence that these systems have contributed to the cohesion and permanence of cultures, while at the same time transforming these individual existences into cosmographical fragments. From this perspective, they are more than simply part of people's lives and minds, since to some degree, they become their true mind and life.

Finally, we may note that because these cosmographic universes associate destinies, providential events, signs of all kinds, symbolic orders, rules or supernatural laws, innumerable myths, mysterious mechanisms, hidden meanings, strange figures, unknowable powers, simple, global explanations, and so on in the minds of their members, they are in all respects fantastic universes. They are fantastic, too, by virtue of the literally incalculable number of imaginary beings (gods, angels, demons, spirits, souls, ghosts, chimeras, genies, monstrous animals, etc.) that humanity has generated in the course of its dreams and nightmares, its deliriums, and its most methodical reflections. And even if we are quite disposed to admit that the ontological space of imaginary creatures is not homogeneous (in the eyes of the believer), it remains on the whole fantastic for all those who view it from the exterior. Fantastic, too, in the strangeness of the practices that are prescribed or described there (mysteries, possessions, mutilations, trances, dialogues with the beyond, hallucinations, ecstasies, interpretive deliriums, ravings, mortifications, compulsive ritualization, superstitions, magic practices, asceticisms, privations, etc.). Finally, they are fantastic in the immense share of the unreal or supernatural that humans have never ceased to discover in the world and to mix into their own lives.

An anthropological study that began with an anthropology of the fantastic would scarcely be exaggerating, for all the rest (social, cultural, or religious anthropology) often represents only the secularized and rationalized version of it that has been gained as the result of analytical work that consists, in essence, of putting the fantastic in parentheses. As if reality, true reality, serious reality, the reality science likes to speculate about, could issue from a simple subtraction: global reality minus fantastic reality equals objective reality (the reality of laws, causal relationships, rational explanations). Contrary to the ideas that unreflective opinion frequently exhibits, fantastic shapes are not something that humanity would, after the fact, have the real world assume in order to make it less hostile or less frightening. Fantastic shapes are rather constituent of the relationship that this same humanity entertains with the world. Using other terms (which have known their day of glory), the superstructures, representations, or ideologies are not added to material infrastructures in order to hide the inadmissible mechanics or sordid aspects, for the former are just as original, as real, and as decisive as the latter. Instead, these simplistic explanations and conceptions, according to which human reality would be subdivided into factual realities and fantastic representations of it, fall into the ambit of the kind of crude explanations that modern science has created to serve its own conception of reality.

A certain kind of humanism and rationalism would have us believe that modern humanity was on the point of fulfilling the program of Lucretius and had finally rid itself of the superstitions and infernal chimeras that oppressed it. But the unreal and the supernatural cannot be summarized in religious beliefs of the Western kind, Christian belief in particular. They also concern mythologies (of love, happiness, wealth, health), fantasy-driven and irrational systems (astrology, tarot, clairvoyance, talismans, horoscopes), apocalyptic concepts, messianic expectations (the Age of Aquarius), new beliefs (extraterrestrials, mysterious phenomena), and radical or utopian ideologies, as well as all sorts of superstitious and magical practices. In our rational, technological universe, "beliefs" of all kinds are no less numerous and no less present than in any traditional civilization. Cosmographic formations are as indispensable here as elsewhere.

These summary remarks, then, apply to all cultures and in the first place to our own.

We ought consequently to be suspicious of those pugnaciously ethnocentric commonplaces that depict the beliefs and behavior of the Other alone as strange, unreasonable, or comic. Ours are no less so, since the world, in this respect, as in many others, exhibits no absolute norms or inviolable models. We should also avoid describing as universal values that the West alone has invented. Since their domain is always fundamentally one of conflict, these values would effectively become universal only when all the others had been destroyed and eliminated—by us.

All orthodox beliefs are equally "right," since all are equally arbitrary, circular, self-fulfilling systems, enclosed within limits that they themselves have defined and erected. Christian theology, the cult of the saints, angelology, the fear of demons, and sorcery open onto universes just as fantastic as those of voodoo or shamanism. In any case, they are no less fantastic and only a tenacious prejudice prompts us to believe that our own creations are distinguished from others by superior spirituality or morality. The creations by which other cultures live are at least as respectable. For the same reason, no criterion (unless it is a criterion sui generis) authorizes us to assert that Christian monotheism represents something more absolute or more complete than Greek polytheism or the asceticism of yoga.

Is it possible to imagine a more surrealist text than the *Celestial Hierarchy* of Pseudo-Dionysius? And the beliefs that this work inspired, the support that it called forth are, after all, just as unusual as those we may observe among the tribes farthest removed from Christianity. The closed world of the Vatican, with its nuns, secret archives, canonists, celibate men, sumptuous ceremonies, secular rites, and exorcists is of little interest to ethnologists, and this is a pity, for it is just as unique and exotic as a community of Turkish dervishes or a Tibetan monastery. The host consecrated by the pope is no less strange than the peyote consumed by the Mexican shaman. The weight of the symbolic charge is identical. Our (Western) world in no way constitutes an ideal reference point in relation to which the others can be assessed. We can only compare them in order to try to discover some common mechanisms. Christian civilization is just as unique and bizarre as any one of its congeners.

As a consequence, no history of religions, and, a fortiori, no critical reflection on it, is possible unless we first abandon the conviction—so Hegelian and so deeply rooted in the mentality inherited from the nineteenth century—that our difference signifies our superiority, and unless we first relativize the range and, in particular, the exemplarity of the Western case.

Religio and Religion

Even today, it is not uncommon for articles or works devoted to religion or to religions to begin with one or two paragraphs intended to recall the etymology—discussed since antiquity—of the Latin word *religio* (the *relegere* of Cicero and the *religare* of Lactantius).[13] This manner of proceeding, so habitual as no longer to cause surprise, is naïve and often driven by ulterior motives that have very little to do with science. On the one hand, this is so because it tends to minimize or cancel out the role of history (with its continuous modifications or shifts), while seeking to preserve an essential (timeless?) tie between the current, living acceptance of a word and its hypothetical first reception, raised to the status of original, founding datum. But in our occidental culture, profoundly marked by a diffuse Platonism, it is often little more than a short step from initial signification to eternal essence. This immutable semantic link thus becomes something transhistorical, independent of the vicissitudes of the real world.

On the other hand, because such a procedure almost always idealizes this first reception, considered original and primordial (while in fact it is always reconstructed in the language of the day), at one and the same time, it retrospectively confers on it a strong, simple, exclusive meaning, devoid of all ambiguity, and recognizes in it some kind of special, almost providential sign—an archetype. Substituted for the confusion between words and things is a more learned confusion between etymological significations and essences. This occurs in our mythic imagination, where origins are considered by many—and often—in an almost spontaneous way as the locus of perfection, of initial fullness and simplicity.[14]

If we distance ourselves from the presuppositions of this linguistic mythology, we observe that on the contrary, the first meaning, the etymological meaning of the word *religio,* even if it had existed in an unambiguous,
transparent form, could only be the initial and very specialized sense of a
rather ordinary Latin word, one that would remain so until the first Christian thinkers seized on it and promoted its exceptional destiny. A destiny
that Saint Augustine at the beginning of the fifth century had not yet dared
imagine, so imprecise did the accepted meaning of the word seem to him:

> The word "religion" might seem to express more definitely the worship due
> to God alone, and therefore Latin translators have used this word to repre-
> sent *threskeia;* [15] yet, as not only the uneducated, but also the best instructed,
> use the word religion to express human ties, and relationships, and affini-
> ties,[16] it would inevitably produce ambiguity to use this word in discussing
> the worship of god, unable as we are to say that religion is nothing else than
> the worship of God, without contradicting the common usage which ap-
> plies this word to the observance of social relationships.[17]

This initial Roman civic sense had no chance of becoming the universal meaning of our word "religion" as it is used today, whatever the accepted, ordinary or more technical meaning associated with it after two
thousand years of reflections and controversies. Only a certain amount of
bad faith would dare to suggest that there is not the least proven continuity between the archaic Latin word, its etymological meaning, its classical, Ciceronian usage, and its progressive Christian acceptance, which lies
at the base of our own accepted meaning, now anthropological and universal. It would show still more bad faith if one asserted that this etymology
penetrated the secret of religion and possessed its timeless meaning: the
old Platonic nostalgia for an improbable universe of essences preceding and
overhanging our own. From meaning to essence and transcendence, the
difference is most often only in a little typographical artifice, the addition
of an uppercase letter, associated with a performative intonation: Religion.

The putative essence of religion that the word would have contained in
its archaic etymology is just a dream, a mystical phantom, ill-suited to subsuming the diversity of human cosmographical productions, even those
that the West has designated religions. If some people, proceeding on this
latter path, more readily imagine that religion, the essence of religion, is
what would be left when all the various religions had been rid of their
noisy ceremonies, exotic details, and exuberant pantheons, they utterly
fool themselves. For religions exist only in the framework of strict seman-

tic dependence, one forged in the West around our word "religion," in the fashion, if you will, of a poetic convention.

Still, let us reflect on the following: if, for a moment, we make an exception of the imperialist, all-conquering destiny of the Christian West, what would be the probability of a term as provincial as *religio* coming to designate something universal that would suit Chinese Taoism as well as Brazilian *umbanda,* pharaonic Egypt and New Age California? What, in other words, was the likelihood of a term from the Latin vocabulary, originally rather technical (whose semantic orientation was then deflected toward a very particular meaning by the first Christian thinkers writing in the Latin language), having the least chance of designating a concept central to modern anthropological thought? How was a typically Christian notion, initially used in a very particular, anti-pagan polemical context, able to become a scientific concept suitable for use in the framework of a vast, crucial anthropological reflection? Did it suffer profound readjustments, radical redefinitions? Or, on the contrary, was it used in only its most general indigenous signification, with a view to furnishing a convenient concept, one that corresponded to common intuition? This would mean (and the paradox is not a trivial one) that one of our major anthropological notions is, in the final analysis, possessed of only a rather vague definition, derived through successive reductions and simplifications from its Christian usage. One of the principal difficulties that we have to explore is to be found right here, in this set of questions, and not in the invocation of a very improbable—and in any case elusive—essence.

Religion, in its capacity as a concept designating, in Émile Benveniste's forceful definition, a "distinct domain," even profoundly distinct, radically separate and different from what surrounds it, is the exclusive and original creation of the first Christian thinkers writing in Latin (Arnobius, Tertullian, Lactantius, Saint Augustine, and others), one that has continued in this shape to our own days. With time, this orientation was confirmed and imposed, while, in parallel, a movement issuing from Saint Paul and never contradicting the preceding one, tended to consecrate religion to the sphere of faith, that is, individual conscience—to the point where religious life has often become a private domain, strictly personal, for our contemporaries. On these two counts, such a conception could never have been born in the mind of a Plato or of a contemporary of Cicero, for whom the worship of the gods was an eminently public and civic matter.

This *religio,* as it was rethought by Christian thinkers, was defined from the very outset by its claim to difference, by its opposition to all other cults, and by its separation from all that was not it, as it defined itself in this fierce movement of self-foundation. This process doubtless summarizes its deepest orientation and its fundamental disposition. This difference, that is, this rupture or systematic opposition, made into a constituent principle, shows itself in several ways. First, it is *nostra religio* in opposition to *vestrae religiones,* our religion versus your religions, as it was for Arnobius.[18] This opposition is immediately repeated in another, principal one: true religion (since the only religion of the true God) is opposed to false religions that address false gods or impious demons.[19] Naturally, we should understand that to the extent that one religion is the true (or right) religion, it is also *the* veritable religion. We should not, however, forget that it is this "true" religion that made religions out of these other cults and beliefs—but in the same breath denied them this same status, that is, of being capable of possessing the truth.

The true religion is in essence the only religion, the perfect and consummate religion. Reciprocally, the latter is incarnated exclusively in the true religion, the Christian religion. False religions are not simply religions that are in error, they do not truly merit the name "religion," or only claim it without justification. Addressing false gods as they do, they do not participate in the dignity of *the* religion. Only Plato and his work, we know, escaped the anathema uttered by the first great Christian thinkers. This clear-cut attitude, which arrogates to itself an absolute superiority, is naturally accompanied by an obsessive, intransigent dogmatism that ceaselessly tracks down heresies and deviations. The Christian religion, in its capacity as true religion, initially distinguishes itself from the others, which it rejects and casts into the void. Subsequently, in the modern era, this feeling of superiority based on an irreducible difference would persist in the European consciousness and, what is more troubling, in European epistemology.

Last, to the extent that the true religion addresses itself to the only true God, the unique divinity, religion tends to valorize this link that ties (*religare*) human beings to God according to the celebrated etymology proposed by Lactantius: "It was here that Plato went astray: he lost the truth which he had seized on at the first, for, as touching the worship of that God whom he admitted to be the Architect and Parent of the Universe, he was silent. He failed to comprehend that man was bound to God by links of loyal affection (hence the origin of the word 'religion'), and that this is the one and only ground for souls becoming immortal."[20] This ultraspecialized orientation imposed on the stance of the believer, inseparable from monotheism and the exclusive faith in the one true God, would be taken up later by Saint Augustine and would win general acceptance:

> We are enjoined to love this good with all our heart, with all our soul, with all our strength. To this good we ought to be led by those who love us, and to lead those we love. Thus are fulfilled those two commandments on which hang all the law and the prophets: "Thou shalt love the Lord thy God with all thy heart, and with all thy mind, and with all thy soul"; and "Thou shalt love thy neighbor as thyself." For, that man might be intelligent in his self-love, there was appointed for him an end to which he might refer all his actions, that he might be blessed. For he who loves himself wishes for nothing else than this. And the end set before him is "to draw near to God." And so, when one who has this intelligent self-love is commanded to love his neighbour as himself, what else is enjoined than that he should do all in his power to commend him to the love of God? This is the worship of God, this is true religion, this right piety, this the service due to God only.[21]

By making an exclusive claim to the lived relationship that a person has with his or her God for itself, Christianity established two principles that would survive into the future and that would characterize religion as a Western Christian concept.

On the one hand, theology in its capacity as a science of the unique divinity and, on the other, faith as the specific link uniting human beings with that divinity together constitute the inalienable and most significant nucleus of this concept—which never can be neglected or devalued, at the risk of obliterating the notion itself. And it is also in relation to this doubly inviolable datum, and to the evaluations implicit in it, that other religions are most often examined and classified. In the global perception of the latter, the practices or acts (worship, sacrifices, asceticisms, disciplines, ecstasies, or deliriums) and the organizations (brotherhoods, priesthoods, communities) will always occupy an inferior position, subordinate to this absolute, this transcendence.

The influence of monotheistic theology in its joint capacity as mode of knowledge and argumentation and as a centripetal vision of the world has probably been spread very far from its origins, perhaps as far as our most positivist epistemological and cosmographical models. The preferred status and privileges accorded to explanations founded on the recognition of an exclusive cause, to processes underpinned from end to end by a single force, to clear-cut oppositions (God versus humanity: soul versus body, etc.), to cosmogonic "Big Bangs," and to linear and uniform evolutionary theories—are they not to some extent secular translations of a schema of thought dominated by the constant but implicit reference to a world ruled by a transcendent God, omnipotent, creator of all things? While it is clearly difficult to determine the scope of such a hypothesis or measure the influence of such a diffuse general schema, the fact remains that the repugnance felt by modern science for constructivist epistemologies, recursive phenomena, or complex structures (which we must, of course, compare to the opposing favors enjoyed by centripetal and monothelite models) can perhaps be explained by the presence of this powerful theological model behind all our efforts to find a global explanation.

This narrow specialization of the field reserved for the religious sphere virtually isolates the space of the nonreligious, of the profane. In order for the latter to be created and to expand, would it not be necessary for the possibility of engendering it to exist at the heart of the religious, as the West conceived of it? And it is indeed because the Christian religion was originally founded in a long series of oppositions to what it was not (pagan, heretical, atheistic, skeptical, etc.) that this possibility must be considered inherent in its own unfolding. The definitive difference and superiority that it claims for itself as true religion—reserved for the true God—and that absolute uniqueness that it ascribes to itself as a "distinct domain," a pretension that it would go on to try to justify in dogmatic terms, actually demands the necessity of the profane world. Nevertheless, the transcendence and omnipotence recognized for the one true God just as vigorously denied that the existence of the inferior world could be attributed to the action of some evil demiurge, as the Gnostics and Manicheans would have it. Destined to serve religion, to exalt it, the profane could not become the ontological antithesis of the religious. That is why it was necessary to distinguish what in the world and in the life of humanity belonged to religion and to the one God, while avoiding a dangerous pitfall: the dualism that would put in opposition to religion an adversary of the same or comparable rank. Pantheism, which negates the transcendence and activity of God, would never constitute as dangerous an adversary for THE religion; it was too foreign to its spirit.

Considered at sufficient distance, such a configuration is immediately seen as quite original. Moreover, it does not possess any equivalent in other cultures. What do we observe elsewhere? To the extent that the term still possesses any meaning in this context, religion nowhere appears as a "distinct domain." The Christian complex that groups theology, belief, the priesthood, and ritual (all four have to be there together in this form) does not exist elsewhere in this capacity and does not form a homogeneous, independent world, separated from the rest. This four-part complex is apparent only to the Western eye, which delimits it and arbitrarily excises it from a vaster reality, a vaster continuum. Would this justify us in saying that in other cultures *everything* is religious? But we can see that in choosing this aberrant solution, we disassemble the notion of religion by seeking at any price to save it. For to what would we make it henceforth correspond if we asserted that in one civilization and in it alone (the very one that invented the notion in question!), religion forms a "distinct domain," and everywhere else it exists only in a diffuse and elusive fluid state? Such a choice would almost inevitably lead to an all too familiar conclusion: Christianity is the only religion worthy of the name. It alone incarnates religion completely.

And since the "distinct domain" of religion does not exist in all civilizations, the oppositions cited above (false religions versus the true religion; religious versus profane, etc.) disappear. These oppositions are then inherent in the Christian conception alone. Elsewhere, where its influence was modest or nonexistent, the relevance of these oppositions is illusory. "Our" religion, for example, as the one true religion, is not absolutely opposed to "other" religions considered "false." The gods of foreign peoples are not denied as such. This difference alone ought to prompt us to regard exotic cultures with a curious eye instead of persisting in describing them by means of our unique religious code.

Let us recall that the Romans, through the ceremony of *evocatio,* sought to co-opt the goodwill of the gods of an enemy city that they were on the point of conquering. And that the Greeks spoke of the Egyptian gods with the greatest respect. It was admitted that each people had its gods, as it had its institutions and customs. This attitude was equally true of the Jews of the Old Testament (see, e.g., Gen. 35:1–5; 2 Kings 17:24–34). But let us not call this attitude tolerance, for tolerance is also an idea that is inseparable from the intellectual history (and the recent intellectual history) of the West. For the same reason, and in just as radical a fashion, we cannot isolate a domain for the profane in these cultures.

Finally, in non-Christian terms, the preeminence that we attach to theology and to faith, which seems to us so obviously enthroned at the heart of religious matters, would disappear. Their interrogations, claims, and definitions are, for example, quite foreign to the teaching of the Upanishads, the practice of yoga, and Confucian morality; as for Buddhism, it is founded on other assumptions. It would be only too easy to multiply other important examples.

The history of religions has not really taken into account all these difficulties, for they would have obliged it to question afresh the presuppositions that are most deeply buried in its universalist plan. It has preferred, as a good daughter of the West, to grant a religion to each people and culture, and this despite the anachronisms, absurdities, and paradoxes to which this ethnocentrism led it.

Texts, Corpora, and Hypertext

We hardly ever speak of religion or of religions themselves, that is, of immanent reality itself, of the states of things thus conventionally designated. Most often, we paraphrase, through translation, commentary, or free improvisation, preexistent texts that are judged *religious* (these are the great, celebrated "sacred texts," "holy scriptures") or texts that themselves deal with subjects that are also considered religious (since when? by whom? to what extent?). These attributions and classifications are themselves justified by other texts, which maintain complicated relations with them that it would require focused historical studies to disentangle.

Here (as elsewhere, but perhaps still less than elsewhere), it is not possible to speak of the thing itself (religion, a given religion), seen with full objectivity, in its unique, contingent reality. For this thing probably does not exist outside the texts that lend it a certain consistency.

In fact, the word "religion," whatever its assigned definition, retains a particular, synthetic symbolic function, charged with subsuming a great number of heterogeneous phenomena, the choice, nature, and disposition of which vary considerably from one civilization to the next. If we add that its relevance is probably very slight, we would have a supplementary reason for saying that the corresponding object or objects have only an unsure or improbable existence. Would they have one at all, moreover, if they remained inaccessible to the sharpest scrutiny, like the innumerable imaginary beings that populate religious universes, which are also nothing more than purely verbal creations? But this takes nothing away from the solidity of the beliefs that they generate—quite the contrary.

It is then within texts that the various conceptions relative to what religion is find their coherence and homogeneity. Thus, as we have long known, it is in a series of texts written by some of the first Christian authors that the Western Christian notion of religion was forged. Initially grafted onto a Latin word that meant something else, it was the result of an audacious textualization. In order to define Egyptian religion, to oppose religion to magic, to assert certain things about religion in general, one had to compose one or more texts, that is, engage in a series of very complex intellectual operations that concluded with the creation of a verbal complex made homogeneous, ordered, and coherent by the combination of themes, style, and genre chosen.[22] And it was this convergent series of architectonic characteristics that would be retrospectively ascribed to the object that they thereby created.

This situation is complicated even further by a fact as important as it is unsettling. How can we (that is, we Westerners, although we are not alone in this difficulty) claim to conceive of the idea of religion or of a given religious fact with any objectivity when we (our very selves, our ways of thinking, our most common perceptions) are immersed in a language in which there preexists the concept of religion and, along with it, a multitude of often very ancient connections and semantic networks, even if they have ceaselessly been revised?

In reality, has not the greater part of our intellectual culture, our common language, and our conceptual apparatus been shaped by two millennia of Christian civilization—simply because they were intimately intertwined with this history? Because they are essentially Christian, bearers of a Christian ideology, our language and, with it, our ways of thinking the world, humanity, history were thereby organized around the word "religion" and all that it represents and presupposes. And they have remained so. Atheism and modern scientific thought (especially when it addresses humankind) are no less indebted, since they are defined in relation to what the word means. Thus, Western atheism represents the very faithful antithesis of Christianity, not of Buddhism (the Buddha would, moreover, likely have rejected both the European believer and the atheist as being in the same category, that of victims of metaphysical illusions) or of Taoism (for which this notion would probably seem incongruous and incomprehensible).

For the modern French or English speaker, the word "religion" evokes, for example, the terms "God," "church," "faith," "prayer," "paradise," "providence," "crucifixion," "communion," "sin," and so on. But these very terms, far from being isolated one from another in our mental dictionaries, on the contrary weave a very tight but flexible fabric, but one that is relevant only within the context of Christian civilization. This series, God, church, and so on, to the extent that it implicitly designates a homogeneous whole, would have signified absolutely nothing to a Buddhist monk, a contemporary of Asoka, or a Greek philosopher. How, to begin with, would they have translated the sequence and, furthermore, according to what criteria would they have associated its terms? The configuration that the words form, which even average Westerners would probably so closely associate with the term "religion" that they would fuse and confuse them, is relevant only in their (Western) languages. Unfortunately, it is impossible for the West to avoid this impasse in order to think of the world in a different way, that is, with the aid of other concepts. So true is it that our language is also our world, the two coextensive one with the other (the aspects of the world that our language does not know do not exist and, symmetrically, what exists for our language exists equally for us in one way or another). The ultimate paradox is probably this: does something that does not exist but that we can name, thanks to our language (the soul, angels, and so on), not still exist in a certain way for, or in, our minds, actually more than what truly does exist but that our language ignores? Let us not be afraid to assert that we are dealing here with a remarkable aporia, a magnificent obstacle set in the path of all modern epistemologies.

Our language, in parallel with its lexicon and its grammar, its modes of social use and its various codes, contains a formidable reticulated memory, organized around generic notions such as, for our present purposes, religion. And, naturally, it is not enough to decree gravely and emphatically that we are going to engage in the history or science of religion to make these presuppositions disappear, inscribed as they are at the heart of our language in the form of radiating networks. This effort is even less possible since the history of religions (like so many other human sciences) cannot avail itself of some advanced metalanguage that would allow it some distance from the configurations contained in ordinary language. The nomenclature employed by historians of religion is so little different from that employed by ordinary language that we pass without difficulty from one register to the other, albeit at the cost of great confusion and deception.

The repeated use of these imprecise and approximate general terms contributes to maintaining a fuzzy semantic sphere, which, however, has the inestimable advantage of being shared by a large community, to which we belong. Now, a collective illusion certainly has more value than an undeniable reality that is known to only one person. This is a situation disregarded by the biologist and the physicist, for whom the conventional configurations associated with everyday language are completely useless. But else how are we to imagine some kind of metalanguage capable of analyzing phenomena so completely buried in linguistic matter, so constrictively imprisoned in the mesh of our texts that they draw their essential being from them, since this essential being is never anything but an illusion generated by a network of verbal coordinates?

When we view the formidable mass of texts that the West has composed and that relate in one way or another to its own notion of religion, it is tempting to regard this corpus as an immense hypertext.[23]

In a hypertext (although the preposition "in" is quite unsuited to the description of such an "object"), we have neither up or down, interior or periphery, first or second. The traditional historical frameworks also lose the greater part of their value: who prevents us, in the course of a thought, from going from Bergson to Plato, then from the latter to Boethius, finally to jump back to Porphyry? Each point, text, or fragment of a text is at the center, since each new text redefines the global configuration at each moment. But how are we to represent the figure generated by the association of all these contemporaneous or successive states of the hypertext in perpetual metamorphosis, since each of these texts, partial or complete, is susceptible, in theory at least, of being connected to any other text, without this liaison (that is, its nature, its points of contact, and the moment of its realization) being in any way predictable?

A hypertext does not, properly speaking, have a structure of its own. It is rather defined as a type of unpredictable functioning within an aleatory field, where intertextual events, resulting from numerous, always complex processes, are exclusively produced. The logic that would account for these events would doubtless have to abandon the marvelous certainties forged since Aristotle. Here, all forms of connections, synapses, interfaces (translations, transpositions, expansions, distortions, etc.), of contiguity or of attraction, all the rules of accessibility are mixed together according to the modalities that go from the most approximative to the most detailed, from the most unstable to the most rigid. A hypertext is the undefined possibility of creating new texts, which in their turn modify less its unimaginable configuration than its richness, which in turn permits new and unforeseen creations.

In reality, things are doubtless somewhat less anarchic and subversive than has been asserted in this attempt to summarize the thesis of Pierre Lévy.[24] That is to say, their order and their interplay, as always, refer simply to a type of unaccustomed complexity and functioning. That is why this first vision of the hypertext should immediately be corrected by a few remarks, which in turn will lead us to address the notion of corpus.

Because it is a locus that unceasingly permits the realization of textual creations, a hypertext cannot at the same time be an indescribable chaos, in which case it would be inconceivable and incomprehensible. This is so for at least two complementary reasons, as follows:

— Given that they concern texts and only texts, the mechanisms that are activated and the events that occur within a hypertext are obliged (because they are bound) to conserve intact an immutable form, that of the text. They respond on every count to the imperatives of a very fertile textual function. Whatever the level or the plane that one chooses for observation, they offer the same fundamental isomorphism, that of textual order. This constraint appears as the indispensable condition that allows the hypertext of a culture (or the culture itself, to the extent that it is also a hypertext) to exist and to remain open to this function, since it gives the hypertext an unchanging orientation as well as points of reference—and rules. In similar fashion, the connections that are established between texts can very well display all the characteristics and all the shadings that one could imagine, since they can be established only among texts and with a view to safeguarding their incomparable architecture. These last two conditions counterbalance the centrifugal influence that these connections would exert by forcing them to align themselves in order to produce only recognizable, comprehensible textual forms (that is to say, paraphrasable textual forms).

— On the other hand, as we everywhere observe, these connections form associations among themselves in order to make up networks (here we are not far from the idea of corpus) and all the (textual) elements that make up such networks should, they, too, (try to) mirror the same isomorphism, the same overall coherence. Each individual (or group of individuals) stores in memory several of these networks as realized in the past; it is thus that we partially know those that the Greeks composed, while we would be quite incapable of reconstituting the status of the hypertext of their era. Inevitably, we then compose our own by moving about in (what is for each of us) the current status of the hypertext, but drawing our inspiration from those paths (consecrated by usage and tradition) that marked the way of numerous itineraries (that which goes, for example, from religion to metaphysics, or the other that allows us to return to morality after pausing in philosophy, etc.). And it is very often these reassuring, familiar routes that we take in our turn while waiting for the day when we are bold enough to venture off the beaten path. To summarize: if, in the open field of the hypertext, an undetermined number of connections and creations are theoretically possible, the fact remains that the latter obey and will always obey a very precise anthropological and poetic finality, which for its part entails a rigorous constraint: the composition of texts, the ones paraphrasable by the others, because they are all subject to the same constitutive principles. To define the hypertext in terms of function would then be to state only a banal truism, if we did not immediately add that this function is subordinate to an exclusive end and to rules that are for the most part immutable.

A hypertext, or whichever state of one that we might chose as example, invariably offers this paradoxical character: in theory it is open to all kinds of play and every sort of adventure (why not go from metaphysics to economy or from mathematics to lyric poetry?). In practice, only some of these itineraries are adopted, and it is in the course of them that, with a great deal of caution and after having assured ourselves of our right to do so, we may launch a few new connections. Just like the majority of travelers on a major railway line who know that other lines exist and that other connections are possible, we always take the same routes.

As a consequence, the hypertext then has a reverse side that is better known to us: the corpus or corpora (corpuses if you like). These are the two inseparable faces of the same textual reality. The hypertext is the domain of the virtual, the corpus that of the actual, the known, familiar, fixed network. This is why the one is a priori unpredictable, while the other is a posteriori intelligible.

The constitution of a corpus, that is, the transformation of a group of scattered texts into an ordered whole, and the homogenization of the latter, depends above all on our capacity to paraphrase. Active, effective, tireless, the paraphrase is omnipresent, since it is the sole means of effective expression for the textual function that conditions the production of texts. And it is paraphrase that permits the composition of a group of new texts, which display, because they will have been created to this end, a close thematic and stylistic kinship (theological or juridical texts, for example);

it also permits the possibility of combining them, coordinating them with others that are complementary or implicitly understood (theological texts *and* philosophical, juridical, or ethical texts, etc.).

This creation of new texts is effected by following all the paths of paraphrase, none of which is exclusive in relation to the others. Among them, we encounter commentary, interpretation, exegesis, glossing, imitation (plagiarism, pastiche, quotation, the loan, etc.), transposition, refutation, discussion, translation, adaptation, and so on—in a word, all the possibilities of conversion offered by the textual economy (but let us not overestimate the quality of their results, for the psychological modalities that accompany them very often limit their fruitfulness and originality).

The fact remains, in any case, that a text (or a set of texts, it scarcely matters here) is always convertible to a new text, since the limits (possible, plausible, credible, traditional, or whatever) within which this operation unfolds are drawn by this new text, even if it were intended only to reassert the relevance of those that earlier prevailed. It is in fact its own coherence that lends them their existence or reaffirms it, an existence no less arbitrary on that account.

On the other hand, it is obvious (and perhaps it is not a bad idea to recall it) that these numerous conversion mechanisms are not all triggered at the same moment or at the same rate. They unfold in time, but at speeds and with forces that can be very different one from another (let us think, from this double perspective, of all that distinguishes the Marxist corpus from the Christian and Buddhist corpuses).

The reduction, expansion, complexification (abstraction, schematization, rationalization, conceptualization, etc.)—and simplification—are based on the same mechanisms. Finally, in a corpus, there always coexist some very general and also some infinitely detailed texts, some very long, others quite brief. As regards order, coherence, and isotropy, a one-page text summarizing a much more substantial text is not fundamentally distinguishable from the latter: from the one to the other, we frequently observe no entropy, since the quantity of its ordering principle (that is, its principal intrinsic quality) remains constant.

The great variety of means and objectives offered by all the procedures of paraphrase, far from introducing and continuing an indescribable confusion, rather permit very different kinds of orderings to coexist at the heart of one and the same corpus: hierarchizations, articulations, syntheses, subdivisions, overlaps, exclusions, oppositions, and so on. But it is precisely their diversity (and here we observe another interesting paradox) that makes them complementary and mutually paraphrasable; no doubt because the number of points of contact, exchange, transfer, and transposition increases in very exact proportion to this diversity. These orderings make a valuable contribution to the solidity of the corpuses, as if they themselves resulted from the crisscrossing of their elements and the links that exist among them.

Still, if we view our own textual tradition (or memory) from some distance, we note, with no great surprise, that the hypertext in which we navigate daily, from which we draw our references and our arguments, in relation to which we attempt to elaborate an intellectual plan that is the least bit original, is primarily made up of references that, in one way or other (or in several ways simultaneously), almost always have something to do with religion. Our most massive corpuses (theology, morals, philosophy, law, literature), which on their own amount to thousands of texts, also follow the same model. Whether we speak of God, mankind, life, the beyond, destiny, sin, the body, happiness or pleasure, love, or providence, we Westerners are continuously referred back to this central notion, the veritable hearth around which the Western tribe has gathered for almost two thousand years. And we cannot even exclude from this aggregate of texts those of antiquity, whether pre-Christian or contemporary with the first Christian thinkers (principally Platonist, Stoic, Aristotelian, and Neoplatonist), so decisive do we know their intellectual contributions to have been to the construction of the gigantic Christian corpus.

This is why today's individual, our contemporary, who believes him or herself to be definitively rid of all religious scruple, continues nonetheless to think of the world and the self by means of (fragments of) texts borrowed from this Western religious tradition or composed according to its canons. And many human sciences, starting with the history of religions, have unknowingly contracted the same constituent debt. When they think, they never do so but in a learned language that, far from having been conceived to do science, was in the main elaborated within the framework of controversies over questions of religion.

Cosmographical Issues

Religion was intimately linked to the principal events and to the major orientations of our intellectual history (when it was not literally identified with them), because it has impregnated and often guided most of our ways of thinking, because it has defined the sense and the disposition of a great number of our conceptual networks, because it has continuously occupied our language and nourished our vocabulary, because it has contributed for centuries to the discipline of our bodies and our minds, because it has lent a particular orientation to our sensibilities, because it has nourished and organized our memory, because it has given our intelligence an unprecedented form, because it has been present for centuries in each of our arts, because it has influenced the design and patterning of our cities, because it has cultivated our manner of looking at the world, because it has doubtless also contributed to modeling our mental activities, and because it has been put at the heart of the principal debates and controversies affecting the definition of humanity as well as the destiny of the world. So religion, as outlined above, must be considered the locus in which the identity or figure of the West has in principle been constituted and defined.

We would be wrong to consider this identity simply from a differential or comparative point of view, for it displays, adjusted over time, a series of traits and characteristics that, taken together in their complementarities and their mutual articulations very clearly draw the lines of a profoundly unique configuration. Identity and singularity mingle here, for the former is never more that the effect produced by the sum of the jumbled elements that constitute the latter. But this identity is also to a great extent our own, the one that animates our minds or defines a certain way of being in the world. This means that the look we direct at ourselves or toward the world is the fruit, long in ripening, of a particular historical construction (and not the result of an objective, invariable mechanism) and that this same view is somehow condemned not to see or not to recognize anything but the forms and colors that are familiar to it. The gaze of European historians or ethnographers can discern religious phenomena only where they perceive facts that recall or evoke, from whatever distance and in however approximate a form, those that the European mind cannot designate otherwise. What other name could be given them? But once they have been called and classified as religious, is it possible to analyze them and interpret them other than by having recourse to the explanations that the West has conceived of with the aid of elements drawn from its own culture, in order to account for what was most inherent in its very self?

This omnipresent and architectonic influence of religion on the whole of Western culture over the past two millennia then displays another aspect, which is of even greater import for the history of religions.

Whatever term we choose—weltanschauung, cosmography, vision, conception, figuration of the world, and so on—the fact remains that all global conceptions of the world, all utopias, all messianic movements, all theologies, all the imaginary worlds that the West has conceived of (and eventually tried to impose) have always been realized by taking as model (whether it was admired, envied, hated, imitated, deformed, or denigrated) that or those promoted by the Christian religion in its capacity of appearing to offer the most complete, most hegemonic conception of the world.

Yet let us never forget that the dominant conception of the world that members of a community share is not and cannot be simply a kind of intellectual construct that each of them would have the leisure to contemplate by situating him or herself outside it. This global conception, capable of defining each aspect of individual life is, for this reason, incarnated in each person; it equally well represents the living community itself, which quite simply would not exist without it, because there is a consensus that such a community cannot prosaically be reduced to a collection of solitary, disempowered individuals.

We must consequently admit, to the degree that the idea of religion has served, explicitly or not, as a reference or model for most of our cosmographic plans, that for Westerners this notion carries a disturbing ambivalence (and no doubt we ourselves, faced with it, are in a comparable situation). In fact, we are condemned to try to think our own cosmographies by using concepts that belong to these very same cosmographies—and that are inscribed in their architecture. Similarly, we can conceive of ourselves, we who are so largely constituted by them, only with the aid of the notions with which they furnish us. How, for example, could we think of human beings or think of ourselves as human beings without employing the categories deriving from a Christian anthropology? Body, sense, mind, and soul. Do we have a competing model available? And has not the set of relations that transform this group of elements into an intelligible system dominated Western anthropology and, with it, most of the controversies that have issued from it?

Perhaps we can now better measure the difficulty that accompanies any attempt at a conceptual innovation—for example, a scientific innovation—that claims to free itself from all prior cosmographical presuppositions, especially in the domain of the human sciences, a domain characterized by the diffuse influence of traditions issuing from the past.

In this universe of representations, each thing is at one and the same time constituted by everything that surrounds it and is itself constituent, since it is always capable of intervening in this environment by relocating or imperceptibly modifying itself. That is to say—and this is the essential point—no representation exists on its own in autonomous, unchanging fashion. Every ontology could readily be summarized in this fashion and limited by this observation. These remarks, which lighten and simplify the list of our metaphysical interrogations, on the one hand, complicate the task of the history (and inevitably of the historian) of religions, on the other.

From the moment one admits (1) that the notion of religion is a typically Western creation; (2) that it has, moreover, supplied the nucleus about which the West has constructed its own universe of values and representations; and (3) that in this capacity, it has influenced the totality of our ways of conceiving and thinking the world, how can one imagine that the history of religions, inasmuch as it too was born in the West and associated from the outset with this idea of religion, could escape its influence? In fact, as is shown below, the history of religions, despite its scientific pretensions, initially appears in the intellectual history of the West as the heir to a Western vision of the world and of humanity that was itself determined by its Christian antecedents.

Before even thinking of untangling this fascinating imbroglio, we must initially show in what manner religion, because it not only represents one of the central concepts of all Western thought, but at the same time constitutes a paradoxical subject for contemporary anthropological inquiry, is another typically Western creation.

2 | A Paradoxical Subject

Religions or Religious Phenomena?

Drawing up a list of all the events, ordinary or solemn, public or private (and for the latter we would immediately have to distinguish among those that concern the intellect, psychological life, conscious or not, affective life, and so on), all the persons, real or fictional, all the objects or facts (ceremonies, behaviors, neuroses, beliefs, and practices) seen under one aspect or another as religious, or having been so identified by this group of people or that, in this age or another, would seem an interminable task, and the mere mention of it may engender dizziness and unease in readers who, like science, abhor metaphysical malaise. I shall therefore limit myself here to examining a fragment of this unavailable ideal list:

— The trance of a participant in a voodoo ceremony
— A Benedictine monk praying in his cell
— A Brahman bathing in the Ganges
— A Christian's examination of his conscience before confession
— The butchered victim of an Aztec sacrifice
— The conclusions of a canonization process
— A Byzantine icon
— The prayer wheel of a Tibetan pilgrim
— The myth of Oedipus
— The pope's ban on contraception
— The cabbalistic exegesis of a verse of Scripture
— The solitary practice of yoga by a devotee of Shiva
— An extract from Hesiod's *Theogony*
— The morning breathing exercises of a Taoist master
— Peasants' midsummer festival and bonfire
— The personality cult devoted to the emperor of China
— A Roman seer reading the future in the entrails of a dead bird

— A pilgrim in Mecca
— The Buddhist expression sarvaṃ duḥkham, "all is suffering"
— The cosmogony outlined in Plato's *Timaeus*
— The symbolism of the Sacré Coeur cathedral
— The collective suicide of the members of the Order of the Solar Temple
— The genealogical list of Egyptian pharaohs
— The gnosis of the Upanishads

The elements that comprise this list are obviously so disparate (gestures, attitudes, persons, situations, and so on) that they draw the contours of an inconceivable galaxy in our mental spaces. Doesn't this heterogeneity throw down a sly challenge to the capacities and resources of our understanding, our most general capacity to sort and order cultural phenomena? Doesn't its unclassifiability make this enumeration seem ironic? Yet each of these data (admittedly chosen for this purpose, while ambiguous or equivocal data on the edge of or outside our native categories have been excluded) is so suitable for inclusion in a textbook on the history of religions that its presence there would surprise no one. Can we see what they have in common? Can we identify a common denominator, kernel, or "religious constant" that they share or express, each in its own fashion? In short, to make this clearer, can we just wriggle out of it by exclaiming, "Holy! Holy!" and invoking some utterly mysterious Beyond? Or are we capable of going beyond the confusion of a vague intuition in order to utter this word "religious," in the name of which all these data have been assembled?

Let me respond at once to those who would object that I have purposely chosen isolated, elementary data, divorced from their contexts, and that calling the complexes from which they are drawn "religions" is a simple lexical operation that resolves nothing. But if these elements are seen as religious because they belong to religions, should they not, each on its own level, possess or present, sui generis, some religious aspect? If not, this would mean that only the all-encompassing complexes—religions in the strict sense of the word—would be religious by nature. Unfortunately, the limitations, the distinctive contents, the laws of composition of these supposed complexes and, even more hypothetically, the structural homologies that they display (but on which level?)[1] are even less sure and until now have never been the object of rigorous definition or description that might be capable of guiding us in our exploration.

This observation should not surprise us. We need only remember that the selection and recognition of the facts identified as religious (operations that only Western science saw fit to undertake) have always depended on criteria borrowed from our indigenous tradition. Thus, the confrontation of our initial list with what, in this same tradition, best personifies this notion of religion (for simplicity's sake, let us list them: God, immortal soul, prayer, providence, sin, faith, rite) reveals that only those examples taken from Christian civilization presuppose this familiar series of concepts or can be referred to it without great difficulty.

Conversely, the complete irrelevance of several elements of our list with regard to these less than universal criteria is just as obvious. The ascetic who devotes himself to yoga would in the best case recognize only the notion of soul (ignoring the existence of the six others), but for him it would be so different from what it is in the eyes of a Christian that without some awkwardness, it would be difficult to ascribe the same name to such dissimilar concepts and entities. And the inevitable and constant recourse to the French or English translation of Sanskrit, Chinese, or Nahuatl terms erases all significant differences, calibrates the concepts to the same standard dimensions and, finally, promotes the fallacious illusion that we are everywhere on "familiar ground." In the same way, the central concept of Upanishad gnosis, the impersonal Absolute of Vedanta, entails neither ritual, belief, nor divinity. On what grounds do we still call it religious, seemingly ranking it along with offerings made to the pope? And this notion of soul or substantive absolute disappears entirely in Buddhism, along with those of God the Creator and universal providence. We do not hesitate, however, to call the teachings of the Buddha religion and to classify as religious facts the rigorous praxis of yoga, even though the latter aims at an annihilation of all mental constructs and formations responsible for individual feelings: beliefs, representations, sentiments, and so on! The Confucian conception of the world—and Confucianism, too, is classed among the great religions of humanity—comprises none of these central elements. The world, according to this doctrine, is neither divine nor sacred and presupposes no transcendence at all.

The differences that we observe in this summary comparison of yoga, Buddhism, shamanism, Confucianism, and the rest are neither anecdotal nor marginal. Nor are they variants that human fantasy or ingenuity would have added to some immutable kernel. We are, in any case, incapable, as is science, of saying what this timeless nucleus is, or of what it is composed. Let us rather consider the differences with equal measures of moral respect and epistemological astuteness in order to convince ourselves that ours is no less different, and that it can in no case set itself up as a universal point of reference.

As for the criterion "worship," it is often too sensitive for effective use. In all civilizations but our own, the distinctions we make between "political," "religious," "social," and "civic" ceremonies scarcely have any meaning.[2] Such distinctions, when they exist, are in any case based on other criteria and do not by contrast serve to isolate a "distinct religious domain."

On the other hand, if you will, Platonic cosmogony, an isolated, speculative construction that does not properly belong to what we call "Greek religion," displays numerous aspects or themes with which Christians have felt in perfect agreement. Would we say that Plato's thought, which is not and does not depend on any religion, is nonetheless more religious that Confucian thought, which is not religious yet is considered a religion? It would be easy here again to add other examples, just as paradoxical.

With this last example, we can better make out the inconsistency in our way of seeing things. On the one hand, in the name of a vague universalism, which is doubtless only the most visible counterpart of our pretension to think the world according to our criteria alone, we feel ourselves obliged to attribute a religion to every culture, even there where our traditional criteria for the religious are absent. Conversely, when some of these criteria do appear there, we gladly qualify speculative works or individual thoughts as religious. As we have just seen, Plato offers quite a good example. The first Christian thinkers (e.g., Saint Augustine or Eusebius of Caesarea) annexed Plato and made a proto-Christian of him (one supposed to have been secretly initiated into the teachings of Moses in Egypt), simply because they found motifs in his work (in particular, the immortal soul, the creative Demiurge, and supernatural providence) that in their eyes could only have a divine origin and were therefore religious. Thus we reach this double aberration: on the one hand, we call religions those cultural configurations that are indifferent to any concern for transcendence (as we observe in Confucianism) and, on the other, we are ready to receive into the bosom of religion certain philosophical works, even when they never founded the least sort of collective belief and never generated any kind of liturgical practice. Where, in the first case, would we say that the religious stops, and where, in the second, that it begins?

The propensity of Western thought to discover the religious everywhere (from the caves of Lascaux to the coast of California) is too systematic not to appear suspect. Beyond its incapacity to bespeak the difference in the Other and perhaps also because of a certain intellectual laziness, the compulsive movement that this propensity exhibits probably betrays its inherent ambition to model the human kingdom on its own image and set itself up at the center.

Historians of religion who draw their inspiration from phenomenology, and on this count invoke the inalienable, timeless, and universal meaning of religious facts, would also have difficulties in justifying all the items on our initial list as religious. For in the name of what transhistorical "signification" and what definition of the "sacred" would they say that the Aztec priest who cut open his victim, the Roman soothsayer who observed the entrails of a fowl, and the interdiction against contraception pronounced by the pope constitute, on any grounds at all, a homogeneous set founded on an unvarying principle? This may prompt the retort that perhaps some of the facts considered religious are less religious, less essentially religious, than others. And that some others, for their part, are totally or intrinsically religious. But which, and on which criteria that are not typically Western would we base the effort to isolate them? On what immaterial borders are these fragile ontological limits drawn? And what sense are we to give this hierarchy—which almost recalls those of Pseudo-Dionysius?

From the vantage point of common sense, whose summary interventions are not entirely absent from the reflections that are prompted in some historians of religion even now,[3] the ultimate argument perhaps consists of saying that what in the end is religious entails one form or another of the beyond or of transcendence and a relationship or interaction with it. In this approach, religion is reduced to its ultimate metamorphosis, to its most stripped-down quintessence: the vague and perfectly unutterable "something" that must exist "up there" or elsewhere. This would be a kind of zero degree of religion, beyond which all returns to silence and to nothingness. Isn't this supremely banal argument still the hardest to counter?

Presented in so crude and skeletal a form (which makes it no less apt to waken many echoes in the minds of our contemporaries), it is true that it initially seems capable of disorienting critical thought, which is so little accustomed to face such disincarnate adversaries. What can we object to, with what analytical methods and concepts can we counter such an elusive, formless statement?

If common sense had ever had the ability to justify a scientific undertaking or to reject it, this would have been known long ago. Common sense, as has been repeated since Aristotle, will never be able to generate anything but capricious, changeable opinion. Its seductiveness depends on the weakness of our critical sense, not on the superiority of its initial intuitions.

A conception as vague as this is in no way sufficient to draw the boundaries of this celebrated "distinct domain" (yet it is there that the principal argument of the defenders of a universal specificity for religion lies; otherwise, as already noted, the latter would dissolve into an amorphous continuum of practices and beliefs), any more than it can offer anthropological thought a criterion (or set of criteria) that permits us to put it on a solid theoretical footing. For example, it lumps together all forms of metaphysical speculation that have postulated the existence of another form or other forms of reality. And again we find the philosophies of Plotinus and Plato on (or in) our way.

Moreover, there are numerous forms of the beyond that have illumined the dreams and fantasies of human beings but have nothing specifically religious about them: all utopias and forms of exalted aspiration for a world that is a little more just, or a little less ugly, bear witness to this. In what sense is hoping for a paradisal existence after death specifically religious in nature—unless most of our ideals and all our mad longings could also be so qualified in one way or another? Conversely, the shaman who travels in the world of spirits goes there with the intention of controlling them (through ruse, force, or negotiation) and, as a consequence, returns from that world with his task accomplished.[4] He experiences no nostalgia for this Beyond. And it would be anachronistic to see in every shaman a savage, exotic disciple of Er the Pamphylian in Plato. In addition, the topography of these shamanistic Beyonds is not laid out in the same way as our European Beyonds (the Bible's, Dante's, Hugo's), and we should use the same word in both cases only with reluctance, for such a confusion creates an anthropological illusion a little too cheaply.

Conversely, numerous cosmographic formations habitually viewed as religious (e.g., Confucianism, Taoism, or Buddhism) are founded either on respect for "cosmic" laws or "natural" correspondences to which humans should subject their bodies and minds, or on the denial of all transcendence, seen as a source of illusion and suffering. What would we call, or would our predecessors have called, a community of the disciples of Lucretius living in poverty and ascetic discipline? A religious community? Would we say the same of the first Pythagorean communities? And if these wisdoms, these human wisdoms, are actually so little devout, or are so only in an anachronistic manner, it is simply because their basic orientation—their original ways of envisaging the world and the best fashion to live there—quite simply do not correspond to those of Christianity? For our strict and rigid model of religion is given us, has been inculcated in us, by that faith.

As a consequence, if it is perfectly allowable to envisage the creation of an anthropology of transcendence that would study all forms of the beyond, all the categories of imaginary beings, all the messianic utopias, all the systems of cosmic laws, all the ideal moralities intended to bear up the weight of living, such as humanity has imagined them, it would be imprudent, and scientifically unsatisfying, to recognize in these only the exotic variations of an obscure religious instinct. The notion of cosmographic formations has precisely the goal of subsuming this totality of human creations in a scientific project that does not itself presuppose specific orientations or values.

If a superficial comparison of the terms of our list with those that Western common sense has long had the habit of spontaneously associating with the word "religion" does not permit us to discern (or even glimpse) in what the *religio* of religion consists, there remains another way, which consists of turning toward the kinds of solutions that modern anthropological thought has developed.

Mindful of our double ambition to arrive at these celebrated universal invariables, and also to escape the relativism and skepticism that would condemn to impotence the scientific thought that elected the study of mankind as its object, this thought may be directed either toward another, more abstract level or toward challenging the very idea of religion.

In the first undertaking, several options, sometimes complementary, sometimes opposed, are possible. At a minimum, they agree among themselves in recognizing that what is essential here escapes direct observation. To succeed in this, to grasp this level (which can only be revealed through analysis), we must somehow extract from the real those general, universal rules (exchange and reciprocity, etc.), structures (subjacent to totemic classifications, to ideologies, etc.), praxeological schemas (the "techniques of the body," ritualizations, etc.), transcendental categories (like those of "mythic thought"), classes of homogeneous phenomena (myths, symbols, magic, and so on), and specific enunciative modalities (such as those employed in prayers addressed to supernatural beings or to a powerful person).[5] Behind the enumeration of this inventory, we may recognize the names of Mauss, Dumézil, Cassirer, Lévi-Strauss, and Bourdieu.

But this procedure meets two major objections. On the one hand, its findings do not specifically concern religious facts, which, moreover, they do not seek to isolate on the basis of indisputable criteria. They view the totality of symbolic productions or activities observable in each society in a much more general fashion: the rules, structures, ritualized practices, transcendental categories, and specialized enunciative modalities in one capacity or another address all aspects of social life and not just those habitually called religious. Yet—and this point has already been made— anthropological thought gains nothing by retaining an artificial opposition in which the religious would be, in our Western civilization alone, a "distinct domain" and, everywhere else, from primitive cultures to oriental civilizations, would never exist except in some diffuse manner.

On the other hand, scarcely are they discerned than these great abstract categories inevitably pose the question of their origin, with the supplementary risk of referring researchers back to endless theological quarrels. In fact, our epistemological debates, as soon as they address the question of origins, begin in many respects to resemble our theological debates. And they are almost as sterile.[6] These debates are closely tied both to our traditional divisions of the sciences (psychology, sociology, history, and so on) and to some major explanatory positions (functionalist, structuralist, symbolist, idealist, relativist). It is thus, after this lengthy detour, that we can discern modern anthropological thought grappling with a limited system of grandiose contrary metatheses (Freudianism, Marxism, historicism, constructivism), comparable on many points to that which the Greeks, for example, imagined in order to explain the origin of belief in the gods (Critias, Gorgias, Epicurus, Sextus Empiricus, Polybius, Plato, Plutarch, and others).

The second procedure has become quite typical of a certain approach to cultural facts; it draws its inspiration from the position defined by Mauss in 1902: "There is not, in fact, a thing, an essence called Religion: there are only religious phenomena [i.e., representations, practices, and organizations], more or less aggregated into systems that are called religions, which have a defined historical existence among specific groups of people and at specific times."[7]

However subtle and shaded this distinction (Religion/religious phenomena) may be, I must admit my inability to see its heuristic advantages. We can certainly admit that there is no *essence* corresponding to what we conventionally call religion, since we are not even sure that religions actually exist everywhere. But then, why continue to call certain phenomena religious? For we do so at the risk of maintaining an annoying confusion and find ourselves asking: "In what then does the *religio* of your religious facts consist?"

The distinction made by Mauss is relevant to the philosophical debate only so long as it authorizes us not to confer on the word "religion" a status that in some way or another would transcend all historical and anthropological determination to become a kind of atemporal Idea or Essence. But the distinction quickly proves inadequate if we believe that through it we can reach a heuristic level situated (on the vertical scale of our old metaphysics) halfway between Platonic essences and trivial realities.[8] In fact, to get out of this fix, it is enough to abandon, along with this vertical vision, forever tied to our philosophical and religious tradition, the words pertaining to it and substitute in their place a horizontal conception, immanent in the human world, such as that summarized here in the idea of cosmographic formations.

The phenomena of which Mauss speaks do not profit very much by being called religious. Not only, as he rightly thought, because they do not refer to an atemporal essence called religion, but in particular because the religious does not in any case represent a category adequate to and fruitful enough for anthropological thought, which continuously runs up against its imprecision, against the Western presuppositions that it implies, and against the absurdities or paradoxes that it bears along with it, in the wake of religion.

In the face of the many sterile misunderstandings that they sustain, the rare advantages that the words "religion" and "religious" offer are conventional only in the sense that they allow us, in the framework of our traditional division of knowledge, to designate globally, in ordinary conversation (shorn of all epistemological objectives), a region of human activity. Their use can then only be provisional, since these advantages are wiped out as of the moment we try to assign to these terms the capacity to resolve the difficult theoretical questions tied to their use in a scientific context.

In the list presented at the beginning of this chapter, two characteristics may have caught the reader's attention:

— All the data listed exclude irony as much as they deny despair. In compensation, if you like, they are all inscribed in vaster complexes in which each of life's elements connects with the others. In this respect, these cosmographic complexes allow the real and very corporeal individuals that they involve to transfigure their present condition, however they conceive of it: limited, uneasy, contingent, disoriented, blind, perishable, ephemeral, absurd, imperfect, or painful. All the techniques or practices and all the creations that were alluded to have the capacity to modify the nature of immediate experience, simply by replacing it at the heart of an ordered, all-encompassing world, endowed for this purpose with the capacity of giving it a significance, a finality or a value. This subsuming of the isolated act into a totality is a cosmographic operation. It is even the most common form of such.

— These same facts, and a good many others along with them (whether we call them "political," "symbolic," "artistic," "ethical," or whatever), themselves always presuppose very broad conceptions of humankind and of the world. In short, cosmographies. It matters little whether these do or do not imply the existence of powerful gods, immortal souls, extraterrestrials, or a solicitous providence. A cosmography that is atheist, racist (of the Nazi type), naturalist, or astrological, alchemical, or mythic, or still others that are founded in warrior heroism, an altruistic morality, yoga, divination, the teachings of the Buddha, the harmonious equilibrium of the breath of life, or the five elements—these are no less comprehensive than a religious cosmography. In all these cases (which might, moreover, be more or less combined among themselves to generate unique or monstrous syncretisms), the quantity of order and meaning, accessible through paraphrase, remains the same. The ultimate finality of a cosmographic formation is never THE truth or THE meaning, but its own truth or meaning, even if, naturally, all claim to possess the one true and exact vision of things. If we were suddenly to divest them of this constituent paranoia, all cultures would immediately collapse into themselves.

History or Histories?

The English and French phrases used to designate what some other languages call the "science of religions" (e.g., German *Religionswissenschaft*) have at least the merit of calling attention to what we call "history" and to what we understand by historicity, with the understanding that "historicity" here designates the fundamental character, and thus the least debatable one, of all human fact, and that "history," which is somewhat ambiguous in my native French (*histoire*, "story, history"), refers to intelligible structures that may emerge from this historicity and, simultaneously, to discursive productions that textualize them in one form or another, as consecrated by the learned rhetorical tradition (books, articles, textbooks, and so on).[9]

Starting out from this sound, hardly debatable—because its terms are so obvious—observation, we are inevitably led to question the validity of the following formulations, taken in their conventional meanings:

1. The historicity of religions (or of religious phenomena)
2. The historicity of religion
3. The history of religion
4. The histories of religions
5. The historicity of the history of religions (as an academic discipline)
6. The history (or History) of the history of religions

If we admit the radical historicity of human phenomena and religious phenomena in particular (1), then the historicity of religion (2), understood as the Western concept of religion, entrains the very idea, immediately desubstantialized, of religion.[10] From this point on, the question "Has the substance of religion always and everywhere remained invariable?" raised by Alfred Loisy at the beginning of the twentieth century becomes meaningless. If many things are already in movement and are being ceaselessly transformed on the tumultuous surface of history, how could a regional concept born almost two millennia ago in very particular circumstances claim to designate a major anthropological fact?

With the disappearance of the unchanging idea (or essence) of religion, the phrase "the religions," conceived of as so many hypostases of this religion, also loses most of its relevance. This definitive loss can naturally not be compensated for, as we have noted above, by the use of the phrase "religious phenomena"; for to what could the stable, common referent of religions or religious phenomena correspond if, to whatever degree (sociological, psychological, anthropological, etc.), there was nothing that we could universally call religion?

As a consequence, there also disappears from the debate the assertion that we are justified in trying to retrace a history of religion (3), that is, to find in history something like a theodicy of the idea of religion.

And from this same perspective "histories of religions" (4) is an expression that scarcely has a meaning beyond the tables of contents of textbooks that conventionally list various monographic studies (not always very historical, for that matter).

Despite its radical and even nihilist character, this starting point opens the door to two paths of inquiry.

The first consists of trying to discover at the heart of those facts called religious a trait or a series of characteristics that is universally valid. But it meets, as has already been shown and as will be confirmed somewhat more fully in the next chapters, a substantial difficulty, irreducible in many respects, which is the inadequacy and imprecision of the Western term "religious" for any procedure that lays claim to an anthropological objective. This handicap is explained in turn by the excessive number of typically Western prejudices and presuppositions that are present in this only too familiar term.

The second, which will be defended here, makes a complete reversal in relation to the preceding, in that it consists of replacing the Western notion of religion and, with it, everything that is conventionally attached to it, with a vaster anthropological perspective dominated by the concept of cosmographic formations. This permits us to subsume the totality of human activities whose objective is the creation, preservation, or consolidation of all-encompassing symbolic universes, capable of receiving and lending sense (value, orientation, and a rationale) to the totality of human facts. In this new conception, religious facts and religion itself would be no more than the expression or the Western equivalent of cosmographic formations, whose various expressions and modalities anthropological and historical studies would have the objective of determining and then comparing systematically.

Even if we doubted the scientific relevance of the word "religion" and, as we are doing here, asserted that the history of religions, in its capacity as a field of specific learning, fully belongs to history (5) on the same grounds as its improbable subject, we would however still be authorized to study the history (or History) of the history of religions (6).[11] Clearly, one might quite logically object that that history ("the historiography of the history of religions") risks being nothing more than a supplementary meta-stage on a path leading to skepticism or, at least, to disappointment. I do not deny that. But each of us can still admit the following:

That this history was poorly written or written too long ago, when the discipline was scarcely out of its credulous childhood, and that it thus warrants being rewritten, or rather rethought, even if it is fated to know only a brief existence.[12]

That when it was written—captive to its Western ethnocentrism—it was without interrogating the very notion of religion, which everyone took as self-evident.

That in rewriting it today, and thanks to the distance created by the time that has passed, we have a right to hope to throw some new light on its presuppositions and its methods and thus perhaps contribute to gaining recognition for the idea that the history (or the history of the history) of a discipline can be conceived of as the critical moment in its redefinition.[13]

Yet this redefinition, if it is simultaneously oriented toward the object and toward the gaze leveled at this object, is capable of proposing, even if only exceptionally, not new ways of thinking (this would be too ambitious) but at least new dispositions of ideas and objects, capable of disabusing us of those that have (mis-)shaped our minds.

On the condition that the critical gaze and historicist point of view are constantly and, if possible, dialectically counterbalanced by the categorical imperative of an anthropological perspective (itself sustained by a comparative methodology as bold as it is vigilant), it seems to me now possible to address the idea of religion, this time as the history of religions has conceived of it and, dare I say, defined it.

3 | An Uncertain Anthropological Calling

A Nebula of Definitions

To begin with, I invite the reader to review some more or less ancient definitions that follow below, to retrace their various filiations, and thus to discover unexpected family resemblances.[1] It will immediately be seen that none of these definitions challenges the very idea of religion, even when the definition is prompted by incredulity. Many of the "scientific" definitions do not truly distinguish themselves from the others: philosophy, theology, and the history of religions spontaneously return to the same general arguments located at the heart of the same topical complexes. Finally, the majority of these definitions have as implicit model the Christian conception, but reduced in some fashion to its "ideal type," to its stripped down quintessence (which, I must emphasize, makes this spiritualized and minimalist version even less open to universalization, even if, at the same time, it seems to us Westerners more relevant and closer to our most familiar common intuition).

This ideal definition advances a psychological and profoundly individualistic vision. It reduces religion to an interior sentiment that is inevitably born of the experience of transcendence, whether the latter be called God, the sacred, the beyond, power, mystery, or the like. This conception, which would be rediscovered in the twentieth century in the wake of the phenomenological movement, owes a great deal, as does the latter, to theological theses of Lutheran inspiration: Johann Herder, Friedrich Schleiermacher, Benjamin Constant, Auguste Sabatier, Cornelius Tiele, Rudolf Otto, and many others less well known have contributed, since the end of the eighteenth century, to the success of this eidetic pseudo-reduction. I write "pseudo-reduction" with no qualms, for it completely disregards (as if this disregard were sui generis to it) the diversity of cultures, the uniqueness of other human beings, and, with the same carelessness, the formidable work of history. Its *eidos* is scarcely more than a rhetorical artifice. In this domain, the transcendental error consisted—and today still consists—of seeing as a universal notion what is after all only the purified version of one of our old native categories.

But can we, for all that, dispense with asking ourselves: how can such numerous definitions, arising from such different eras and temporal horizons, inspired by opposing opinions and at times promoting contending theses—how can they despite everything be brought so easily into agreement, apparently without it even being necessary to raise this point, to admit that something called religion, for better or worse, exists in most, if not all, human cultures? This amounts to admitting the idea of a humanity —and human beings—who are fundamentally religious. Otherwise, the deep disagreements, clearly expressed, could have gradually led to a challenge to the received idea of religion, where, conversely, its general recognition ought to have opened a door to the discovery of some undeniable universal trait or characteristic. These seem to be the two extreme options involved in the choice with which this strange situation confronts us. But what, curiously, do we be observe? That disagreement finds expression, admittedly, but without ever quitting a kind of preestablished framework in which this notion seems obvious, irrefutable, as if the word and the thing "went without saying." No doubts, no reservations are expressed with regard to them.

But, at the same time, as we have seen, this tacit agreement hardly goes beyond a schematic definition of religion, about which the least that one can say is that it is content to express, with no little naïveté and conviction, the narcissistic ambitions of an ecumenical Christianity—to such an extent and so thoroughly that we cannot very well see what other civilizations would have been or would be capable of recognizing themselves in it. It is true that Western thought has never been very concerned with this aspect of things, the paradoxes that it could contain, never having asked other cultures what they thought of the concepts that it imposed on them. In a fashion that we might qualify as compulsive, this symbolic violence was always followed or accompanied by very real violence. It cannot be too strongly stated that since the end of the fifteenth century, the West has associated its imperialist perspectives and conquests more and more explicitly with its own conceptions of mankind with a view—if the neologism may be permitted—to "anthropologizing" these conceptions, to making them an absolute and universal point of reference. This process culminated in the second half of the nineteenth century, the period in which the history of religions was born.

This fundamental agreement, the fact that all European thinkers, or nearly all, judged the idea of an eminently religious human being to be just as obvious as the idea of religion, is a fact of primary importance. It proves that religion is inherent in Western culture, that it is situated in its very foundations, there where the deepest structures of thought are elaborated. As always, we must initially call attention to the cultural weight of the Christian religion in any reflection concerning religion (its definition, nature, or attributes). No discussion, no intellectual controversy on the subject ever proceeds other than within its own limits, with the aid of arguments and ideas that were fashioned by it or in its interest. This soothing procedure, although it avoids the most striking contradictions, is surely condemned to add nothing new to its own presuppositions. For (as a variant on Gödel's theorem) one cannot speak analytically of a form of knowledge with the vocabulary of that knowledge, a fortiori when it has borrowed its nomenclature and a good share of its essential conceptions from the sphere of the object that is supposedly under study! Discursive circularity (speaking of things in the language of these same things) is guaranteed.

In addition, who cannot see that disagreements on the nature or role of religion are in reality engaging in another debate, one more metaphysical than scientific. Behind it, it is in fact (to be brief) a question of the existence of God, since, for many Western minds, denying the idea of religion is tantamount to denying the existence of the divinity. (In the Christian conception, is not religion the eternal, unchanging bond that unites the creature with his creator? In this perspective, human beings, religion, and the divinity form a unique, indivisible ensemble—they mutually imply each other.) The presence of this theological equation has continuously sidetracked all debate. A regrettable confusion constantly arises between religious ideas and ideas about religion. We could not talk about the one set of ideas without these opinions reverberating noisily among the others.

Nothing authorizes us to claim that this equivocation has dissipated today. The modern history of religions has too often remained captive to these same metaphysical controversies, in which it could only become mired down. And although it has stimulated a certain number of opinions and an even greater number of discussions, it has not generated many original analyses or fertile reflections. Most have remained prisoners of its religious past.

> And in these four things, opinions of ghosts, ignorance of second causes, devotion towards what men fear, and taking of things casuall for prognostiques, consisteth the natural seed of religion, which by reason of the different fancies, judgments, and passions of several men, hath grown up into ceremonies so different, that those which are used by one man, are for the most part ridiculous to another. (Thomas Hobbes, *Leviathan*, 1651)

> We may conclude, therefore, that in all nations . . . the first ideas of religion arose not from a contemplation of the works of nature, but from a concern with regard to the events of life, and from the incessant hopes and fears, which actuate the human mind. (David Hume, *Dialogues on Natural Religion*, 1757)

> In a general way . . . we designate as religious the relationship of man with the sacred, which is expressed, as subjective religion, in veneration and adoration and which is incarnated, as objective religion, in confession, in speech, in acts . . . and in law. (*Dictionary of Theology* [1960s])[2]

> But when religion—consciousness of God—is designated as the self-consciousness of man, this is not to be understood as affirming that the religious man is directly aware of this identity; for, on the contrary, ignorance of it is fundamental to the particular nature of religion. To preclude this misconception, it is better to say, religion is man's earliest and also indirect form of self-knowledge. Hence, religion everywhere precedes philosophy, as in the history of the race, so also in that of the individual. (Ludwig Feuerbach, *Das Wesen des Christentums*, 1841)

> The wretchedness of religion is at once an expression of and a protest against real wretchedness. Religion is the sigh of the oppressed creature, the heart of a heartless world and the soul of soulless conditions. It is the opium of the people. The abolition of religion as the illusory happiness of the people is a demand for their true happiness. The call to abandon illusions about their condition is the call to abandon a condition which requires illusions. (Karl Marx, *Zur Kritik der hegelschen Rechtphilosophie: Einleitung*, 1844)

> Religion is (considered subjectively) the recognition of all our duties as divine commands. (Immanuel Kant, *Die Religion innerhalb der Grenzen der blossen Vernunft*, 1793)

> The essence of religion consists in the feeling of an absolute dependence. (Friedrich Schleiermacher, *Christliche Glaubenslehre*, 1821)

Religious feeling is born of man's perceived need to enter into communication with invisible forces. (Benjamin Constant, *De la religion,* 1830)

Religion, therefore, as I now ask you arbitrarily to take it, shall mean for us the feelings, acts, and experience of individual men in their solitude, so far as they apprehend themselves to stand in relation to whatever they may consider the divine. Since the relation may be either moral, physical, or ritual, it is evident that out of religion in the sense in which we take it, theologies, philosophies, and ecclesiastical organizations may secondarily grow. In these lectures, however, as I have already said, the immediate personal experience will amply fill our time, and we shall hardly consider theology or ecclesiasticism at all. (William James, *The Varieties of Religious Experience,* 1906)

Religion is intimate prayer and deliverance. It is so inherent in man that he would be unable to tear it from his heart without condemning himself to be separated from himself and to kill that which constitutes his very humanity. (Auguste Sabatier, *Outlines of a Philosophy of Religion,* 1897)

[Religion] is a commerce, a conscious and willed relation into which the soul in distress enters with the mysterious power on which it feels that it and its destiny depend. (Auguste Sabatier, ibid., 1897)

[Religion is] the manner in which man realizes his relationship with superhuman, mysterious powers on which he believes himself dependent. (Eugène Goblet d'Alviella, *Introduction à l'histoire générale des religions,* 1887)

Summing up in the broadest possible way the characteristics of the religious life, as we have found them, it includes the following beliefs:

1. That the visible world is part of a more spiritual universe from which it draws its chief significance;
2. That union or harmonious relations with that higher universe is our true end;
3. That prayer or inner communion with the spirit thereof—be that spirit 'God' or 'law'—is a process wherein work is really done, and spiritual energy flows in and produces effects, psychological or material, within the phenomenal world.
   Religion includes also the following psychological characteristics:
4. A new zest which adds itself like a gift to life, and takes the form either of lyrical enchantment or of appeal to earnestness and heroism.
5. An assurance of safety and a temper of peace, and, in relation to others, a preponderance of loving affections. (William James, *The Varieties of Religious Experience,* 1906)

[Religion] consists of two parts: the first an easily definable, if not precisely specific feeling; and the second [of] certain specific arts, customs, beliefs, and conceptions associated with this feeling. The belief most inextricably connected with the specific feeling is a belief in spirits outside of man, conceived of as more powerful than man and as controlling all those elements in life upon which he lays most stress. (Paul Radin, *La Religion primitive*, 1941)

In short, religion can be looked upon as an extension of the people's social relationship beyond the confines of purely human society. And for completeness' sake, we would perhaps add the rider that this extension must be one in which the human beings involved see themselves in dependent positions vis-à-vis their non-human alters—a qualification necessary to exclude pets from the pantheon of gods. (Robert Horton)

I shall define "religion" as an institution consisting of culturally patterned interaction with culturally postulated super-human beings. (M. E. Spiro, *Anthropological Approach to the Study of Religion*, 1966)

Religion signifies the totality of relations that exist between man and the invisible world. (Benjamin Constant, *De la religion*, 1830)

Set of doctrines and practices that constitute the relationship of man with divine power. (Émile Littré, *Dictionnaire de la langue française*, 1872)

Specific set of beliefs, moral rules, and cultural practices through which man establishes his relations with the divinity. (*Grand Larousse de la langue française*, 1977)[3]

Religions diametrically opposed in their overt dogmas, are yet perfectly at one in the tacit conviction that the existence of the world with all it contains and all which surrounds it, is a mystery ever pressing for interpretation. (Herbert Spencer, *First Principles*, 1862)

Religion is the determination of human life by the sentiment of a link uniting the human spirit with the mysterious spirit whose domination over the world and over himself he recognizes and with which he is pleased to feel himself united. (Albert Réville, *Prolégomènes de l'histoire des religions*, 1881)

A set of scruples hindering the free exercise of our faculties. (Salomon Reinach, *Orpheus: Histoire générale des religions*, 1909)

In its objective aspect, active religion consists, then, of attitudes, practices, rites, ceremonies, institutions; in its subjective aspect, it consists of desires, emotions, and ideas, instigating and accompanying these objective manifestations.

The reason for the existence of religion is not the objective truth of its conceptions, but its biological value. This value is to be estimated by its success in procuring not only the results expected by the worshipper, but also others, some of which are of great significance. (James H. Leuba, *A Psychological Study of Religion, Its Origin, Function, and Future,* 1912)

Religion consists of three elements: (1) the natural recognition of a Power or Powers beyond our control; (2) the feeling of dependence upon this Power or Powers; (3) entering into relations with this Power or Powers. Uniting these elements into a single proposition, religion may be defined as the natural belief in a Power or Powers beyond our control, and upon whom we feel ourselves dependent; which belief and feeling of dependence prompt (1) to organisation, (2) to specific acts, and (3) to the regulation of conduct, with a view to establishing favourable relations between ourselves and the Power or Powers in question. (Morris Jastrow, *The Study of Religion,* 1901)

We shall say then that there is religion everywhere and only where there is, implicit perhaps but certainly present and displaying its natural effects of seriousness, submission, fear, the transcendent nature of the Being who is the object of prayer, rite and sacrifice. Religion is then defined by the group of beliefs, feelings, rules and rites, individual or collective, directed toward (or imposed by) a Power that man currently holds as sovereign, on which he as a result depends, with which he can enter (or better, has entered) into personal relations. More briefly put, religion is the conversation of man, individual and social, with his God. (Léonce de Grandmaison, *Christus: La Religion chrétienne,* 1916)

On one hand, religious facts make religion manifest, one and indivisible, and the goal of history would be to reveal, in the phases through which it must pass, its permanence and identity. On the other, religious facts are the whole of religion; they can maintain a relative independence and can be studied for their specifics; this is the case in the present history. We obviously prefer this second method. (Henri Hubert, "Introduction" to *Manuel d'histoire des religions* [French translation of *Lehrbuch der Religionsgeschichte*] by P. D. Chantepie de la Saussaye, 1904)

A religion is a unified system of beliefs and practices relative to sacred things, that is to say, things set apart and forbidden—beliefs and practices which unite into one single moral community called a Church, all those who adhere to them. (Émile Durkheim, *Les Formes élémentaires de la vie religieuse,* 1912)

By religion I do not mean religious practices or specific beliefs, which so obviously vary from one social state to another. But true religion is surely

incapable of being born of any social connection; for there is in it a fundamental negation of all exterior givens and thereby a breaking away from the
group as well as from nature. The religious soul seeks itself and finds itself
beyond the social group, far from it and often against it. (Jules Lachelier, in
Oeuvres, vol. 2, 1913)

Men expect from the various religions answers to the unsolved riddles of
the human condition, which today even as in former times deeply stir the
hearts of men. (Vatican II, "Nostra Aetate," 1965)

We have determined the sphere of the phenomenon "religion": we have
included . . . beliefs, actions, institutions, behavior, etc. that, despite their
extreme variety, appear as the products of a particular type of creative effort
by various human societies, by virtue of which these societies strive to acquire control over that which, in their concrete experience of reality, seems
to escape all other means of control. (Angelo Brelich, "Prolégomènes à une
histoire des religions," in *Encyclopédie de la Pléiade*, vol. 1: *Histoire des religions*, 1970)

One fact can be established immediately: there is no common Indo-European term for "religion." (Émile Benveniste, *Le Vocabulaire des institutions
indo-européennes*, 1969)

Religion (from Latin *religare* "tie") is the bond that ties man to the sacred
and that prevents him from feeling lost in the midst of a world that he will
never totally dominate. It is then to be hoped that the crisis of agnosticism
through which Western civilization is currently passing will soon lead to
an authentic religious revival that will deliver us from our solitude. (Jean
Delumeau, in *Le Fait religieux*, 1993)

Religion is a mental faculty or disposition, which, independent of, nay in
spite of, sense and reason, enables man to apprehend the Infinite under different names, and under varying disguises. Without that faculty, no religion, not even the lowest worship of idols and fetishes, would be possible;
and if we will but listen attentively, we can hear in all religions a groaning
of the spirit, a struggle to conceive the inconceivable, to utter the unutterable, a longing after the Infinite, a love of God. (Max Müller, *Introduction to
the Science of Religion*, 1873)

[According to religion] all things are manifestations of a power that transcends our knowledge. (Herbert Spencer, *First Principles*, 1862)

The fundamental dogmas of religion are two in number: (1) the existence of
God, a living, perfect, all-powerful God; (2) the relationship, equally living
and concrete, of this God with man. (Émile Boutroux, *Science et religion*,
1908)

This metaphysics, which we might call popular metaphysics, is religion. However, religion consists of something more than the metaphysical ideas of the masses; it contains the capability of discerning the means and directions for arousing in a strong and lasting form the religious sentiment with this metaphysics for its foundation, —that is to say, religious cultus; and secondly, religion contains the deductions drawn from this metaphysics for the practical conduct of men; in other words, religious ethics. (Eduard von Hartmann, *The Religion of the Future,* 1900)

It is the realm where all enigmatic problems of the world are solved; where all contradictions of deep musing thoughts are unveiled and all pangs of feeling soothed. . . . The whole manifold of human relations, activities, joys, everything that man values and esteems, wherein he seeks his happiness, his glory and his pride—all find their final middle point in religion in the thought, consciousness, and feeling of God. (G. W. F. Hegel, *Philosophy of Religion,* 1840)

The result is that religion, as an integral part of human nature, is true in its essence, and that above the specific forms of the cult, necessarily marred by the same defects as the times and countries to which it belongs, there is Religion, the clear sign in man of a superior destiny. (Ernest Renan, *Études d'histoire des religions,* 1857)

Religions are groups of religious phenomena; Religion is the disposition of the human spirit that engenders these phenomena. (Eugène Goblet d'Alviella, *Introduction à l'histoire générale des religions,* 1887)

Religion . . . is a careful and scrupulous observation of . . . the "numinosum," that is . . . either a quality of a visible object or the influence of an invisible presence causing a peculiar alteration of consciousness. (C. G. Jung, *Psychologie und Religion,* 1958)

For religion is, as a matter of historical and psychological fact, always metaphysical. It is always a naïve or reasoned theory of reality. It is an attempt to explain human experience by relating it to invisible existence that belong, nevertheless, to the real world. (G. T. Ladd, *Journal of Philosophical, Psychological and Scientific Methods,* 1904)

In the sphere of religion the emotion consists in the consciousness that we are in the power of a Being whom we revere as the highest, and to whom we feel attracted and related; it consists in the adoration which impels us to dedicate ourselves entirely to the adored object, yet able to possess it and be in union with it. (Cornelius Tiele, *Science of Religion,* vol. 2, 1899)

In every religious belief, two things are necessarily included: an intellectual element, i.e., an item of knowledge constituting the object of the belief; an affective state, i.e., a feeling which accompanies the former and expresses itself in acts. (Théodule Ribot, *La Psychologie des sentiments,* 1896)

In all religion the endeavour is made, with the help of the exalted spiritual power which man adores, to solve the contradiction in which man finds himself as part of the natural world, and as a spiritual personality which makes the claim to rule nature. (Albrecht Ritschl, *Die christliche Lehre von der Rechtfertigung und Versöhnung,* vol. 3, 1874)

In the broadest and most general terms possible one might say that the religious life consists of the belief that there is an unseen order and that our supreme good lies in harmoniously adjusting ourselves thereto. This belief and this adjustment are the religious attitude of the soul. (William James, *The Varieties of Religious Experience,* 1908)

Religion rests above all upon the need of man to realize an harmonious synthesis between his destiny and the opposing influences he meets in the world. (Albert Réville, *La Religion des peuples non-civilisés,* 1881)

By religion, then, I understand a propitiation or conciliation of powers superior to man which are believed to direct and control the course of nature and of human life. (Sir James Frazer, *The Golden Bough,* 1900)

[I]ts function is first to validate and fortify authority, consequently to make the strong and powerful more strong and powerful . . . but second, it goes very far in protecting and supporting the weak, notably women and children, old age, widows and orphans. . . . The influence of the first function is eminently political, while the second may be called ethical. (Ferdinand Tönnies, "The Origin and Function of Religion," 1906)

Religion is at the core of it, for religion is the connection of man's life with the absolute, and the moral law is an absolute law. (Felix Adler, *The Religion of Duty,* 1905)

All religion begins in cosmic emotion. (R. J. Campbell, *The New Theology*)

[Religion is] the sane and normal response of the human spirit to all that we know of cosmic law; that is, to the known phenomena of the universe, regarded as an intelligible whole. (F. W. H. Myers, *Human Personality*)

This universal postulate, the psychic origin of all religious thought, is the recognition, or, if you please, the assumption, that conscious volition is the ultimate source of all Force. It is the belief that behind the sensuous, phenomenal world, distinct from it, giving it form, existence, and activity, lies the ultimate, invisible, immeasurable power of Mind, of conscious will, of Intelligence, analogous in some way to our own; and—mark this essential corollary,—that man is in communication with it. (Daniel G. Brinton, *Religions of Primitive Peoples*)

All ideas and feelings are religious that refer to an ideal existence. (Wilhelm Wundt, *Ethik,* 1886)

It is important to distinguish two meanings for the word "religion." The one, subjective, envisages religion as an attitude of the soul; it concerns above all the psychologist. The other, objective, sees religion as a reality exterior to individual conscience; it concerns in particular the historian.

In the objective sense, trying to encompass in the definition all the traits most commonly admitted as characteristics and to set aside the solution of contested problems, it seems that one could say: religion is a collection of beliefs and practices (or practical attitudes) concerning a reality, personal or impersonal, unique, multiple or collective, but in some fashion supreme, on which man in one way or another sees himself as dependent and with which he wishes to enter into a relationship. (Henry Pinard de la Boullaye, *L'Étude comparée des religions,* 1925)

An Absence of Criteria

If the search for a rigorous, coherent definition of religion meets with powerful intellectual prejudices stemming from the Christian tradition and, in a certain way, from the banality of all those that have been proposed for more than a century, one could think that this failure resulted from several factors, foremost among which we see the absence of any systematic thought aimed at determining satisfactory analytical criteria capable of winning unanimity among scholars, simply (and even if this seems surprising) because we have witnessed no true effort aimed at defining what should be the status and function of these criteria. However, for such a sensitive question, it would have been, and still remains, indispensable to ask (beyond the illusory comfort offered by superficial comparisons limited to summary statements or misleading schematizations), what kinds of criteria should have been chosen for this purpose. But the determination of such criteria presupposes that we have defined an exact protocol for research, which then would have reviewed and carefully examined the different options available (conventional, heuristic, empirical, logicistic, deductive, and others), that would have distinguished different possible levels of intervention (factual, structural, functional, symbolic, formal, transcendental, etc.), that would have tried to excise or at least call attention to its most operative presuppositions, and that finally would have specified where the epistemological conditions and limitations for their use are situated.

But instead of this, what have we seen and do we still observe today? In a general way, that people have casually chosen the Western Christian model as reference, reduced to what is considered its central framework in order to make of it a kind of ideal, intangible norm. What do we most often find in this doxa? Essentially, three things, of which one, the first, is already familiar: (1) the affirmation of the existence of God and of the living link that unites the mortal creature to him; (2) a Church or priestly organization; and lastly (3) sacraments and ceremonies, that is, according to the nomenclature proposed by Hubert and Mauss, beliefs, institutions, and practices.[4] We may note in passing that this tripartite assemblage is to be found almost everywhere (what class of social phenomena does not entail the concomitant action of beliefs, institutions, and practices?), and that as a result it is difficult to recognize any religious specificity here.

But the anthropological illusion began, as noted above, when complexes were distinguished within the continuum of other cultures that consisted *grosso modo* of the same elements but lacked precisely the essential element, that is, of existing as an original structure within these cultures. Admittedly, it is fairly easy to isolate, for example, in the mass of known ancient Indian facts (for example, in the Rig-Veda), a series of apparently comparable elements (gods, a priesthood, and sacrificial rites) and to consider them religious. Yet by so doing, we forget to stipulate that this complex is, in India, artificial, that it corresponds to nothing, since, from the Indian point of view, it refers to no distinct domain or notion.

Let us imagine the inverse situation and ask what we would think of a learned Hindu pandit who eruditely questioned whether the public ceremony celebrated in France on July 14 [or on July 4 in the United States] could be called a *yajña*—a matter of some significance for anyone trying to define the essence of *yajña* (usually translated as "sacrifice"), and who might suppose that it was to be found, albeit in less complete or, frankly, primitive form, among all peoples. Would we for all that admit the universality of the term and, with it, the profoundly yajñic character of humanity or human cultures? How would we feel about this Indian ambition to found a yajñic anthropology conceived in the image of, and as a rival to, our religious anthropology? Mightn't we call it a caricature of a comparison, and indecent or even sacrilegious? But is what Western scholars have been doing for centuries with the term "religious"—most of them without the least embarrassment—any less ridiculous or pretentious?

Thus the Aśvamedha [horse sacrifice] and Rājasuya [coronation sacrifice], those great royal rituals of Vedic India, are classified among the most spectacular liturgical celebrations in Vedic religion.[5] But how are they more essentially religious than our ceremonies of July 14 and November 11 [Armistice Day], even when the latter are accompanied by a memorial service? For Vedic thought, one of the essential oppositions was between public rites and private rites (between rites that did or did not include the recitation by Brahmans of texts drawn from Śruti)[6] and not between religious and political rites, since the latter two general categories do not exist as such, even implicitly. In the eyes of the ancient Indians, the totality of elements and events of the world depends in any case on an impersonal and probably uncreated cosmic order (*ṛta* or dharma).[7] On what grounds could we assert that some of them were more religious than others? And what definition would then have to be given to this qualifier?

But, in a way that is to some degree itself dictated by the implicit reference to the Christian model, the Vedic example offered above (gods/priesthood/solemn rites) constitutes a case relatively favorable to the Western thesis. In reality, if, beside the gods, we do not forget to cite all the varieties of demons, of supernatural powers and beings, to call attention, with regard to the gods themselves, to their differing ontologies; if, further, we do not neglect to ascribe to the Brahmans the totality of their functions and attributions (poets, jurists, pedagogues, counselors, etc.) and, lastly, if we do not forget that the great, solemn Vedic rites (against which no doubt, innumerable magic practices competed) are more concerned with the permanence of the cosmos and of society than with the obligation to devote an exclusive personal cult to this or that god—then, the tripartite block (gods/priesthood/public rites) established in the Western pattern would be bound either to shatter or be substantially distorted.

Moreover, it is the very existence of this triform block and its relevance that must be questioned afresh here, because the Indian elements noted above, completely reestablished, would show that they are closely associated with others that we call "social," "economic," "juridical," "political," and so on, which, together with them, constitute an original culture founded on principles worth as much as our own. This does not, however, authorize us to dismember them, to extract them arbitrarily from their context and, finally, to redistribute them in our own mental space.

If we do not respect the structural uniqueness of each cultural continuum, all cultures in effect become comparable, but at the price precisely of that which made them unique. This tendency is accentuated even more by the substantialist approaches or conceptions of religion, according to which it is understood that every religion ought to possess just such a series of elements (of the gods/priesthood/rites type). But here we face a super-annuated conception, the distant heir of scholastic Aristotelianism, which disregards all those more modern conceptions that assert that the essential is situated elsewhere, not in these series of discrete elements, but in net-works of relationships, in structural homologies, in information systems, or in symbolic representations and functions.

On the other hand, the arbitrary dismemberment that results from fol-lowing the Christian norm leads to absurdities or disfigurations that are difficult to accept. Did the warriors of that far-off Vedic era who asked the god Indra for victory in combat and fabulous booty experience sensations similar to those described by Bernadette Soubirous and Thérèse de l'Enfant-Jésus at the end of the nineteenth century? Doesn't the very question seem absurd to us (which in no way prevents us, however, from considering all these facts as religious phenomena)? Nevertheless, if the pragmatic con-texts are dissimilar,[8] if the supernatural interlocutors involved are very dif-ferent from one another,[9] and if, finally, the sentiments felt and the emo-tions experienced by the human actors are strangely different, how can we say that despite everything, these situations are all equally religious? By reason of the origins that have given it such an original profile, the con-cept of religion is incapable of integrating or explaining such differences. Its capacity to subsume or encompass this diversity in pertinent fashion without disfiguring or impoverishing it is, in reality, very slight.

In order to create the possibility for it to be universally valid, the notion of religion has often been reduced, as we have seen, to a kind of simpli-fied schema, a minimalist definition. Unfortunately, even in this abstract, quintessential form, we are no more successful in locating it in other hu-man cultures. Thus, we have already called attention to the case of religions (with the understanding that it is we who call them so) that do not pos-sess a significant god or gods, similarly to the Epicureanism of antiquity (Confucianism and Buddhism, for example), religions without true specific institutions (the majority), or show beliefs and practices that are as much political as religious, and so on. Are we, moreover, capable of determin-ing exactly where in traditional or ancient societies the limits of the corre-sponding domains lie? But this, of course, involves our own conventions.

Would we be exaggerating in saying that the Christian model is with-out doubt the *least* exemplary and that, had it not been for the support lent it by Western cultural and military imperialism, it is probably not the point of reference that modern anthropological thought ought to have chosen? But it is equally true that the latter is one of the purest products to emerge from this hegemonic stance.

Lastly, we should not fail to note that all these discussions or controversies have occurred only in the West (or in imitation of the West) with the help of *its* categories and *its* terminology alone—no account was ever taken of the others, all the other peoples. If the West has willingly spoken of the religions of the Chinese, Inuit, Papuans, Bororos, and so on, it has never permitted the latter to speak of them in their own tongues. Its few, rare lexical loans from exotic cultures ("mana," "tabu," "totem," "voodoo," etc.) never served for more than the description or explanation of religions or religious phenomena it considered primitive. No important concept was borrowed by the history of religions from any foreign cultural sphere at all!—as if it were self-evident that the Western, Christian, Platonic terminology ("god," "soul," "faith," "belief," "rite," "church," "priest," "providence," etc.), specific as it is, held the power to describe everything and understand everything, starting with mankind.

In the same fashion, people speak of Greek or Roman religion, doubtless without noticing in the case of the latter that, as Georges Dumézil observes, "Latin has no word to designate religion. *Religio, caerimonia,* the latter of obscure origin, do not cover the semantic field; both are frequently used in the plural."[10] But what were the content and structure of this pre-Christian religious field? Was it more or less religious (on what grounds and to what degree?) than the one that would succeed it? In order better to measure the ironic scope of this last question, let us try to imagine what would be entailed, solely from an intellectual and psychological point of view, in personal "conversion" to the Roman paganism of the age of Augustus. Must we admit that something, religion, could have preexisted its appearance in history, that it could have preceded the technical acceptance of the word, which is contemporary with the invention of the thing in question? Committing such an anachronism is possible only by tacitly admitting that the word actually refers to something atemporal that appears in all cultures (but a "something" that would assume its consummate form in our civilization alone). Otherwise, if we wish to use the word "religion" as a simple, conventional designation, consequently shorn of all scientific value, it would first be necessary to divest it explicitly of all specific characteristics intrinsically tied to its Western Christian meaning.

Can we imagine for an instant that Western thought could borrow "its" anthropological criteria intended to define religion from sources other than itself? This would be equivalent to recognizing its inability to conceive of the universal, while taking the additional risk of recognizing that these criteria are not suitable for Christianity or, worse, that they reduce it to the status of an aberrant or monstrous example. The risk that is run is in any case purely imaginary, for, it must be asked again, how could Western epistemology ever accept or even conceive of a universally valid terminology that did not originate within itself and that might have been arrived at, for example, on the basis of the terminology of Chinese, Quechua, or Dogon? Under the heading of "universal," invented by us and reserved for our sole use, we arrange facts and attitudes that are at best only abstractions constructed on the very limited basis of our own categories. This is why we so easily manage to convince ourselves that these abstractions are present among us in their most perfect form.

Thus the irreducible specificity of the religious and its universality, so often proclaimed, are perhaps nothing more than an empty core around which the West has wrapped its discourse on religion, on *its* religion. The imprecision and plasticity of the concepts that it has used for this purpose have doubtless assisted, as have the endless interpretations appearing in all the texts that, with the aid of enigmatic symbols or elaborate allegories, evoke the origin of the world or the status of humankind.

And when, more recently, some European thinkers have tried to substitute for the concept of religion some notion judged by them more essential, they neither propose a more radical change of perspective nor renew the received conceptual apparatus. On the contrary, they are content to go searching in the heart of the traditional religious for something susceptible, according to them, of transcending it, such as faith (according to Karl Barth) or the notion of the sacred (according to several contemporary phenomenologists and theologians). Could we conceive of a vainer campaign than this tireless effort devoted to greater and greater absorption in the Western adjective "religious," in its own narcissistic categories? And to believe that one is escaping history when in fact one submits oneself entirely to it. As Ernesto de Martino so correctly wrote about the ahistorical theses of Mircea Eliade: "Eliade asserts that man is opposed to history, even when he strives to make it . . . but the truth is that man is in history even when he claims to escape it."

Far from opening itself to others or looking to free itself from its theological origins, Western thought directed at religion seems incapable of pursuing other avenues or of looking for other issues than those that invariably bring it back to its lonely face-to-face encounter with itself.

Imprecise and Shifting Boundaries

If there is one point on which history and anthropology can understand each other and agree, it must be this: every human group, in order to exist and to perpetuate itself as such, is obliged to develop and preserve a set of ideas, opinions, and diverse theses, themselves passed on and deepened by images, symbols, and myths concerning humankind, the world, and society. And this complex set, formed of a tangled multitude, is so indispensable, so intrinsically tied to the existence of the group itself that it finally appears (even if it is, from a metaphysical point of view, perfectly contingent) as its exclusive reference. A fortiori, this illusion is fundamental for its proponents, who have no other way to think themselves and the world than to draw from its own repertory of ideas and notions.

According to the times and cultural shifts, but especially according to the argumentative models that are adopted, the French and English languages, each in its way, have given different names to these complexes, names that extend from the humblest prescriptions associated with everyday life to the loftiest philosophical flights. Depending on the case, people speak of ideology, doctrine, cosmology, global vision or theory, or philosophy, when it is the *speculative* intellectual aspect that is privileged. On the other hand, in conformity with an old dichotomy that was already well known to Greek thought, when the practical aspect is in view, an equivalent is sought among the following terms: wisdom, morality, art or manner of living, discipline, ethics, path, road (*odos* in the New Testament, *tao* in Chinese, *mārga* in Sanskrit).

Our word "religion" (independently of its most specifically Christian characteristics) to some degree signifies all this at one and the same time. On these grounds, it would be more judicious, as has already been proposed, to include it in the vaster, more intelligible category of "cosmographic formations." This term, freed of all religious concern and all Western prejudice, has the advantage of calling attention to the fact that the formations in question possess a global coherence and are at the same time positioned with respect both to representation, that is, weltanschauung, and existence, individual or collective, in which the corresponding ideas are incarnated in the form of practices, institutions, ways of being, observances, rules for life, and corporeal expressions.

Since there is as yet no history of cosmographic formations, but only a very Western epistemology or history of religions, it is the limits (if there are undeniable limits) that the latter have attributed to religion(s) that must be identified. But here, too, and just as before when we addressed the questions of definitions and criteria, the inquiry soon meets with disappointment.

We note, to begin with, that limits, however arbitrary and fluid they may be, are indispensable to the exercise of all communication and thought. This is why, while admitting that we are incapable of defining in rigorous fashion what philosophy, religion, or literature might be, we regularly use these terms, which, in this limited general use, have proved to be irreplaceable. This then means that even if the words "philosophy," "religion," and "literature" have no corresponding definitions or stable referents (which would make them, at least on the scale of European culture, universals of a kind), it would still be true that here and now these terms offer numerous advantages, both practical and institutional (what would our schools do without them?), so true is it that, inserted between imprecise limits and the total absence of limits, the conventional nature and pragmatic function of language has made such general terms indispensable.

On the other hand, as we often observe in the human sciences (where supposedly "scientific" terminology is frequently drawn from the vocabulary used by each of us in everyday language) that the hegemony of ordinary language does not permit us to make an easy distinction between casual language and its more idealist uses, or to imagine that any critical function could be assigned to it: the common standard use of the word "religion" does not preclude us—quite the contrary—from giving it a significance that Cratylus would not have disowned (that is, religion, the absolute idea or essence supposed to be present in every religion); this is why this confused situation makes difficult (except at the cost of endless redefinitions and precautions) any hypothetical, experimental—that is, heuristic—use of this same word.

It is undeniable that several effects complicate this matter, none of which facilitates the task of scientific inquiry. John Locke deplored this at length in the third book of his *Essay Concerning Human Understanding*, and we can only follow his lead: (1) in order to think and to speak, according to the well-known principle of economy, we need general terms; (2) these general terms exist; (3) unfortunately, each of us constantly uses them ("religion," "philosophy," "literature"), both in everyday language and in scientific terminology; (4) in addition, spheres of knowledge, fixed by definition and used in the schools, correspond to each of these three terms; and (5) their limits, although quite imprecise and in any case unstable (when they are examined over a lengthy period), apparently correspond to a certain way, conventional and thus arbitrary, of dissecting and organizing the world of intellectual productions.

In this regard, it is even allowed to be quite categorical, since these general terms, and with them their empirical domains and their limits, scarcely have any equivalents beyond the West. How could we consider literature or religion to be universals? To put it another way, these conventional limits (like most limits in this respect) have only a very approximate scientific value, a value that is admittedly most often quite problematic. They too have been produced—and neither immediately nor once and for all—not by a timeless objective mind, concerned uniquely with scientific rigor, but by a historical community preoccupied above all with a concern to preserve the order that dominates its own conception of knowledge about the world and, eventually, with the ambition to impose it on others.

This is why, once we venture beyond Christian cultural space, the use of the word "religion," and in particular the need to say what the term covers, leads to banalities (since there doubtless exists no element, in a premodern society, whose description does not include some supernatural intervention, irrational belief, or symbolic signification, so we quickly find the religious everywhere for lack of being able to define the proper sphere of religion) or we find absurdities. Let me briefly cite a few examples, which return to or advance the observations made above.

By which rigorous criteria—that is, criteria employable in scientific argument, or at least in a serious conversation—can we distinguish what in Plato's work belongs, respectively, to philosophy, theology, and religion? Would we have to agree in advance on what is meant by the word "philosophy"? Would we use it in its modern meaning or as used in antiquity (whether pre- or post-Platonic)? These do not have much to do with each other. But then in the name of what (which history or which concept?) do we group in the same class "philosophers" as different as Iamblichus and Wittengenstein, Pythagoras and Sartre? And we should not forget that "our" Plato is very different from the Plato of the first Christian thinkers who willingly appropriated him, only too happy with the windfall, by making him a disciple of Moses or the Hebrews, just as he is different from that of Proclus, their pagan contemporary. Let us recall that at the time of Proclus, the fifth century of our era, the study of Plato followed that of mathematics and Aristotle and was preparatory to a consideration of the Chaldean Oracles and the Orphic writings. Could we today imagine a more surprising fate for the work of one of the greatest Western philosophers, thus reduced to serving as propaedeutic to an esoteric theology?

The Stoics pose a problem no less troublesome than Plato, for their teachings, as Émile Bréhier so clearly emphasized, seek precisely to transcend the various arts, sciences, religions, and social obligations in favor of a practical wisdom in conformity with the intuitive grasp of a cosmos, an intelligible and providential nature. And this Stoic ethics coexisted in Rome with civic cults, beliefs that had come from the Orient, mysteries, divinatory arts, an incalculable number of superstitious practices, and the ever-powerful magic. Where, under these conditions (and whatever our definition), are the beginning and end of the religion that we would ascribe to Rome at the beginning of our era? On the other hand, would we say that the official, public cult was more, or less, religious than the conscience of a Seneca? But can we exclude the latter from the moral history and thus, in more than one respect, from the religious history of the West?

Still looking to Rome, to what (in our idea of religion) would we refer the opposition established there between *sacra* and *auspicia*?[11] Is this dichotomy any less relevant (and if so on what grounds?) from the semiotic point of view than the opposition, more familiar to us, of the sacred and the profane, the basis on which so many fine minds have established what they consider to be the foundation of all religious attitudes? The structural organization of a vision of the world founded on the opposition *sacra/auspicia* is as valid as one based on the pair sacred/profane in the sense that both relate to and have value only in the worlds that are built on them. What is universal in this case is not the one rather than the other but the fact that both display the same bipolar organization.

These unstable and intellectually unsatisfactory divisions engender orphans and bastards as well. Does philosophy or religion claim the right to study hermetical writings or the corpus of esoteric works? Who, on an even more general level, is ready to admit that the "occult sciences" (magic, sorcery, astrology, divination, superstition, spiritualism, and the like) effectively represent—in addition to official religion and philosophy, those noble and worthy fields of knowledge—the current that has surely counted for most in the mental history of the West, pagan and Christian? In most cases, the human sciences almost always disregard them or grant them at best a marginal place—like that always ceded to them by official religion, and it is the latter that has drawn the limits and pronounced the anathema that epistemology, much later, would adopt. But what is the value of a division of learning founded on such debatable grounds?

Similarly, in the name of which scientific criteria has it been decided that magic, divination, astrology, horoscopes, pharmacology, alchemy, sorcery, and secret initiatory teachings do not belong to the religious sphere? In point of fact, no scientific criterion can be invoked. For here again, epistemology has assumed official Christianity's execrations and prejudices. It and it alone has arbitrarily excluded magic, divination, alchemy, and the rest from the religious. It is enough to think of the importance that divination had in Rome; alchemy and the techniques of long life in China; Indian or Mesopotamian astrology; or the magical practices that can be observed (almost) everywhere to understand to which degree these "techniques" are absolutely not dismissible or marginal. In what way is a conception of the world ruled by the movement of the stars, the equilibrium of the five elements, the powers of jade, or the flight of birds less moral, less reassuring, less human, less fantastic than the conception of the world ruled by an ineffable God who expresses himself through winged angels, or seraphim?

But we soon see the threat and danger posed by taking these techniques into account: either Western epistemology, for whatever reason one chooses to imagine, includes them in its canonical definition of the religious, and it would then be our habitual designation that would prove incomplete or false (for we have seen that our own anthropological and sociological conceptions of mankind depend on it), or it excludes them from its definition, but then runs the risk of remaining captive to its contradictions and the Christian heritage. At bottom, it has only two ways in which to be mistaken, either through dogmatic unfaithfulness or through excessive faithfulness, but always in relation to this traditional notion.

The exterior limits recognized for religion are in fact so problematic to define that even here, in the West, the most eminent jurists and most expert theologians prove incapable of saying what distinguishes a religion from a cult, while at the same time appearing to insist on this distinction and at times being prompt to declare it undeniable. Is there no difference between them? some ironic spirits will ask in the face of this hesitation and discomfort. In reality, this uneasiness is fairly readily explained. Latin *secta* did not have a pejorative coloring, and the word did not acquire one for a long time. Moreover, the first Christian thinkers used it to designate their own community: religions and sects have often been associated. What would American Protestantism be without sects? Contemporary sects draw their inspiration, to the point of simulation and even caricature, from the dogmas and ceremonies that can be observed in the various Christian denominations. What is held against the one greatly risks rebounding against the others (in what way is the Roman Catholic catechism taught to young children less divisive than the gospel of the Reverend Moon?). In fact, sects lack only one thing, which is not in itself a defect and is not situated on the level of definition or principle: participation in, or better still, representation of the dominant vision of a large community of individuals. With this they would cease ipso facto to be considered occult, minority groups.[12]

If we really move away from the West, the contradictions and aberrations become so ridiculous that they paralyze all serious reflection. Let's begin again by examining a few examples from a rather different angle.

On what grounds would we say, for example, that the teaching of the Indian Upanishads is religious, since (deliberately putting itself on a level of the gnostic type) it is uninterested in rites, is attached to no church, and is ignorant of any idea of a divine being? Is a metaphysics that leads to practical wisdom a religion? The same question, now asked of yoga, creates the same difficulty: practical philosophy or ascetic wisdom (rather like the Pythagoreans)? Individualist religion? It is, however, true that the Upanishads and yoga do not have exact homologues or equivalents in Western culture (which does not prevent us from thinking—again—that our Western concept itself might have an incontestable universal purpose), any more than the corresponding conceptions of mankind on which they are based.

We have already, with so many others, mentioned the case of the Buddha. Where shall we situate his teaching, which denies the existence of the soul (as individual, immortal principle) and the transcendence of the gods, but which stimulated the birth of various cults around the figure of its author? If these cults merit the term "religious," then so would many heroic cults, ancestor cults, or the one that Mao Tse-tung tried to impose, because associated with these cults were real conceptions of the world and mankind, incarnated in institutions and possessed, as well, of an ethics, a cosmogony, and an apocalypse. On what level are the cults of exceptional persons different—substantially different—from a superstitious believer's worship of the relics of a prestigious saint?

Would we agree with Pinard de la Boullaye that Buddhism is an "atheist philosophy"? But we immediately see that it would follow that a good part of Western philosophy would have to be qualified as theist, counting, as it does, so many theologians and spiritualist metaphysicians in its ranks. And if we decided that the dividing line finally runs between "philosophies," theist or otherwise, that have engendered true collective belief, and "philosophies," theist or not, that have remained simple speculative works, we would have served our idea of religion in no better fashion, for this is a distinction that it accepts only on the condition that theism and atheism not figure on the same side of the dividing line. If it is true that our idea of religion does not admit that a religion can be individual, it is just as inadmissible that it could be atheist.

The best-known paradoxical example remains Confucianism, which the West stubbornly insists on classifying among the great religions of humanity, while in the opinion of the most authoritative experts this "religion" has no "religious basis":

> The revelation to which it refers is not divine but human: it is the fruit of the remarkable wisdom of the saintly kings of antiquity, armed with quasi-scientific techniques of divination. . . . These texts then treat of something very different from religion: basically, they deal with all Chinese culture as the particular form of a certain approach to the harmony of society and its positive integration into the entire universe, on the basis of a conception of mankind and the world, of a construction of values and morality, of an organization of institutions and the economy to which China has attached its tradition.[13]

Beyond the contradiction, amusing to note (how can we effectively speak of religion in instances where precisely our most important criteria for the religious are lacking?), it is the "why" that is important. And the response to this question is to be found in the intellectual attitude adopted by the West and by Western anthropology vis-à-vis other civilizations. We prefer to attribute to them a religion (which will in any case be "exotic," "primitive," "uncontrolled," "inferior," "imperfect," "abnormal," or "ignorant," etc.) tacitly conceived on the Christian model, though lacking precisely its constituent characteristics (a unique, omniscient God, the soul, the Church, faith, and so on), rather than challenging the foundations of *our* anthropology. For among this anthropology's principles is precisely the religion that we have already shown to be intrinsically tied to the fate of Western thought and peoples. Quite clearly, this attitude has nothing scientific about it, since in its own way, it expresses the persistence of an attachment to a concept and way of apprehending the world and humanity in which the West recognizes itself, even as we recognize ourselves. Nor can atheism, conceived in terms of negations of, or antitheses to, religion, make us any less Western.

Arbitrary Typologies

It is in keeping with the spirit of a signal confusion (whose pernicious character has been noted more than once) that if the history of religions is completely unable to assign precise limits to religion or to the sphere called religious, whatever the extension given this concept, the limits of the history of religions are themselves even less certain, since added to the imprecise boundaries of its object are those of its own scholarly undertakings, these associated in turn with various auxiliary sciences. The philological analysis of a passage of the *Iliad* is counted here just as well as the archaeological study of Germanic bracteates, a philosophical meditation on the notion of the sacred, a sociological investigation into the use of hallucinogenic substances in a Californian sect. Yet each of these approaches at times possesses, along with of a specific philosophy, its own analytical instruments, its own intellectual tradition, and, doubtless, its own way of reconstructing reality.

The taxonomies (admittedly summary) that the history of religions has developed over more than a century in order to try to classify various religions betrays an inefficiency no less great and an ethnocentrism no less fervid. It is perhaps in them that we are best able to observe to what extent Western epistemology, incorrigible as it is, has always under cover of classification created a cult faithful to itself by raising its own prejudices to the rank of universal or absolute categories. But since these prejudices are shared by the majority of Westerners—both scholars and the general public—this illusion is probably destined for a long life.

These successive classification projects, from Hegel to Ricoeur, can be summarized in two great models, which themselves find expression in different ways. The first, binary in nature, is content to contrast and (by the very fact of its choice of descriptive terms) to hierarchize, two types of religion. The second model is evolutionist and allows of several types, although most often just three types, of religion.[14] Here are the best-known examples that correspond to the first model; in some cases, the initial proponent of the distinction can be identified:

— True religion (note the singular)/false religions[15]
— Revealed religions/natural religions

— Founded religions/ popular or traditional religions
— Monotheistic religions/ polytheistic religions
— Dogmatic religions/ mythological religions
— Universal religions/ Local and ethnic religions
— Civilized religions/ primitive religions
— Historical religions/ cosmic religions
— Prophetic religions/ mystical religions (R. C. Zaehner)
— Religions of the spirit/ religions of authority (Auguste Sabatier)
— Religions of proclamation/ Religions of manifestation (Paul Ricoeur)

Now the most celebrated formulations of the second taxonomic model:

— Natural religion, artificial religion, absolute religion (G. W. F. Hegel)
— Fetishist, polytheistic, monotheistic religions
— Naturist, animist, mythological, polytheistic, legalist, and mono-theistic religions (Albert Réville)
— Religions of nature, or morality, or redemption (Hermann Siebeck)
— Natural religions (polyzoolatric, polydemonic, and polytheistic), ethnic religions (national or universal) (Cornelius Tiele)

Of the reflections that these two lists inspire, let us outline only the most obvious, which annul or condition all the rest. Whether they oppose two types or have several ascending stages succeeding one another, these classifications agree on one point, which when all is said and done is the only one that counts. The positive pole of the opposition or the supreme stage of the evolution is in each case occupied by a type of religion identified with Christianity. The combinatory model, whatever its terms, always shows the same winning side: the Christian West carries off the victor's laurels each time. In the first series, for example, the adjectives successively cited in the first of each pair (the left-hand column if you like) (true, revealed, universal, civilized, and so on) are intended explicitly or in a scarcely indirect way, to designate Christianity, and most often it alone. Whether they view religions from a typological point of view or from a chronological (that is, evolutionist) one, these classifications agree in placing the type of religion with which the West identifies itself at the summit or at the end, the present, of the history of humanity. Thus the well-known opposition of polytheism to monotheism is resolved chrono-logically, because polytheism is followed and superseded by monotheism.

In the circumstances, it would be vain to confront these classifications with the facts of history or of ethnology with a view to trying to evalu-ate their relevance or correct their reductive, not to say naïve and jejune, character. None of them has the least scientific value.

From all this, let us draw at least three partial conclusions.

Despite its scientific trappings, the production of these concepts, tax-onomies, and evolutionist schemes is not the prosaic result of ideological preoccupations. It even seems not to have any other objective. Its degree of correspondence with reality, whether in the effort to describe it or to understand it, is subordinate to an infinitely more gratifying end, which is to advance a division and organization of the world that, whatever the criterion selected or the point of view adopted, always leads to the same re-sult: the religion of (or religion according to) the West invariably occupies the most advantageous and prestigious position.

Ethnocentrism can then be seen as much more potent and insidious than the rules of any scientific protocol. One might even ask whether epis-temology has not served (as here under the cover of objective neutrality) to give it what appears to be the most undeniable support. This means as well that the relationship that links the West and epistemology is based on an ideological perception of the world that is not fundamentally different from that met in that other pair, the West and religion. In both cases, and by paths more complementary than contrary, the originality and superi-ority of our culture are clearly stated and proclaimed.

If people today have generally abandoned the project of classifying religions according to their greater or lesser degree of perfection,[16] it is not at all certain that the influence of this ethnocentric prejudice has disap-peared from Western consciousness. Does not the diffuse, subterranean action of its mode of classification persist in our ways of thinking? Does it not subsist, partially unaltered, even into our learned terminology? Is it not with the aid of the latter that Western epistemology represents and thinks the "real" world of beliefs and fictions? Who would dare to claim that the pairs "primitive/civilized," "monotheism/polytheism," "revealed/ popular," and "religion/magic" have left no trace in our mentality and in our schoolbooks?

A Scattering of Monographs

The difficult anthropological objectives of the history of religions, already compromised by the history of its strictly European origins, must confront another difficulty, after all those that we have so far examined. The problem is not exclusive to it, since it is common to all branches of the human sciences, but in the history of religions, it takes on a more pronounced character than elsewhere, one linked to the ambition of its discourse and to the paradoxical nature of its object: analyzing religious phenomena or religions is an activity that almost always brings into the discussion or demonstration theses as general and unverifiable as those of which theology and metaphysics are so proud.

The most undeniable fact tied to the existence of these theses in the field of the human sciences concerns the rather radical division of intellectual work that they sustain and doubtless even stimulate.[17] Although this is not habitually recognized, and its weighty consequences are often not assessed with precision, it must be noted that all the work published in this field obeys a very rigorous principle of classification, which it is probably not too much to say is as old as the Western intellectual tradition (philosophical and theological in particular). As a consequence (here as in many other situations), modern scholarship has been content to perpetuate a model or style of intellectual work without really seeking to validate it or substitute another for it.

On the one hand, we have the thinkers, creators of these general theses, followed by their interpreters (students, disciples, and heirs, gathered or not into schools, networks, and circles), prominent among whom are those who have been in personal contact with the master (the magical sign that is interpreted as proof of orthodoxy and exegetical competence).[18] From the cosmographical prestige generated by their works comes the use of the quotation, the tutelary invocation, we might rather say, which signifies allegiance, adherence to a unique vision of the world. For, on its own, the quotation proves nothing. The immense Western corpus provides enough to guarantee any imaginable opinion or assertion.

On the other hand, there is the nameless proletariat, more and more numerous, of dissertation and article writers, little read, never commented on, and quickly forgotten beyond a narrow circle of specialists.[19]

This division of labor then has its exact counterpart on the level of intellectual production: on the one hand, we have the original works that play the recognized and authorized role of global cosmographies (the status of religion, description of humanity, signification of culture, role of history, structure of society, or origin of art) and that are admired less for the accuracy and certainty of their information than for their globalizing and totalizing ambition. Improbable, indemonstrable, and, most of the time, unverifiable, the general theses that they defend put them, as Karl Popper saw, beyond the reach of all refutation.

Assertions such as "the unconscious is structured like a language" or "the sacred reveals itself in the world" are gratuitous propositions impossible to confirm. Conversely, to the extent that they allow us to characterize reality by conferring on it a certain signification or general value, they possess undeniable cosmographic effectiveness. However, by virtue of their laconism and their frequent obscurity, these assertions almost always call for extensive clarification. This is why such propositions bring in their wake so many exegeses, commentaries, and controversies, the majority of which are almost as vain as the theological quarrels that stirred the cloisters of medieval universities: Is the unconscious structured like a language or not? Is class struggle the motor of history or not? Is the id really in charge? Is the sacred the opposite of the profane? Is the structure binary?[20]

Asking whether the human mind is as impersonal as it is structural, or perhaps dominated by an insecure, terrifying, libidinous unconscious is in reality a false dilemma, since, presented in these terms, the question that it poses can be resolved only by an arbitrary choice, itself dictated by certain metaphysical preferences. In addition, the apparent rationality of the corresponding concepts ought rather to be compared to that of the autochthonous or indigenous concepts that are the mark of every culture. Their value and signification are never fully relevant except within the limits of their world. Values and significations never exist save as a function of these limits, and the converse is true as well, since they are mutually self-constructing.

Such works, and this is another of their remarkable characteristics, propose only exclusive, isolated, and incomparable visions of their worlds. Closed, deaf worlds. The world according to Marx and the world according to Jung are two incommensurable universes, forever alien to each other— two worlds that it is impossible to inhabit at the same time. And if a third work, at the cost of who knows what effort, advanced a synthesis of them, it could do so only by imagining a third world.[21] The unconscious of Lévi-Strauss and the unconscious of Freud are in the same way two radically distinct entities. This is why it would be vain to seek to correct these works on this point or other, or to improve on them without affecting their premises.

But it would be just as illusory to propose a modification of these premises. What sense is there in correcting a myth or a theological assertion?

Inevitably, facing these canonical mammoths distinguished by their personal style (another decisive criterion), there are a host of learned works written in a duller, impersonal, almost "gray" style—a color taken as proof of objectivity, without the contradiction really surprising anyone. The quality of the latter's information is often superior, and their findings are often more trustworthy, but these qualities unfortunately do little to counter an insurmountable defect: these studies cannot respond to any of the essential questions, such as those concerning the origin, meaning, or function of the complexes to which the objects and individual facts that they examine pertain. In addition, in order to fulfill the mandate that all serious scientific work today imposes, they must increasingly specialize and—a constant corollary—pulverize the study of reality and reality itself into domains and specialties that are more and more microscopic. The monograph contributes to the analysis of reality, to its decomposition, while the canonical text, the scripture, seeks on the contrary to encompass it in a single theory.

This fragmentation or atomization of the real is effected without there symmetrically being any comparable effort (actually it would have to be much greater) intended to counterbalance the influence of these learned studies by trying to utilize them as a basis on which to reconstruct and re-think intelligible syntheses. Today, we infinitely multiply the number of dissertations and monographs without seeking at the same time to conceive of models (heuristic or problematic) destined to permit the systematic (and not simply cumulative) recapitulation of their results. In return, and with disconcerting ease, the totalizing theories contained in the scriptural works are capable of assigning a place, a status, or a meaning to specific facts, while these, as numerous as they may be (and especially when they are) and however detailed their description (and especially when it is) are incapable of generating, through simple summation, such a global vision. This is why visions of the whole, general explanation, the unveiling of origins, or the attribution of an unchanging meaning finally fall to the master works alone, whose most evident and perhaps sole decisive contribution this is.

Because they are above all represented by such learned, atomized research, many disciplinary fields, in their global representations of these fields and their corresponding domains, maintain in parallel fashion veritable doxas, whose scientific relevance (nature and definition of concepts, rigor of protocols preceding demonstration, heuristic value of the perspectives thereby opened, etc.) is very weak, if not practically zero, though one might find a certain philosophical or poetic charm in them and recognize that they are indispensable in a certain way, since they alone allow us to conduct the necessary operation of subsuming the particular under the general. These general doxas naturally have intimate ties to the great works mentioned above, since they frequently offer schematic versions of them, reduced to two or three central themes.

If we can easily cite several reasons at the origin of this separation, this division of intellectual labor, we also see very clearly the most disastrous consequences that follow from it. The requirements for rigor that contemporary epistemology imposes, the pitiless constraints of learning and modern methodologies, the dizzying growth in the number of publications along with the obligation to publish quickly and at length, the compartmentalization of scientific disciplines and—let us state it bluntly—the absence of intellectual originality imposed by the composition of an academic dissertation, all this prompts researchers to choose objects of study that are increasingly narrow and circumscribed. But this tendency, which we observe in all scientific branches, but especially in the human sciences, leads to disaster, for, pulverized into fragments isolated from one another, reality as an intelligible whole disappears (if, indeed, reality is intelligible). It is as if it escaped our grasp the more attentively we studied its multiple elements. We have an apparently insurmountable paradox: the more a scientific discipline breaks up into numerous subspecialties, the more the field itself and the reality supposed to correspond to it fade away as totalities.

Contemporary epistemology, then, finds itself confronted with two kinds of dissimilar writings, the fragment and the whole, whose results and conclusions, far from adding to each other or correcting each other, most often remain mutually indifferent. On the one hand, learned monographs that do not dare to address a general problem, a crucial question (the domain reserved for the "thinkers" on whom the epigones will tirelessly comment in their seminars); on the other, ambitious syntheses, cosmographical "isms" (Freudianism, Marxism, phenomenology, and so on) that do not hesitate to take a stand in the most irresolvable debates, but to which the facts assembled in monographs correspond in only partial and imperfect fashion. The heuristic concepts common to these two kinds of works are rare indeed, and the rifts that separate them are ever deeper.

The history of religions cannot escape this dismal division. The majority of the learned works that it stimulates divide up fairly clearly into these two categories—and without it being necessary ever to raise insoluble metaphysical problems.

On the one side, we have a few great, general theories of religion, probably fewer than a dozen, that have over time become exemplary and emblematic.[22] Their general premises, which can only be void of scientific value, transcend the results of learned monographs by offering intelligible global visions, since this intelligibility concerns, if need be, the overall signification of history just as much as it concerns the vital destiny of humankind. These few global theses (relating to the origin of religions, their nature, and their status) draw their premises from conceptions that are in the final instance metaphysical in nature. According to the individual case, they address the innermost part of human beings, social life, or the unreal world of mystical inventions. The manuals and treatises reproduce and unflaggingly comment on these theses, while their authors have accepted the notion of religion as self-evident, a priori and without the least critical examination.[23] Moreover, they have never attempted to give the history of religions trustworthy methods, usable within the framework of a debate or a scientific program.

On the other hand, we have impressive numbers of monographs, characterized by fragmentation, dispersion, and erudition. All seem determined to isolate fields or objects for study that are more and more cramped and heterogeneous but at the same time challenge the indexing and storage capacities of modern databases. For their part, the separation of disciplines (philological, historical, archaeological, sociological, etc.) and the rival methods that inspire them (descriptive, interpretive, structural, hermeneutical, etc.) do little to make these monographs any less disparate. It is enough to go over the tables of contents of a few specialist journals in the history of religions to measure the degree to which modern epistemology, in its most learned productions, has become atomized. The heterogeneity, quantity, and dissemination of articles and collected materials are such that they prevent any effort to construct a global synthesis of any kind. Specialized analysis, decomposition, and fragmentation have reached such a stage, have developed techniques so radical, that rethinking totalities on the basis of their results has now become illusory.

No human mind would be capable of absorbing "in real time" the sum of the annual publications produced by historians of religion (let alone all those written over the past fifty years!), much less make a synthesis of them. On the other hand, each of us can gain an idea of the origin and status of religion by reading or rereading Lucretius, Hobbes, Spinoza, Feuerbach,

Freud, or Marx. Another major point: it is obvious that no person, even an honored academic, can do without such a global vision. Is it not such a vision that so often dictates the choice and the manner of interpreting this or that fragment, when the latter is not the object of a strict and considered description?

If it is clear that such a global vision of the world or of religion has no great scientific merit, conversely we must immediately recognize that it is practically impossible to think outside such a synoptical representation, or *übersichtliche Darstellung* (Wittgenstein). These main alternatives (learned blindness on the one hand and metaphysical vision on the other) doubtless represent the major paradoxes confronting the perspicacity of modern epistemologists. Academic studies, doctoral dissertations in particular, whether or not they try to disregard these debates and avoid this fatal choice, have only very limited room to maneuver, perhaps none at all, for are they not finally condemned to show a preference for one of the two following attitudes?

Either they can detach a fragment of the real as minuscule as possible and isolate it arbitrarily from the uncertain whole where it belongs, consequently refusing the (too visible) assistance of any *übersichtliche Darstellung* but nonetheless helping to break up the universe of human experience into innumerable discrete fragments. But by thus fragmenting the world, we render it unthinkable.

Or, there too, they can accept the traditional division of our spheres of learning into "academic disciplines" (literature, philosophy, history), to which those classes of objects or phenomena supposed to posses a particular quality (religious, political, literary, sociological, etc.) have been allotted, and then, within these ideal domains, adopt global, exclusive explanatory positions (historicism, Freudianism, Marxism, structuralism, nominalism, and so on). This amounts in effect to projecting onto our scholarship an essentially Platonic conception of knowledge: to objects and their parallel explanations correspond the ideas and schemas, ontologically pure, now organized into a kind of ideal, timeless world.

But human beings, it is true, cannot easily accommodate themselves to such a sharply divided choice. And so we observe among the most lucid (or the least satisfied) of them that the division of labor sketched above can be found in their own work: scholarly articles are reserved for certain journals or publications, while more general reflections find a place in others.

. Unfortunately, this defensive choice, which makes the existence of the difficulty official instead of resolving it, condemns the study of religions to remain captive to its own contradictions. Such a choice amounts in fact to admitting that the explanation of religious facts could lie elsewhere than in the facts themselves or, if you like, that the explanation of these facts makes necessary recourse to global conceptions drawn from speculative fields that never consider them other than with lofty condescension. Clearly, this situation turns into a windfall for all those who admit or claim, at the price of a tautology that does not frighten them, that the explanation of religious facts cannot, in essence, be other than religious, that is, supernatural. The difficulty or epistemological paradox is then at once transformed into metaphysical controversy. Now of all debates, metaphysical debates are the most conventional, and the arguments and positions taken are the most traditional. Immutability and absence of innovation are the hallmarks. (What unexplored arguments could we add to the providentialist theses the West has used for more than two thousand five hundred years?)

These obstacles are not exclusive to the history of religions, and we easily find them in numerous other sectors of modern anthropological thought, especially when such thought faces up to ultimate questions in which its own scientific legitimacy is at stake. But we know that the history of religions is not a discipline quite like the others. Some of the debates troubling this sensitive field up the ideological stakes of ordinary epistemological controversies. Thus, materialist theses relative to the origin of religions stimulate passionate discussion that goes beyond the history of religions, a discussion the field has only recently inherited, and one that originated in the era of Democritus, Protagoras, and Critias, when the Greeks started raising questions about the origin of the gods. In fact, whether we regret it or not, every thesis of a certain scope, proposed (or redeveloped) within the framework of the history of religions finds its echo in the Western religious consciousness, since the sphere of religious ideas and that of ideas on religion have never ceased to communicate with and influence one another. This confusion is facilitated by the fact that the two employ the same notions, the same vocabulary, and share several common conceptions (on how to think of humanity, the world, society, etc.). Comment on religion in the West, even when it is surrounded by all the necessary precautions dictated by modern epistemology, can doubtless never be made without some sensibilities immediately feeling that they are affected.

This situation, associated with a division of intellectual labor between works offering synthetic explanations and monographs focused on atomized, circumscribed objects, is further clouded and complicated (always at

the expense of our understanding), by the presence of a substantial supplementary obstacle, connected with the existence of "inexplicable disproportions" between "material causes" and "cultural effects."[24] Although
the theoretical difficulties that thereby arise are pertinent to all fields of the
human sciences, these disproportions stand out starkly in the case of the
history of religions by virtue of the fact that in our eyes, its preferred object
often represents the quintessence of the phenomenon of culture. Here we
cannot address every aspect of this problem, and I shall only describe their
general tenor.

However much care they take in fixing their object by isolating and
concatenating the causal relations, the scholarly monographs that have
here been contrasted with metahistorical works cannot, any more than the
latter, avoid noting that there exist "unexplained disproportions" between
the "material causes" and the "cultural effects," and that the cultural effects
do not prolong and do not reflect the material causes. A contemporary an-
thropologist, Mondher Kilani, rightly speaks in this respect of "symbolic
transubstantiation."[25]

Everything in human social life, down to the most elementary needs,
is symbolic in nature, that is, is subject to metamorphoses that transform
and transfigure reality into signs. The food swallowed by human beings is
never a simple material element in a physico-chemical (or economic) process intended to keep them alive; at the very same time, it is invested with
very diverse imaginary and affective values. It is present in a great number
of our myths and works of art; it gives rise to complicated rituals; it serves
family and social cohesion by way of meals in common under various circumstances, solemn or private; it possesses any number of metaphorical
equivalences; it partially calms our anguish, just as it can also haunt our
dreams. And all this does not prevent it from giving us pleasure and keeping
us in good health.

The complex whole, rich with innumerable nuances, that is made up
of all these associations (with the body, life, society, the imaginary, myth,
etc.) allows food, now become a symbolic object, to be connected in turn
with other animated, interlaced expressive networks. Certainly, the image
of a jumble, of an indescribable mix-up, remains the most accurate to evoke
the high degree of complexity achieved by these symbolic networks. But
as if to balance it off, they have a resistant texture, one that is nevertheless
flexible, as well as a stupefying capacity to generate new synapses. This also
explains why the formalization of cognitive and symbolic processes constitutes a formidable logical problem. How are we to describe with algorithms

or mathematical equations an enormous plate of spaghetti that never sits still, that keeps multiplying and metamorphosing?

These significations and symbolic forms are dynamic and possess a considerable degree of morphological autonomy. Unfortunately, the innumerable interactions that are produced among all the domains of human experience (social, psychological, sexual, individual, historical, economic, etc.) and all the registers of symbolic life (objects, practices, gestures, dreams, fictions, discourse, signs, institutions, and so on) also exceed the capacity of our current crude analytical models. This is why epistemology, when it interests itself in the issue, is forced once again to have recourse to vast global explanations intended to simplify and impose order on this complex reality. In particular, these are the explanations provided by the irreplaceable "isms" mentioned above, those grand cosmographical works whose objective it is to tell of the world, history, and humanity, while giving preference (most of the time) to their own version of the symbolic function.

This is why Marxism, Freudianism, structuralism, and so forth are not fundamentally distinguishable, when we consider only their cosmographic aims, from Orphism or Platonism. Like them, they claim to set out a homogeneous conception and to offer a uniform explanation of reality. From the perspective of cosmographic formations, a certain number of distinctions that we Westerners judge to be critical (such as those among the political, philosophical, religious, and even scientific domains) lose a portion of their legitimacy. Their relevance is perhaps neither as absolute nor as universal as we like to think.

In the face of these huge, mobile, and infinitely complex symbolic complexes, the explanations offered by the history of religions often turn out to be feeble. Either they invoke supernatural processes and a mysterious Beyond that is the source and receptacle of absolute signification, or they borrow their interpretations from some other discipline—depth psychology, sociology, or even biology.[26] Eliade is a quite remarkable example in this respect, especially if we recall that he incarnated one of the principal and most powerful currents of thought in the modern history of religions, and that as such he was received and honored by the most prestigious universities.

Today, every general theory of the symbolic function seen in its totality entails, in the first instance, that it address the symbols and define the status, that is, the conditions (social, historical, psychological, ideological, etc.) of their production, their principal semiotic characteristics, their formal and/or logical-semantic properties, possible modes of reading or interpreting them, and, lastly, their multiform role in the lives of individuals and groups.[27]

To these requirements, despite the fact that he put the symbol at the center of his conception of the religious universe, Eliade gave only vague and dogmatic responses, inspired by a summary metaphysics, which, for this reason alone, cannot be subjected to a detailed evaluation or rigorous examination. The responses are rather characterized by a kind of lyrical paraphrase punctuated with mysterious expressions, almost incantatory and clearly endowed with only a weak conceptual value, such as the "deep sources of life," "the act of coming into being," "the sign of the beyond," "primordial religious signification," "mystery of the totality," "superior mode of being," "sacred presence," "mystical communication with nature," and so on.

Moreover, although he was their contemporary, Eliade never discussed modern linguistic, philosophical, or semiotic conceptions at all.[28] Reading him leaves one ignorant of even the names of the authors who have made the most valuable contributions to the comprehension, analysis, and history of theories of the symbol.[29] Similarly, Eliade neglected to face up to the formidable theoretical difficulties that various examples of hermeneutic research have revealed (from Schleiermacher to Dilthey, Gadamer, Husserl, Wittgenstein, and Ricoeur) in an effort to account for the production and interpretation of meaning. This is to be regretted, for it is evident today that the principal issue for epistemology does not consist in naïvely proposing a supplementary interpretation (a fortiori an interpretation based on premises of a mystical type), since it will never be more than one paraphrase among all the others. At issue, rather, is our understanding of the subtle mechanisms that govern the complex processes (poietic, rhetorical, argumentative, pragmatic, and so on) that unfold within the various semantic domains created by human cultures.

These examples are offered to remind us that Eliade's work, even though it may have seduced a good number of academics, keeps a prudent distance from any serious or challenging epistemological debate. Eliade's assertions are rather drawn from the category of poetical, mystical pronouncements, of which one may say, in the best of cases, that they contribute to creating a strange distortion of the world and to disguising reality, but certainly not to understanding them better. In addition, they offer nothing very original. Their implicit model, which consists of opposing the gnosis reserved for the elect few to the trivial knowledge of the vulgar, is situated in the distant exegetical and allegorizing tradition of the Neoplatonists.[30] This is also, from the *Corpus Hermeticum* to the illuminated work of René Guénon, one of the clichés of the Western esoteric tradition.

Arbitrary, Narcissistic Objectivization

The various positions adopted by historians of religions and the debates that divide them reproduce, faithfully enough to be immediately recognizable, those found elsewhere in the philosophical tradition and more generally the intellectual tradition of the West—in particular the cardinal opposition that is illustrated at the beginning of this section in the quotations taken from Plotinus and Lucretius respectively, which might for brevity's sake be called "the great Western paradigm." It is as if the history of religions had condensed within itself the master plan for the West's major intellectual positions and controversies and had not been capable of inventing other substantial debates than those that had preceded it (at times in the far distant past) in the long history of Western thought.

The close, almost incestuous relationship, that unites religion and the West, to the point of making them inseparable, can be summarily explained by invoking the following set of facts:

Religion, that is, the thing that is ours because our history invented it and transmitted it to us, is part of our dominant cosmographic formation. It even represents the core or central axis of it, since it is in relation to religion, to its definitions of the world, humanity, and history that most of the other categories of knowledge are defined. This is why it seems to us as indispensable as it is irreplaceable. None of our books of history, sociology, literature, music, law, philosophy, psychology, or the like can avoid including one or more chapters devoted to religion or to the influences of religion. And when their authors write them, there are few who ask themselves why, or seek to justify this inclusion. For them, it concerns a type of evidence that the philosophers called "apodictic," which does not have to be discussed. On the contrary, it would be prudent to imagine books conceived according to other cosmographical structures and thus ignorant of what we call and classify under the word "religion." The major error that we spontaneously commit (or the transcendental illusion into which we fall) consists in seeing in it the key to all culture, while it in fact is only one very specific way of seeing things, intrinsically tied to the history of the Western vision of things (a vision for the moment considered fairly homogeneous, at least in its special features).

The history of religions has probably committed a capital blunder in unquestioningly adopting a word inherited from tradition, for in so doing it has sided with and become dependent on everything (the concepts, debates, theses, or general conceptions) that supports it and intellectually justifies its acceptance. The first historians of religions in the mid nineteenth century should, at the outset, have reflected a bit more or a bit more effectively, as the true anthropologists or historians that they should have been, so as to organize the nascent discipline around a more neutral concept (in a word, one less European), which might have been capable of subsuming the whole of what are here called cosmographic formations, in order to give the discipline truly universal status. But they were far too European, far too persuaded of their exemplary superiority even to conceive that they might adopt such an iconoclastic attitude. On the contrary, they hastened to generalize, to universalize this indigenous notion (in accord with a movement that followed the last great colonial surge of the Christian West), even if it meant being faced, in their capacity as "scientists," with insoluble paradoxes. I have called attention to some of these above in examining the difficulties encountered in efforts aimed at establishing definitions, criteria, and assignable limits to religious phenomena. But we must assume that an ideological constraint weighs heavier and more decisively than scientific ambitions, especially when the intellectual destiny of a culture is unknowingly at stake. Also at work is the fact that the implied contradiction is easier to bear—whatever the epistemological cost—than the renunciation of intellectual sovereignty, the certainty of being the sole possessor of the truth.

What the West and the history of religions in its wake have objectified under the name "religion" is then something quite unique, which could be appropriate only to itself and to its own history. And with this notion, it was those very intellectual categories of the West that were objectified, raised to the dignity of points of reference or unassailable norms. This is why we can affirm that such an objectification is arbitrary, since it is content to generalize, to extend to all humanity the utility of a concept that is autochthonous as well as narcissistic—to the extent that it recognizes and integrates only its own notions and ways of thinking. This explains why the history of religions (not the only "science" to be the victim of this incapacity) finds itself totally powerless when it attempts to conceive of the anthropologies of other cultures (even when these are called religious). For it, there exist only, for example, the person, body, soul, and human aspirations, in conformity with the model progressively elaborated in the West.

And we should not forget that these notions are included in only a rather limited number of combinations, configurations for debate that are themselves associated with a few major philosophical positions (Platonic, Christian, Kantian, materialist, and so on).

In all these respects, we would not be exaggerating to say that the history of religions is a Western academic discipline or epistemology, in that its methods, concepts, ways of posing questions and formulating problems have meaning only when referred to the West's own history. Must we add as well that the objects and objectivity that such a science recognizes are never different from those that this history fashioned and recognized? Perhaps all culture is no more than this play of mirrors and reflections.

The process that concluded in the formation of this Western epistemology, which somehow transformed its objectives into evidence, rests in the final analysis on three conjoined pillars: (1) The most immediate and least debatable experience reveals the presence of a notion that is both central and diffuse in our culture: religion. This is an undeniable historical fact. (2) Incapable of resigning ourselves to considering that we, our civilization, and this very notion might be unique and contingent, we prefer to think that we are dealing with the privileged expression of something that in fact concerns all mankind indiscriminately, whatever the time and place.[31] This deduction is in turn explained by a fact that is inherent to Western thought, for it alone (be it Stoic, Christian, or heir to the principles of 1789) invented the idea of generic Man (to retain the vocabulary of the times), even if in reality he is not and never was conceived of in other than the very idealized image of his Western model. (3) Whether this common notion is considered an anthropological invariable, a transcendental category (or innate tendency of the human mind), or transcendent essence, it claims an exclusive original cause. This is the most visible result of a positivist epistemology (but one doubtless influenced by the creationist model of Genesis) for which the causal relationship precedes and determines all the others.

As a consequence, the scientific status of the idea of religion is illusory, since it in fact results from a complex process that mixes together trivial observations, deductions founded on our own intellectual prejudices, and explicatory schemas borrowed from the most narrowly positivist epistemologies.[32] In addition and at the same time (the concomitance of the phenomena is of capital importance here), the information drawn from philology, history, and ethnography has been systematically retranslated into the religious categories of the Christian West. This substantial, ceaseless work of acculturation (and falsification!) has had as result the erasure of all strangeness, every alterity. Siberian shamanism, Roman civic rites, voodoo ceremonies, prehistoric rock carvings, and many other phenomena have been indistinguishably "formatted" to the dimensions and calibration of our mental frameworks. We could naturally amuse ourselves by imagining the reverse process: to ask, for example, what the Christian theology of the Trinity would look like if translated into the Algonquin, Quechua, or Buryat languages. To think of the symbols of the papacy or the functions of the exorcist on the sole basis of voodoo categories would be a no less instructive or invigorating exercise.

In all this has intervened another factor whose major influence must not be underestimated. Cultures put in contact with, or under the direct influence of, the West, sometimes for centuries, have been constrained to invent a religion for themselves by taking a leaf from the West's book. This perverse effect, the "religion effect," if we absolutely have to give it a name, proceeds from the acculturation unceasingly exercised by our hegemonic and conquering civilization, since the age of the great discoveries, on a larger and larger number of foreign cultures, which it condemned to adopt terminologies, frameworks of thought, and distinctions borrowed from (or imposed by) the West.

To speak with a Hindu in English of "his" religion does nothing to prove the universality of the phenomenon of religion; it shows only that a concept is capable of traveling, that this idea has a certain flexibility, that the elements of a specific cultural reality can always be redistributed in a more comprehensive general framework (especially when such a framing structure does not exist in situ), and that unforeseen (or even improbable) syncretisms will see the light of day if they are relevant to certain dominant interests. In addition, the idea of religion did not emigrate on its own. Along with it, British India adopted many other ideas that concerned important aspects of its own existence (political institutions, union organizations, economic regulations, juridical statutes, etc.), so that in the end, India constructed a good part of "its" contemporary reality based on the Western model. How could religion not have been included in this process?

In Japan, demand for a national religion that would rival those of the West led the political establishment to reinvent Shintoism, taking its cue from its prestigious Western rivals: "Shortly after the Meiji restoration (*meiji ishin*) of 1868, when the new government was exploring the notion of a religious system that would be proof of a civilized, modern nation, it turned towards Shinto which, for the first time in its history, then rose to the rank of an independent religion."[33]

The invention of a religion, that is, of an organized set of beliefs, practices, and institutions, conforming in broad outline to what the West has conceived by this term, does not represent an extravagant or unattainable goal. This is all the more so when this complex astutely flatters the chauvinistic spirit of a nation or the reflex toward identity-building of a small community that finds itself in competition or conflict, real or imagined, with what this West, so scorned and simultaneously so envied, personifies in its eyes.

That this Western model, so long part of our familiar sphere, has somehow reached the point of generating its own neurotic, stereotyped forms is further proven by the fact that this adventure now attracts so many unbalanced minds and personalities afflicted with megalomania.[34] Nothing in fact combines a greater collection of worn-out clichés than the modern religious sects that compete with stupefying zeal among themselves in the field of bad taste and kitsch. It is no less true that the Western religious imagination has long been living off its assets and has ceased to invent anything new. As for knowing why one of these efforts should succeed while another fails, this is one of the ritual questions that the West has been asking itself for some two thousand years. Saint Augustine had already long reflected on this topic in the early fourth century with his interrogation of the fate of the Roman empire.

How, at a time when the all-powerful representatives of the West were dominating and subjugating them, could the peoples of Africa and Asia have come up with intellectual weapons enabling them to meet the West on its own ground? This acculturation retrospectively gives the West the feeling of having been right, of possessing the truth, or at least the key to reading it, and in any case of itself being the norm with reference to which other cultures ought to be evaluated. The West not only conceived of the idea of religion, it has constrained other cultures to speak of their own religions by inventing them for them. Religion is not only the central concept of Western civilization, it *is* the West itself in the process of thinking the world dominated by it, by its categories of thought.[35]

The history of religions played a role in this process. For did it not, where and as best it could, stand epistemological security for the vast colonial enterprise that finally spread over the entire world? Did it not contribute to hardening and fixing all sorts of original cultural configurations by transforming them, at their own expense, into religions? (As if its own categories had had a retroactive effect on the situation of things by subjecting those things to the definition that was a priori ascribed to them.) Did it not, in other words, privilege Western narcissism by allowing it to find echoes or reflections of itself everywhere? For the West's procedure has always remained the same: find its own image elsewhere, in order not to have to renounce what it thinks are universal categories (which are precisely those on which its own structure rests), but always in another, less perfect form, in order not to be obliged to renounce its hegemonist objectives.

When historians of religion proposed various definitions for religion, when others recognized that they were not capable of defining it, and when still others apparently chose to attack the dominant religion's central reference point, the idea of God, few indeed were those who questioned the very notion of religion itself. Atheist or materialist theses denied the existence of God, but not that of religion. Are not these contrary theses the very ones that cling most fervently to the notion of religion? This proves, if only in paradoxical fashion, the attachment of European scholars to the idea, for it is precisely those who recognize that they are incapable of defining religion, or of saying with any precision in what it consists, who nonetheless continue to maintain the fiction of its existence. And on this pseudo-object are built up competing theses that in turn become the subjects of interminable theological debates.

Why does the word "religion," despite everything, despite all the difficulties that its use raises, continue to be employed so frequently by historians and professional anthropologists? Created by the West, enshrined in Western epistemology, and central to its identity, the concept of religion eventually came to be the core of the Western worldview. Since this notion is intrinsically linked to all the philosophies, complementary or competing, that have been invented in the West, the West cannot, at the risk of its own disintegration, do without it, because these global conceptions would then decompose into scattered or juxtaposed fragments. The same disaster would strike our language, to the extent that we admit that it is not only an assemblage of words but also an organized memory containing semantic networks that are nothing less than cosmographic elements. We cannot use the words "humanity," "nature," "history," and "providence" without the association of ideas bringing up cosmographical schemas deeply buried in our ways of thinking.

Would not abandoning the idea of religion be the equivalent for Western thought of abdicating part of its intellectual hegemony over the world? A world bereft of this idea would no longer be a world that was thinkable and thus controllable by Western categories alone. This is why the West prefers to continue to espouse bad epistemology rather than abandon the description of reality according to its own canons, that is, in a fashion that in the last analysis simply does not work: Western epistemology creates or constructs the reality that it studies, since it does so only with the aid of traditional, conventional notions that it has itself in great part constructed.

Through the idea of religion, the West continuously speaks of itself to itself, even when it speaks of others. For when it does so, it is implicitly in relation to the perfected model that it thinks itself to be. This is narcissistic objectification.

II | Order and History

For the nature of man doth extremely covet to have somewhat in his understanding fixed and unmovable, and as a rest and support of the mind. . . . Therefore men did hasten to set down some principles about which the variety of their disputations might turn.

—Francis Bacon, *The Advancement of Learning*

For, to talk of a man, and to lay by, at the same time, the ordinary signification of the name man, which is our complex idea usually annexed to it; and bid the reader consider man, as he is in himself, and as he is really distinguished from others in his internal constitution, or real essence, that is, by something he knows not what, looks like trifling; and yet thus one must do who would speak of the supposed real essences and species of things, as thought to be made by nature, if it be but only to make it understood, that there is no such thing signified by the general names which substances are called by.

—John Locke, *Essay Concerning Human Understanding* 3.6.43

4 | Christianity and the West

A Unique History

If the use of the term "religious history" seems fully justified when speaking of the West, and may even seem justifiable only in this case (so mutually determined are the two inseparable members of this pair), I must hasten to add that the evidence masks an amusing paradox, which we would perhaps be wrong to treat as no more than a kind of intellectual acrobatics. If we are ready to see religion in general (including the galaxy of notions associated with it) as one of the West's most original constructs, we shall almost inevitably have to admit that this massive, omnipresent idea, which has informed our intellectual history in each of its major expressions, in each of its movements, has oriented all of that history's other products by defining their themes and topics, how to deal with them, and the choice and spirit of their major arguments, or by deflecting the tenor of a debate or controversy in one direction or another. In this capacity, the idea of religion has equally and substantially contributed to fashioning the notions, or conceptual instruments, with which we think history, and in particular the history of phenomena gathered under the aegis of the religious.

At this point, the paradox perhaps stops being amusing and becomes troubling, sufficiently so, no doubt, as to arouse our epistemological anxiety. We are condemned to think a complex intellectual object, religion, while the latter has never ceased to intervene in the choice, constitution, definition, and deployment of the tools, including intellectual tools, with which we are today reduced to thinking about this subject. Nor has it ceased, over the centuries, to shape the real consciousness and existence of individuals (our ancestors and, in so many ways, ourselves today). The Western mind-set has been shaped or influenced for centuries by religious notions, and the world itself, the universe, like each of its parts, has been systematically referred back to them.

Among our universal concepts, our visions of the whole (of mankind, the world, their destiny, etc.), our general topics, our rhetorical strategies, our batteries of arguments, and our major controversies (or simply the terms, the words of our philosophical vocabulary), how many of these developed outside and independently of all influence from the religious paradigm? And how many have simply tried to become autonomous creations, indifferent to all religious questions? Doubtless none, and it would be only too easy to multiply the examples—which, moreover, concern the trivial details of domestic life just as much as great political institutions, the most naïve superstitions as well as the loftiest moral conceptions, and the most trifling maxims as well as the most learned discourse. For centuries on end, the totality of the elements that made up daily existence, mental life, and the intellectual activity of Western civilization have been determined in one way or another by religion. It occupies a central place at the heart of every system, whether it concerns interior life or war, sexual morality or scientific speculation, cookery or the art of torturing infidels.

In the same way, it would be child's play to demonstrate the omnipresence of the notion of dharma in India, not only in all human activities but also in the totality of reflections or discussions that sustain intellectual life. An indefinable notion, literally untranslatable, which covers a limitless domain (law, justice, morals, social life, observances of every kind, etc.), dharma seems to be a notion more functional—even a topic (in philosophical terms)—than strictly conceptual.

In order to constitute themselves and endure, societies, like individuals, need first to imagine their being and their destiny, then to inscribe those within the framework of a global cosmography that is co-extensive with their sphere of the thinkable. Any complex on this scale calls for a "total" concept,[1] one transcendent and inaccessible—at once core and center of gravity—and at the same time able to order in relation to itself all domains of knowledge (the various technical corpuses), all practices, to ensure the coherence and permanence of the group, and lastly to incarnate itself in each point and each instant of the life of individuals (gestures, thoughts, dreams, wishes, etc.): "Dharma is so called because it protects *(dhāraṇāt)* everything; dharma maintains all that is created. As a consequence, dharma is indeed the principle that is capable of sustaining the universe."[2]

Transcendent and immanent, lived as well as conceived, normative but at the same time very subtle *(sūkṣma)*, personally experienced and collectively recognized, dharma also manages to give birth to an order that, infinitely repeated, becomes Order, the model and guarantor of all the others. How, in the circumstances, could a traditional Brahman have thought (conceived, imagined, etc.), beyond the system of coordinates and references centered on dharma, a world ignorant of dharma? And how can we today think of humanity, the world, history without appealing to ideas, to notions that were conceived, elaborated in the mental and intellectual context dominated by our own idea of religion? In both cases, we find ourselves in universes similar to Möbius strips, the internal surface of which gradually becomes the external surface, where the concept that makes it possible to live (in fact) in one certain world also permits us to think *the* world (but can the latter ever be other than that initial world?).

In any case — and this is a major difference that a Western mind ought to try to understand in all its nuances and without forgetting any of its consequences — India has never been tempted or never been able to impose its concept of dharma on anthropological thought as an absolute system of reference. Nor did it ever claim that there was a universal essence of dharma present in all cultures, that every person carried within him or her a *homo dharmicus*. It could doubtless not even have had the intention or ambition to do so, since, from within its own universal, it was never concerned to render other peoples and other cultures alien — something the West, more concerned with conquest and hegemony than with intellectual rigor, has long done spontaneously by considering its universal *the* Universal.

On the other hand, we must take care not to confuse dharma and religion, as do so many superficial observations. Dharma is not the equivalent, and still less the Sanskrit translation, of the word "religion." The idea of an impersonal, uncreated, and unchanging cosmic order to which everything from plants to supernatural beings is subject is not in itself religious.[3] On what grounds could it be said to be? On the other hand, it may readily be admitted that these two notions have, each in its own way, organized around themselves cosmographic formations that probably present a certain number of identical structural characteristics. For it is to this morphological level, freed of all religious or ethnocentric prejudice, that we must raise ourselves in order to seek out unquestionable anthropological invariables.

In fact, if we admitted or postulated that two cultural sets, A and B, were homologous, it would seem obvious and even necessary that the explanation of this homology could not be unilaterally supplied by the intrinsic particularities of A alone (a fortiori if the characteristics of A are selected, defined, and interpreted by the representatives of the examining community).[4] The homology must be found at a more abstract level that encompasses A and B in the same fashion. The subsumption of A and B, if it is possible, exists only on this analytical level, which is not available to common intuition or experience: despite appearances, a crayfish is not a little lobster, and a whale is not a fish. Science alone has taught us that.

To think religion(s) with words invented by religion. This variant on the hermeneutical circle, where the "before" can never be analyzed except from an "after" that is fashioned and conditioned by this "before," the perception of which is dependent on this after, which in turn depends . . . . , this complicates our task a bit more. It ought in any case to prevent us from using an expression such as "the religious history of the West" without preceding it with some verbal acrobatics intended to forewarn the reader that we are not for a moment taken in, but that only a sound principle of economy obliges us to use it (a warning that would have to be repeated every time such a formula or one like it turned up: doubtless a salutary exercise, but one that would make most books deadly boring, if not unreadable).

While fully conscious of this difficulty, we shall, in spite of everything, disregard it, acting as if the expression, "the religious history of the West," could be taken literally, in its immediate, conventional meaning, since in any case we would scarcely use this waiver before immediately recalling— and this is the essential point, beyond the nominalist quarrel—that there is a close, genetic relationship between the historical destiny of Christianity in the West and the construction of the idea of religion with its very specific signification. That each of these is continuously reflective and supportive of the other, and that evoking "the religious history of the West," far from meaning that there concurrently exists such a history, signifies more prosaically that our "scientific" language (in which we can never have too little confidence) is more often the heir of an immemorial history than the result of an analytical procedure.

This general remark also means that innumerable circumstances, ideas, and individuals had to meet and interact for such a unique idea to develop and win acceptance. This ought to be enough to cancel out the reflections and invocations of all those who stubbornly try to discover or name the "essence" of the religious or of Religion. As if, from such a succession of events, such a jumble of unpredictable circumstances, unique accidents, and exceptional situations, there was ever the slightest chance of the appearance of an unchanging entity, one that, perfect and unchanging, could somehow, in some metaphysical heaven, be supposed to have preceded them. Recourse to the idea of an atemporal, immutable essence is intellectually lazy, as well as being a simplistic means of reintroducing a bloodless variant of the earliest philosophical idealism into the sphere of anthropological thought.

The religious history, that is, the Christian history, of the West began with an incomparable, unheard-of event. Let us never forget, for it is a rarity in the annals of humanity, that Christianity was uprooted and exiled at the moment of its very inception. Scarcely had it been born (if it really was) than it developed, very rapidly and in all its essentials, elsewhere, away from its original Jewish site, at the heart of other—especially Greek—cultures. A vast, centralized empire united under its authority, in which had flourished that highest pre-Christian moral or spiritual creation, the Stoic ideal "of a truly universal form of civilization in the sense that it was not limited by any national or local tradition. It addressed itself directly to all humanity because it had faith in the identity of the reason that was common to all and because it took this belief as its reference point."[5]

Here one cannot but recall Saint Paul's bold, inspired decision to turn away from the Jewish world (which he saw as too sectarian and ungrateful), evangelize the heathen, and, finally, go to Rome, the heart of the pagan empire?[6] Without doubt this decision, which inaugurated what in its further propagation would be transformed into a veritable world conquest, must be seen as one of the founding acts of the West, one of those of which we can say with certainty that it influenced the fate of humanity. Is there a single other example in all history where we see a philosophy, system of knowledge, or doctrine leave its culture and native region immediately after its birth in order to undertake the conquest of its neighbors? (The original site, which occupied only a peripheral place and played only a minor role in the empire, did not dispose of the economic and military resources that would have permitted this doctrine to impose itself otherwise.) The exceptional circumstances of this eventful, unforeseeable origin had several consequences that would be aligned with the fate of the West and of Christianity in the very particular forms that the idea of religion would subsequently adopt in its act of self-construction.

Saint Paul's choice, reaffirmed without any reservation or the least doubt at the very beginning of the Letter to the Romans, was tantamount, as we all know, to proclaiming the objectives and asserting the universal claims of Christianity, summoned by this incomparable ideological stroke to transcend the boundaries and differences, ethnic as well as cultural, that until then had always limited the diffusion of ideas. Saint Paul was obliged, as he himself said, to propagate the message of Christ to all men, whoever they were, to the very ends of the earth.

Here too we must try to measure the profound originality of the Pauline plan and the reception that it met. Never before had a man thought of expounding a wisdom, a conception of the world, beyond his country and his people, and also of converting all humanity to a new mode of life and thought by going forth to meet them.[7] And this even if it is true that this choice would probably not have been followed by such effects (and would itself have been inconceivable) if the intermediary of the Hellenized Jewish diaspora had not existed and the conflict that opposed Saint Paul and orthodox Jews had not occurred. The destruction of the temple in Jerusalem and the dispersal of the Jewish people that occurred shortly thereafter also favored this rupture and the autonomy that new Christians would then claim.

Because it was uprooted from the very beginning, Christianity was also, from its origins, confronted with alien conceptions, competing ways of living and thinking. Among these, some enjoyed great prestige (Plato, the Stoics), boasted origins distant in time, and could exhibit an imposing intellectual production. Based on its numerous, lengthy controversies with pagan philosophies, beliefs, and cults, Christianity experienced the need to define in precise, systematic fashion a doctrine that was solidly and firmly constructed (albeit one in which we nevertheless find some borrowings from the detested pagans). Christianity would never cease to proclaim itself the sole true religion (which in a certain ironic sense is quite true), and this dogmatic intransigence extended to the heresies and heterodoxies whose appearance it helped provoke within the Church.

Because Christianity is characterized by its strict monotheism and by the privileged relationship that it sought to establish between humanity and its unique God, theology has always occupied a central place in it. The step from a universalist goal to the spirit of conquest is probably no longer than that which leads from doctrinal rigor to intolerance. Thus we see in the West these dogmatic, conquest-oriented tendencies taking form both on the intellectual level and on the institutional level, in a Church whose power and hegemony they reinforced.

Yet here too we are dealing with two aspects that, far from being common among human cultures or from being inscribed in some order of things, constitute a unique, even notable exception. If religion, as a distinct domain, is unknown from other cultures, there is all the more reason that the idea of a Church devoted to assuring the administration of this unique domain, itself organized around the cult of a unique divinity, should be more than inconceivable, should, in short, be impossible.

The universal objective ascribed to the Christian message; certainty of its radical difference and absolute superiority, leading in turn to dogmatic intransigence, intolerance, and ecclesiastical imperialism; and the preeminence accorded to theology are of no small importance here. In a complex process, these architectonic features of Christianity configured a unique whole about which there was nothing inevitable, whose contours could not have been imagined or its contents conceived of beforehand. Too many heterogeneous, contingent factors have intervened in this genesis and throughout this history for us to be able to recognize today, after the fact, the consequences of any anthropological (pre)determination, inscribed in the very depths of human thought or cultures, of which the West miraculously conceived the most consummate form. On the other hand— again—these same traits define and situate the general framework in which the typically Western idea of religion developed and spread.

If we were to characterize it by a single notion, in order to call attention to its most visible structural characteristic, it would be, as noted, *opposition*. The Christian religion, as much through its acts as in its spirit, rests on a system of antithetical categories or principles. It is par excellence the domain that constituted itself "against" what was external to it (pagans, heretics, atheists, etc.), while at the same time defining itself through a series of clear-cut dichotomies. Of these two complementary orders, the principle expressions have long since been enumerated and have become commonplaces in our anthropological and theological thought: true religion/ false religions; orthodoxy/heresies; soul/body; God/humanity; magic/religion; reason/revelation; knowledge/faith; theology/anthropology; believer/atheist; clergy/laity; sacred/profane or religious/profane; monotheism/polytheism; papacy/empire; religion/science, and so on.

These various formulas never modify or attenuate the sense of this major structural modality; they merely confirm its success and assure its intellectual hegemony. Whereas other civilizations preferentially think/ thought in the modality of harmonious integration, the resolution of oppositions, the rejection of division and separation, the proximity of the other, universal sympathy, noncontradiction, there is no doubt that the Christian education of the West led it to prefer division and controversy as dominant modes of operation, themselves reduced to radical alternatives: providence or materialistic atomism, the soul or the body, God or Satan, science or faith, the imagination or reason, life or immortality, this world or heaven, and so on.

It would be fascinating and instructive to follow, beyond its original context, the diffusion of these ways of thinking and these binary patterns into our conventional ways of classifying knowledge, defining and deploying our concepts, constructing our arguments, or organizing our existences. The frightening technical efficiency of the West, the autonomy enjoyed by scientific thought and political action, the distinction recognized between the private (or interior) sphere and the public sphere, in short, all those aptitudes and arrangements so willingly recognized in the West, are they not in the final analysis explained by the omnipresence of this original matrix? Reflecting on the various points, one will better understand what was meant when it was asserted above that the intellectual equipment of the West was constructed and, above all, shaped in the very particular context of the Christian religion and its theology.

And it is quite clearly this conception, this structure, devoid (need it be repeated?) of all religious character sui generis (given that such a plane quite simply does not exist), that in its turn (albeit much later, when European civilization dominated the world) imprinted itself on the complex of ideas and thoughts that would go on to form the obligatory, principal, and constituent point of reference for the nascent history of religions.

Interiorization and Universalization

Saint Paul's unprecedented pronouncement, his ambitious project of evangelizing the pagans and addressing himself to all human beings without distinction, whatever their origin or status, might have been realized at the cost of a simplification and impoverishment of the evangelical message. For in conformity with the implacable mechanisms of a well-known law, by diffusing itself ever farther afield, among cultures and populations more and more foreign to the Greek language and to the spirit of the New Testament, this message might have undergone sclerosis and very quickly have come to represent no more than a collection of conventional practices and sayings.

Against the very real risks implicit in this threat of entropy, Christianity from the very beginning established an essential principle in opposition, which, because it is central to its history and to its theology, is equally so to the idea (that is, our idea) of religion. Here again, I must reiterate (at the risk of tiring the reader) that we are dealing with a principle and a conception that a priori have nothing necessary or self-evident about them, that are the sign of nothing but their own manifestation. They simply put us in the presence of a unique fact that, elsewhere and most of the time, is not to be found (something easily verified) or present under other forms, colored with a thousand unexpected shadings.

Only intellectual laziness, the legacy of a tradition that profoundly shaped our ways of thinking, and a particularly lively and invasive ethnocentrism authorize some people to transform this uniqueness into an incomparable event, into evidence of Divine Providence. But who can fail to see that in accepting such reasoning, each of the cultures reviewed by contemporary ethnography would be authorized to make its own claim to uniqueness and, on those grounds, to promote itself as the absolute reference and model for all anthropological thought?

The celebrated principle that Christianity associated from its birth in a particularly fortunate way with its claim to a universalist vocation was clearly that of faith. Seen as the ultimate point of Revelation, recognized as the effect of an "interior spiritual grace," placed at the heart of the evangelical message, in particular, the Pauline message, from the very outset it set itself in opposition to the impersonal precepts of the Law as well as to the anticipated, mechanical results of the accomplishment of prescribed acts ("works"):

> Then what becomes of boasting? It is excluded. By what law? By that of works? No, but by the law of faith. For we hold that a person is justified by faith apart from works prescribed by the law. Or is God the God of Jews only? Is he not the God of Gentiles also? Yes, of Gentiles also, since God is one; and he will justify the circumcised on the ground of faith and the uncircumcised through that same faith. Do we then overthrow the law by this faith? By no means! On the contrary, we uphold the law. (Rom. 3:27–31)[8]

Even thus defined and celebrated, the idea of faith alone would probably not have sufficed had it not been supported, animated by a unique process that culminated in the notion, still current, of the human person.[9] This is a phenomenon typical of and proper to the history of Western consciousness and culture, which, moreover, it helped to define by conferring on them so many specific orientations. Although it is difficult to follow its evolution over the centuries of medieval theology, it has undeniably developed and spread since the period of the Reformation and has since then been intimately connected with the rise of modern individualism, which has paid increasingly keen attention to the development of personal consciousness and to the torments of the interior life. The modern vogue for different forms of psychological inquiry and analysis doubtless represents only the ultimate, inevitable consequence.

"Faith in the heart" (Rom. 10:10) would quickly have become an unfelt adherence or simple acquiescence if, being ever more attentive to follow and dissect each of its emotions, each of its spiritual states, it had not accompanied and nourished the Western conscience in its own introspective movement, which the twin proddings of culpability and repentance unceasingly animated and sustained. In sum, faith would have rapidly dried out, emptied of its vitality, if the parallel progress of personal individuation had not allowed it to become increasingly interiorized, to plunge ever more deeply into the innermost reaches of personal conscience. Reciprocally, these developments would probably not have occurred had they not been preceded and supported by this particular attentiveness to the self, to inner life, that the idea of living faith entailed.

This evolution, as it concerns the historian of religions, obviously remains associated with the spirit of the Reformation, with Luther in particular ("Is the essence of God anything other than the essence of faith"), with German pietism, Herder, Schleiermacher, and then, at the beginning of the twentieth century, with Rudolf Otto.[10] Beside the better-known analyses of Puritanism by Wilhelm Dilthey[11] and Max Weber,[12] we might also quote Auguste Sabatier, who, although fallen into obscurity today, summarized the spirit of this inner religion (albeit not without some unfairness with regard to Roman Catholicism):

> Far different is the notion of faith in Protestantism; different too is the notion of dogma. The Reformers caused religion and Christianity to pass from the outside to the inside, from the social sphere to the innermost of the soul. Religion, which in Catholicism was essentially an institution and a priesthood, became a principle of conviction, a moral experience, a consecration of the soul. The Gospel enters and takes root in our heart, not through the effects of a supernatural guarantee but through its intrinsic virtue; it is legitimated by its own content and its intimate power. It is through what it is in itself that it reaches us and wins us over. It illuminates us and reanimates us. Faith is then not an act of submission to some authority. It is a moral act, an act of confidence and love, an interior inspiration.[13]

But this profound evolution, in a vast convergent movement, so fully harks back to the principles of Roman personal law, the examination of the conscience of the wise Stoic, the romantic celebration of the omnipotence of affect, modern individualism, and the concern for the self so characteristic of the Western ethos that we cannot fail to be tempted to see in it a long and lasting tendency that has contributed to define European sensibilities.

No more than the intelligence or the imagination, sensibility must not be conceived of as a kind of original disposition fixed in unchanging form. It has received this form at the end of a complex process that unfolded over numerous centuries. The emotion we feel today before a setting sun has been preceded by a very long history.

Subject to these convergent influences, religion becomes sentiment, and sentiment the quintessence of religious life. Benjamin Constant gave one of the most celebrated expressions of this tendency or orientation in his famous eulogy *On Religion,* where he calls it the "response to that cry of the soul that no one can silence, to that impetus toward the unknown, toward the infinite, that no one can entirely tame, whatever the distractions with which he surrounds himself, however adroitly he deadens or degrades himself."[14] In exaggerated form ("impetus," "cry," "soul," "unknown," "infinite"), we here find summarized and combined the call or aspiration to transcendence, the urgent reference to the most intimate self (in other words, the soul), the rejection of reason, and the exaltation of personal sensibility.

We also see the appearance of a kind of lyrical form, a thematic of the diffuse, vaguely evocative, and the seeking out of a mysterious pathetic quality that will in turn become one of the great topoi in a kind of poetics reserved for religious effusions and flights of fancy. In the twentieth century, Mircea Eliade's works would often be constructed around these facile effects, intended to impress a credulous public.[15] It is only too true that for a certain number of historians of religion, attachment to, a passion for, the words of religion, provides access to paths that lead to transcendence.

When they speak of religion, they like to pause and adopt a grave tone—letting readers know that they are facing essential questions or profound mysteries. This stylistic habit is much more than a clever rhetorical procedure, for it developed around a true, specialized topic (topic in the philosophical sense). There is a religious way of speaking of religion that generates this pathos, frequently solemn, sometimes enthusiastic, a conviction displayed by all discourses in which form and content seem to correspond or coincide.[16] Conversely, the irony that surfaces here and there in this book seeks only to recall the need to keep a healthy distance and avoid any complicity or connivance.

The religious orientation of this individualization of conscience has reached the point today where it is almost everywhere recognized that religion is a strictly private, interior matter, which exclusively concerns personal conscience. Still, in order to assess the complete reversal that has been effected, let us recall that Plato in his *Laws,* for example, firmly condemned every kind of worship in private, for the relations that people have with the gods above all concern the polis and by virtue of this fact are inscribed in the framework of public life.[17]

This is why no one, or hardly anyone, in the West hesitates to classify the withdrawal proper to meditation, the examination of conscience, or internal prayer among the most noble of attitudes, the most elevated on the spiritual level. Moreover, the idea that dance or trance, for example, could ever designate an authentic or praiseworthy religious attitude is here dismissed a priori by use of the word "spiritual." Silence, isolation, monastic renunciation, contemplation, or even mute prayer are, on the contrary, so intimately associated by the modern West with its conception of the human being and of religion that they seem absolute values. In our hierarchy of religious behaviors, the use of powerful psychotropes (hallucinogens intended to provoke states of delirium or trance) cannot for a moment compete with all our received attitudes, expressly centered on the valorization of the individual person or inner conscience.[18]

By simultaneously targeting the universal, in the generic form of the human being, the creature of a unique God, and, in this same human being, an inner point endowed with the greatest personal intensity, Christianity has succeeded by means of individualizing faith in establishing a balance whose success was neither obvious nor guaranteed in advance.

Interiorization, as it concerns faith and sentiment, brings with it affectivity, moral evaluation, introspection, the examination of conscience, existence in its most private and most personal form, and with it engages the fate of what Luther called "the spiritual inner man."

On the opposite tack, universalization, under the cover of the generic human being, the creature of God, seems to imply juridical and anthropological abstraction, the disincarnate idealization of an impersonal being, and the cancellation of various cultural, ethnic, and social points of reference.

On the one hand, there is the most intimate, most personal "self"; on the other, the most abstract, most disincarnate human being.

These two forces seem fated to act in opposing directions, the one centripetal, the other centrifugal. But they end up complementing each other rather than being mutually exclusive or mutually destructive. Indeed, we cannot forget that surrounding the conscience with external constraints, the discipline of the body, the regular rhythm of sacramental life, dogmatic intransigence, in short, the control and surveillance of the Church, have been of no little help in the success of Christianity. Despite everything, they have favored the emergence of an original situation in which these two forces balance each other and cooperate.

The fact remains that the result, on the level of the formation (a word to be read here in its etymological sense) and the education of the Western conscience, is quite remarkable. In fact, the balance that has been achieved (the paradoxical synthesis, if you like) seems to have been more dynamic than stable, more fruitful than precarious. Moreover, it continues to orient a good number of our general figurations: in our eyes, religion and religious life simultaneously concern all humans (whoever they are, from whatever period)—they are what is most intimately connected to our most personal life. There are, then, these two beings, the inner person and the universal person, who are the targets of conversion in the sense that it makes a claim to pertain to every individual and, simultaneously, claims to address only that which is properly his or her own in each person.

This last aspect, the valorization of interior life, which would doubtless raise a smile on the face of a Buddhist, a practitioner of yoga, or a Shankarian philosopher, for whom the inner "self" is the most illusory and captious of phenomenological realities, has become one of the commonplaces of Western ideology. We must speak of ideology here, for we are dealing with a profound tendency, centuries old, that equally affects art, medicine, philosophy, law, and, inevitably, psychology, and that has continuously added increased importance to the smallest perturbations of our spiritual states. The success of Freudian psychoanalysis with the general public may one day seem the ultimate manifestation of this narcissistic culture, this concern with the self that has become obsessional.

Let us also recognize, in good faith, that these tendencies are also at the origin of a very particular form of sensibility and perception of life and, among the most gifted, of a series of original aptitudes for dissecting the most shaded emotional states. This is why, from Marcel Proust to the Impressionists, from Henry James to André Gide, we find them in the multiple expressions of modern art, where they often constitute the principal distinctive feature. Could we today imagine that literary activity or a work of art could be anonymous, impersonal, the result of a collective effort that would forget and obliterate itself in its own undertaking? On the other hand, it is equally true that there is no end to so-called artistic productions that are no more than a vain display of petty manias and trivial egotistical preoccupations. Works that are nothing other than—to borrow Claude Lévi-Strauss's stinging retort—"an undertaking of auto-admiration, in which, not without gullibility, modern man locks himself into intimate dialogue with himself and falls in ecstasy before his subject."[19]

Autonomy and Imperialism

The uniqueness, always present but probably more pronounced today than ever, of this cult of the self, of the individual person, as well as the passionate interest in its impressions, desires, and subjective interior states, now belongs, in near obvious and familiar fashion, to our most general conception of religion, evolved over time into religious consciousness or feeling. How are we to dissociate the two? How can we today succeed in thinking the religious on bases other than this intimate, almost constituent relationship? How could we recover the state of mind of a Plato or imagine that which animates a Zande or Nyakusa sorcerer? Also part of our most general conception of religion, and just as obviously, is the humanistic, universalist project that, despite the fact that it has remained viscerally ethnocentric, nonetheless has the merit of seeking to think of humankind outside its limited and relative worlds (made up of various cultural boundaries and conditionings), and even despite them.

The most distant origins of modern anthropological thought are to be found here, in this preoccupation, and it, too, we must recognize in all honesty, has no comparable equivalents in other cultures. The idea of a generic humanity that is to be found in every individual, made up, as Sartre said in roughly equivalent terms, of all individuals, that is valid for the collectivity as for each and every member of it—this idea is probably one of the finest invented by the West. Its deepest pre-Christian roots are to be found in the thought of the Stoics and in the admirable Ciceronian utopia of a human society made by men and women for men and women:

> It seems necessary, however, to probe deeper into the fundamentals of community and human fellowship ordained by nature. First comes that which we see existing in the fellowship of the whole human race. The bond which unites them is the combination of reason and speech,[20] which by teaching, learning, communicating, debating, and evaluating endears men to each other, and unites them in a kind of natural alliance. This more than anything separates us from the nature of the beasts. We often concede that animals such as horses and lions have courage, but lack justice, fairness, and goodness. This is because they lack reason and speech. This is human fellowship in its broadest sense, uniting all men with each other.[21]

These ideas found an echo (albeit a self-interested one) in nascent Christianity, which would continue to reverberate down to our own day, after being greatly amplified by new political and ideological foundations in the eighteenth century. Among its other, perhaps even more far-reaching consequences, this willingness to think of mankind in general, timeless, universal terms also prompted the peoples of the West to leave their world and go toward others, to study them, but also to "civilize" them.

This original orientation of the concept of religion, tied to the respective developments, centripetal and centrifugal, of Christian theology and Christian anthropology, would probably not have succeeded in imposing itself had it not itself been defined, in minds and in acts, as a distinct domain. It is this that permitted the expansion and resolution of the double tension: toward interiorization, a product of the culture of faith, and toward universalization, by means of the idea of the human being as the unique creature of an equally unique God, with fewer and fewer intermediaries and obstacles intervening between the two. The autonomy of religion and of the religious (practices, beliefs, attitudes, and so on) protected and yet exacerbated these two aspirations, as contradictory as they were complementary, which without such autonomy would have remained fixed firmly in the other institutions of their era and would probably have disappeared with them. But without them the domain of religion would never have won such autonomy. It is in their paradoxical equilibrium, in their double polarity, that its most evident dynamism is based. Religion needed power and found it in these two orientations. In turn, these forces needed a separate world, and religion offered it.

On the other hand, by becoming autonomous and different from everything that surrounded it, the totality of practices and beliefs, ways of thinking and modes of sensibility, mind-sets and various observances, all that would go on to become religion, not only favored the autonomy of other spheres of human or social activity conceived on this model (art, politics, jurisprudence, etc.), but also permitted the creation in the mid nineteenth century of an order of knowledge and learning that claimed to be autonomous on the same grounds as grammar or biology, and whose object ipso facto appeared to be universal. This is so true that at the time no scholar posed the question or asked whether our indigenous idea in effect warranted being applied and generalized to the totality of human cultures and humankind. Quite the contrary. For Edward B. Tylor, considered one of the fathers of modern anthropology, the universality of religious facts left no doubt. With impeccable assurance, he asserted: "[F]or no evidence justifies the opinion that man, known to be capable of so vast an intellectual development, cannot have emerged from a non-religious condition, previous to that religious condition in which he happens at present to come with sufficient clearness within our range of knowledge." This premise is immediately swept away: "Were it distinctly proved that non-religious savages exist or have existed, these might be at least plausibly claimed as representatives of the condition of Man before he arrived at the religious state of culture. It is not desirable, however, that this argument should be put forward, for the asserted existence of the non-religious tribes in question rests, as we have seen, on evidence often mistaken and never conclusive."[22] Tylor is not the only scholar of the era to display such certainty. For the most part, in fact for most of his contemporaries, the Western case was always perceived as the model or the absolute reference. But here too we may entertain the notion that the famous Stoic thesis of *koinai ennouai* (common notions or universal consensus) always exerted a decisive influence on the minds of nineteenth-century writers and scholars trained in the classics. It seems self-evident that the most noble, most remarkable Western creation, to the extent that it had pretensions to universality, could not do other than rediscover itself, in one form or another (albeit in preferred forms) almost everywhere. Peoples who seemed to be deprived of religion were considered ipso facto and without the least question to be the most primitive and degenerate examples of humankind.

The West gave religion to the world, and it was necessary that the world give it back, to the West's greater glory. The universal must be found everywhere, must be valid for all, and to do this, it must retain a familiar profile, its own. But how under these conditions to account for the differences, the alterities, and even the "monstrosities" that a fledgling ethnology was then discovering in such numbers? Were they not a threat to religion, and would they not dissolve it into a multiplicity of unique, incomparable configurations? Here was the germ of what might have been a major contradiction for Western science, for it immediately reduced it to a trifling matter, if it did not obviate it entirely, by associating the idea of progress, irresistible and continuous progress, with this universalist vision. The majority of other religions were thenceforth viewed as rough drafts, archaic or primitive forms of our religion. The universal undeniably exists, but at different stages of development. By having these religions succeed one another along a single temporal axis, where the West clearly occupied the terminal position, the differences that were observed lost all capacity to subvert.[23]

Conceived of from the outset as historical, they never became ontological. It was they that were dissolved in the idea of progress.

At a single stroke, imperialism and colonialism were equally justified and even, with the impetus of missionary activity, received an unanticipated moral guarantee. Under the cover of bringing progress and civilization, it was the vast process of universalization that would be completed by giving it for good measure, along with religion, its highest expression or form. This was a rude blow to fragile cultures that had scarcely come onto the stage of universal history. Most of them died of it; others have been subjugated and deformed.

This implicit deduction, which makes it possible to pass from Christian universalism to the universalism of science, from Christian anthropology to scientific anthropology, is naturally of the greatest importance for our topic. It clearly signifies that the human sciences (and among them the history of religions) have frequently been content, often unknowingly, sometimes naïvely, at other times arrogantly, consciously to revive a prejudice—and one of our dearest native categories. In so doing, do they not "by other ways and with other means" further the movement begun by Saint Paul and continued after him by the Christian churches? To be quite clear about it, the imperialistic impulse demonstrated in Western science was long summarized in the attitude that consists of "universalizing" the categories and values issuing from our cultural tradition alone. And this is still too often the case today, unless "cultural relativism" gains the upper hand. Does this attitude not consist of somehow appropriating and a priori alienating the image or idea of humanity of which it claims, however, to be making an objective study?

Just as it can never encounter religions other than those that display forms inferior to those prevailing in its own culture, Western science never conceived of anthropology in any form other than that most familiar to it. In both cases—the history of religions and anthropology—it was its own image and its own ideals that it projected onto the world.

Is it necessary to add that in the context of the late nineteenth century, colonialism, the missionary spirit, and capitalism found nothing objectionable in the approaches taken by these "sciences"?

5 | Continuities

A General Topic

We have just seen that religion was too specialized, too unique a notion to legitimate the ambitions that anthropology had for it, that it was too intimately associated with history, that is, with the cultural formation of the West and of Christianity.

It was also shown that what this notion covered, the attitudes and behaviors commonly called religious, had evolved toward forms that represented quite remarkable cases, exceptions among all those that various human cultures permit us to observe. In particular, the interiorization and individualization of feelings called religious, the autonomy of the corresponding sphere in its capacity of "distinct domain," and the proclaimed will of the West, scientific as much as Christian, to universalize the idea of religion by associating it with the totality of human societies—all these appeared as so many unprecedented facts, comprehensible only in the light of an original history, that of the West itself. It also dictated that we not seek in this evolution and succession of unforeseeable events the expression of any religious universal.

Under these conditions, how are we to view this gigantic assemblage of ideas and unique facts? Just because it was constituted on the basis of an unforeseen history, does it escape a certain regulation, and to what degree? At first sight, one might think so and conclude that disorder reigned everywhere. History, then, if it is capable of generating such incomparable singularities, should at the same time and in almost inevitable fashion stimulate works and thoughts as original as they are unpredictable. Under these conditions any retrospective look must reveal tortured landscapes to our horrified minds, true challenges cast down before the skills of the most astute cartographers. This discouraging, apocalyptic conclusion rests on a superficial confusion, one that starts with the term "singularities," or one of its synonyms, and then deduces that the phenomena observed, as well as the corresponding connections, must be devoid of order and, as a consequence, of intelligibility. This is an erroneous deduction. In addition, did we not note at the time that as concerns religion, a very great number of opinions, as diverse as they are opposed, had been expressed and that these, with the network of controversies associated with them, furnished the richest and best-organized repertory of ideas that Western thought had ever conceived in two thousand years, a repertory that influenced all other forms of artistic and intellectual production? An element is "structuring" precisely to the extent that it itself rests on a rich and abundantly ramified organization. It is this architectonic function that religion filled in the West.

It is clear from the examples of the various human cultures known today that orderings, arrangements, and classifications dominate everywhere, and that they concern the totality of social activities and preoccupations equally well. There is no doubt that the most universal and distinctive character of these cultures in fact lies in this. And, in the case that interests us (which is far from being an exception), such order is no less present over time, throughout the course of history. For intellectual history in a given civilization draws sustenance from revivals, commentaries, and reinterpretations, in short, from traditions that make up so many specialized complexes that endlessly back each other up. Nothing is less subject to entropy than a culture, than the degree of order that rules there.

This is why the history of religions and the vaster historical complex of ideas and themes that preceded it merit being placed in this larger and more encompassing totality, the history of Western thought, in order to give us one of the keys to their reciprocal comprehension.

We shall consequently see that over time a vast general topic has been built around the nucleus of religion.

In many respects, this concerns the history of ideas as much as the more specialized history of religions. This should not surprise us. It has already been noted that the latter was often only the heir and successor of the former. This topic no doubt also represents one of the most durable and best-structured systems that are to be found. For example, reflections on the universality and origin of the belief in gods, the presence or absence of a benevolent divine providence, or the type of interpretation that could be applied to myths began in Greece long before the birth of Christianity and were revived later by the first Church fathers. As for true innovations (provided that such innovations, until then absolutely unheard of, ever saw the light of day), rare indeed were those that were not obliged to position themselves with regard to, or take a stand on, one or the other of those great questions that rapidly became traditional.

I offer no original contribution here to the definition of the term "topic" [*topique*]. On the contrary, I am content to take it in the most ordinary sense, which is also the most practical (according to Port-Royal logic, the loci [*lieux*] that form one topic or another "are certain general heads to which may be reduced all the proofs we employ in the various matters of which we treat"). In order better to measure its heuristic potential, I shall simply begin by first putting this topic back into a broader problematic, which is consubstantial with it in many respects and for which I propose to reserve the phrase "poetics of knowledge."[1]

The texts, theses, and various works published by specialists in the human sciences cannot be summarized as impartial presentations, objective descriptions, or rational analyses of hypotheses, facts, and perfectly identifiable and circumscribed objects on whose nature and significance the scholarly community finds itself in spontaneous agreement. This is because (among other better-known reasons) the fields of knowledge corresponding to these worlds of discourse are subject to numerous complex, independent constraining rules, which have nothing to do with observation, reasoning, or explanations of the scientific type, but rather with an original poetics that succeeded in putting the most diverse rhetorical procedures to work in its own creative activity (*poiesis*).

The most general and constant characteristics of this poetics equally affect the totality of verbal productions that a culture devotes to the conception, composition, and transmission of its bodies of knowledge, whether or not they are learned and, if they are, whether or not they are scientific. For through their discursive productions, whose forms and contents are themselves closely codified and catalogued, all cultures unceasingly work toward the solidification of their systems of knowledge. In the richness of their poetic structures, in their very high degree of thematization, and in their multiform influences on the life of human societies, such bodies of knowledge are actually complex organisms, saturated with order and meaning. And it is in this capacity that they intervene in the corresponding culture to organize conceptions or representations of the world. But as the world in such cases becomes their world, these bodies of knowledge contribute to form these same cultures as noncontingent complexes. In the circumstances, we should perhaps take one further step and say that the ultimate substratum of human cultures is intimately linked to principles, rules, and productions of a poetic nature.

If bodies of knowledge in the human sciences, like that in the history of religions, have a poetic structure, it is due initially to the fact that they result, like any kind of knowledge present in any culture, from the implementation of the general procedures of textualization.[2] Confronted with the puzzling richness and complexity of the "real" world or history, the clearest features of textualization, such as unity, coherence, order, and homogeneity, have little chance of possessing any great objective value, because they correspond only too well to certain requirements of our minds. In fact, by what miracle would such artificial constructions represent accurate descriptions or explanations, in exact conformity with one or other given state of affairs? What is left, for example, of the vitality and diversity of a confused era when it is presented in the form of a dissertation organized around two or three major ideas that themselves belong to our traditional repertory of loci, be they descriptive or interpretive?

In the face of the damage done by this tenacious illusion, we must reassert that language, a fortiori when it proceeds to the composition of developed texts (themselves subject to constraining writing rules that have been sanctioned by academic authority and tradition), must absolutely not be seen as a kind of photographic instrument, capable of delivering or faithfully stating reality such as it is (or was).

A text, especially if it claims to be perfectly objective, is always the result of innumerable intellectual operations, among which those referring specifically to its creation do not simply complete that rigorous rational process (observations, critical analyses, reasoning) to which the decisive part of any scientific project would be entrusted, since textualization not only informs each of these stages but equally well intervenes from the outset, at the very moment of the conception of the project. It is this textualization that determines the scope, tone, and style, sets out the major argument, and through a thousand channels links it organically to a learned tradition, to the spirit of an era, to a field of intellectual controversies, and so on.

To this must also be added, on the simple level of style (of the utterance properly speaking), the repertory of tropological operations, such as the transfer and metaphorization of concepts, which, calling on the most accessible resources of the language, create effects of meaning, perhaps even effects of the real, that have no other existence than a verbal one.

The least debatable data (observations, descriptions, etc.) are in addition simultaneously subjected to the complementary demands of discursive genres that preexist them, such as the historical book, the philosophical thesis, or the philological article, whose almost unchangeable (on the scale of a human life) norms are always under the care of traditions that are as vigilant as they are inflexible. It is not without reason that they are called "disciplines." These are genres that determine the choice of data, their treatment, and their concatenation within discursive wholes, whose intelligibility concerns, not reality as such, but rather our conventional ways of apprehending it and translating it into terms we find meaningful. Is there a single history [*histoire*] (the history of law, of painting, of France) that amounts to no more than a dry enumeration of a multitude of undeniable facts, that is not, in other words, also a story [*histoire*]?

In any case, it is enough to try, in exhaustive and objective fashion, to describe an object, a fact, or an event at a point in time (an apple placed on a desk, a cigarette burning down in an ashtray) to see to what extent such a bit of reasoning—the simplest imaginable, moreover—at once runs into innumerable constraints and is repeatedly reduced to making decisive choices of a rhetorical nature, consubstantial with the very act of description. In the use of a language, all language, we dispose of only an extremely reduced freedom, perhaps even none at all in many cases. And scientific writing (with its models, traditions, demands, ethics, proprieties, tacit rules, etc.) cannot escape this law, which rests on so many conventions whose history it would be hazardous to retrace without having recourse to the discursive schemas that this same history has bequeathed to us.

Within the framework of a culture, as within the framework of a scientific discipline, these fields of knowledge are, on the other hand, always dependent on a topic, that is, an inventory of ideas and general positions that themselves thematize our access to reality. This access actually never appears as an immanent, spontaneous, unmediated relationship. It is always subject to very precise rules, the complex heritage of a more or less ancient intellectual tradition, a great number of whose elements have survived into the modern *epistēmē*. This last remark is particularly valid for the history of religions, which has erected itself on the fossilized strata laid down by the long Christian tradition.

This general topic contains schemas that define, firstly, the loci from which we speak and the objects of which we speak to the exclusion of all those, just as plausible, that could have been substituted for or associated with them. In a given period, the status of a system of knowledge, like that of modern science, can be compared to a combinatory system that contains a certain number of exclusive observation points (structuralism, Marxism, functionalism, historicism, Freudianism, nominalism, etc.), from which alone the conceptual exploration of the surrounding world is conducted.

In addition, this exploration is always preoriented for another reason, for this surrounding reality is itself thematized around a certain number of exemplary, exclusive objects (myth, language, symbolic function, meaning, the imaginary, the hypertext, etc.). In other words, the realities with which the human sciences are confronted are already constructed, textualized, classified, and arranged as functions of this double combinatory system (the loci from which we speak and the objects of which we speak).

As a consequence, in order to understand the state of things that surround us or that have preceded us, in order to contemplate them as they are or as they have been, it would be absolutely indispensable first to acquire the means to understand and analyze the preexistent, systematically thematized networks that intervene between them and us. Unfortunately, this radical step is not easy to conceive of, for it would likely itself be no less thematized and ordered than the domain it intended to analyze.

In the circumstances, some will perhaps think that the greatest scientific revolution would consist in leaving our texts behind, in transforming ourselves into simple observers. In reality, such an objective is not desirable either, for such observation would inevitably be restricted to the sole, contemporary here and now of its ephemeral manifestation.

We may also associate with this overall topic the majority of the hermeneutical schemes that govern our conceptions of meaning and truth, which are in the same way the result of unique thematizations. This means that our own conceptions of truth and meaning, to which we are nevertheless tempted to assign an absolute or invariable value, are just as fully the result of specific historical constructions, tied to certain usages and intellectual practices that together define a certain type or types of explanation. Nor do the conceptions that we might have of meaning and truth ever proceed from an immediate relationship with reality; they are defined within a culture by rules that this same culture has recognized as orthodox. This orthodoxy equally defines, in an admirable reflexive movement of autofoundation, the axis delimiting the domain of the true, which will always only be true for itself.

This is also generally true of our celebrated scientific objectivity, for its goal can at best never concern anything but fragments of reality (those associated with the observations famously called "scientific"). Reality considered in its totality—the only one that has any meaning for humanity—is not a scientific but a philosophical problem, since in its capacity of "world," it cannot fall within the reach of scientific observation or analysis. In this respect, we could doubtless assert that, as we see today, traditional cosmographies (conceived on the basis of myths or beliefs, ideologies or revelations) have nothing to fear from the progress of science. Indeed, they alone possess the capacity to integrate certain of its results into their own constructions.

Interpretation of the works of Plato has varied over the course of history and will continue to change, not merely because we continue to learn more about him but even more because the art of interpretation and commentary, which comes down to the question of meaning and truth, presents itself differently in each era. Even so, this variability does not create an anarchy or disorder that the mind cannot cope with, because there is also a thematization of controversies and debates in any given culture. Seen from a distance, each culture offers only a limited number of theses or adversarial positions, all perfectly mapped: Plato versus Aristotle, Plotinus versus Lucretius, Locke versus Bossuet, Marx versus Freud, Heidegger versus Bourdieu, and so on. And these theses and stances in turn become symbolic. Nor is it uncommon for them to be cross-disciplinary and common to several fields of knowledge or that they group together to form vast, durable paradigms (idealists or theists versus materialists). And it is almost always on the level of these global structures that the general orientation and fundamental position that are at the basis of the work of interpretation are determined.

In any case, the omnipresence and vigilance of institutions (schools, universities, churches, academies, journals, and scientific societies, etc.), as much in the transmission of knowledge and the definition and codification of learned discourse as in the ideological control of what is or is not acceptable, enable these topics and great thematizations to organize intellectual life and production. We observe this in contemporary academic notions, which in so many respects often still remain conventional: how many scholarly interpretations can we count for each original thought?

What we might call the rhetorical treatment of reality then owes very little to impartial observation and analysis. In fact, it would seem that the description of an object, the narration of an event, the stages of an argument, the modalities of an utterance, and the use of tropes make up so many artificial, codified, but still perfectly indispensable instruments that we are constrained to use in order to analyze any single particle of reality. It is then proper to seek to understand what these procedures add to it, how they subject it to stereotyped forms that will thenceforth be those through which we apprehend it. Keep in mind that, contrary to what has long been supposed, we read reality much more than we see it.

If simple, real objects as described in books must already be conceived of as problematic, unique constructions that have required the deployment of perfected poetic means, we shall all the more readily recognize that the narration of a history—the coordination of arguments in a proof—are intellectual operations that show similarities with the structuring and composition of works of fiction that are too obvious for us not to be at least bothered by the resemblance. On the other hand, how, in a comparison or explanation, could we abandon the rhetorical procedures, perfectly inventoried and known since antiquity, that allow us to attract the attention and win the agreement of the reader?

Reduced to a logician's strict, intractable analysis (of the type, if p, then q, where p and q as well as the nature of the inference are perfectly known),[3] that is, in favorable cases where their presentation at least permits us to undertake this salutary exercise, most of the general explanations provided by the human sciences reveal that they are founded on poetic instances, themselves constructed in texts (the Oedipus complex, class war, structure, the opposition between the sacred and the profane, and the like) and seem convincing only because they will in turn be used in exercises of paraphrase and interpretation. And these exercises are also subject to very precise rules.

Because they, too, exploit to maximum effect all the resources of poetics and rhetoric, we would unhesitatingly classify all global theories (concerning the world, humankind, history, art, natural or symbolic languages), all visions that rest on a unique, originary explicative instance (the myth of Oedipus for Freudianism, the binary system for structuralism, class struggle for Marxism, the sacred for the phenomenologists, etc.) in the same register. This attitude is still to be found among all the modern conceptions and "isms," as well as among the numerous schools of thought that played a major founding role in the nineteenth century, when the epistemological frameworks of the human sciences were erected.

As if that were not enough, we must also point out that this vast domain of the human sciences is not isolated. The division of fields of knowledge, whether useful for the individual or for society, is effected within a vast complex, of which these sciences represent only one sector. Among all these bodies of knowledge, there are contacts, for example, between the pseudo-sciences and the sciences, or between the latter and literature, as well as reciprocal influences and interferences. It is very instructive to observe how, in contemporary Western civilization, knowledge is divided up between literature and anthropology. Curiously, dealing with the problems most relevant to the lives of human beings, to their troubled and ephemeral real existence, falls to the former, to literature, as if the human condition in its most concrete, most vital aspects were an object of study too trivial (or too embarrassing?) for science. But to whom or to what are we to attribute the exclusion from the human sciences of humans' most ordinary "lived experience"? To what ancient and venerable division of the fields of knowledge? Analogously, although there have long been chairs at universities devoted to the phonology of archaic Greek dialects, there are none, as we all know, devoted to the study of human cruelty and barbarity. But we might just as well ask ourselves in what sense "humanity according to Lévi-Strauss" is more anthropological than Heidegger's view of it or less philosophical than Cassirer's.

On the periphery of the human sciences, literature (again), philosophical speculation, various ideologies, and mythic thought all construct other general topics. And influences and exchanges are continuously at work among them. Thus the human sciences offer surprising analogies, exemplary in more than one respect, to mythic thought.

Like myths, the human sciences, with some rare exceptions, do not speak of the production of their own discourse. Such discourse always seems "decontextualized," external to the history (social, economic, ideological, institutional) of its own formation. On the other hand, these same discourses willingly and systematically associate themselves with distant ancestors, founders, and eponyms (e.g., Plato, Marx, Freud, Heidegger).

Once they become interested in origins (of humanity, language, religion, power, etc.), or try to summarize or explain complex processes, or look for exclusive, uniform causes, specialists in the human sciences readily turn to the old mythographical reflexes. For the human sciences are not just content to speak in the fashion of myths, to adopt their terminology. Sometimes they also borrow characteristically mythographic elements. The study of certain "objects" gives the human sciences other opportunities to plagiarize mythic discourse. Among these, let us mention the instances and notions (originary, central, essential, and so on) invoked in a number of works (on meaning, language, form, essence, the unconscious, evolution, dialectic, etc.) or entities that are difficult to apprehend in their totality (the world, mankind, society, history, mind, etc.). In all discussions referring to them, mythical reflexes and mythic content are effortlessly substituted for the deficiencies of scientific knowledge. Mythic "thought" seems capable of spontaneously filling all the gaps left by scientific thought, and it is unfortunately when it comes to providing global explanations—visions of the whole—that the insufficiencies of the latter appear most tellingly.

The fact that the heuristic hypothesis of a general topic associated with a poetics of knowledge may be capable of assisting us in better appreciating certain complex intellectual phenomena does not relieve us of trying to inventory the elements that make up the specialized topic that concerns us here, centered on the idea of religion.

The history of the West, considered in the intimate, organic relationship that it maintains with Christianity; the even vaster history of ideas relative to what this same West has admitted, at times retrospectively and anachronistically, as relevant to the domain of religion; and, lastly, more recently, the history of the history of religions also comprise bitter controversies and debates. Let us then consider this topic, constantly bearing in mind the idea that its constituent elements, or in any case most of them, never appear except in polemical or confrontational relationships. And that it is these same relationships, provided we view them globally and from some distance, that perhaps give this topic a coherence and tighter texture, to the extent that it is probable that controversies and debates, through the unceasing exchange of arguments and ideas about the same "nodes," seem to weave a fabric as solid as it is immaterial.

We should not neglect to add that this topic comprises everything from the most trivial commonplaces to the most subtle metaphysical arguments. This is doubtless the surest indicator that it belongs to a particular culture, the totality of whose attitudes and intellectual positions it espouses. Its task is to establish bridgeheads, lay out corridors between these different levels.

On the first level, we initially encounter the things of which we are speaking, which in the final analysis are not all that numerous. A retrospective look over our past history reveals in fact that discussions have crystallized around a few indigenous subjects (in particular the soul and the body, the existence of God, faith, myths, magic, providence), which in our eyes often make up the very idea of religion.

The things about which we speak, we must immediately note, are also the only ones of which we are capable of speaking, given that associated with them are the handful of ideas and concepts adapted for their evocation. Thus, it is very easy for us to initiate and promote a discussion on the interpretation of myths, for here we find ourselves on familiar ground, worked over in every direction for twenty-five centuries. On the other hand, we have a bit more trouble defining the specificity of religious phenomena in a given African tribe or in the China of a distant era. And so we do this only at the cost of numerous inaccuracies and ridiculous anachronisms, which we do not easily perceive, since our language (the one that is speaking at this moment of Chinese religion) is the same one that has spoken for centuries of religion itself as an obvious and natural thing.

A topic concerns not only the objects of which one speaks, along with the usual words in which the agreed-on utterance is expressed; it also encompasses the schemas or frameworks of thought by means of which this speech act is organized as discourse, as an exposition of arguments. Thus, for us Westerners, the proofs of the existence of God comprise a traditional locus, long known and carefully catalogued, the different elements of which have given rise to many detailed inventories. And, clearly, the same is true of proofs to the contrary.

These repertories of arguments, associated with this or that question, are themselves made up of very ill-assorted materials. Found there are many general opinions (concerning the world, mankind, the fate of societies), clichés, and commonplaces, as well as demonstrations conducted with the greatest care and most remarkable erudition. And it is not because they belong to differing levels of abstraction or development that they mutually contradict or exclude each other. On the contrary, it is certain that between these various levels continuous exchanges are effected and modes of coexistence established. Thus, it is not uncommon in an article on the history of religions to observe a mixture of data displaying the most rigorous scholarship along with the most banal opinions on "the essence of religion."

An intellectual tradition is not a massive heritage, growing weightier from generation to generation by the superimposition of fossilized strata. It is a "dialogics" ceaselessly revived, renewed, reactualized, but always within the framework of a combinatory mode that is modified only very slowly. A tradition is always alive, even if its life is essentially composed of resumptions, commentaries, and interpretations of the works of the past. Western thinkers confronted with the questions (in any case stereotypical) posed them by the idea of religion have never ceased to comment on the opinions of Plato, Saint Augustine, Spinoza, Marx, Feuerbach, and Lucretius, and—to put it a bit maliciously—have often done no more than that.

In reality, for each culture, even one as vast and ancient as ours, there exist only a small number of exemplary theses dealing with the world, mankind, their origin, or their fate. Intellectual life, no matter how rich it may be, never develops except within its own creations, from which it cannot easily escape. The creativity of the human mind, unless we are speaking of simple ingenuity, is deployed especially in ornamentation, shading, scrollwork, coloring. As regards the overall architecture, the disposition of mass and general orientation, it most often remains attached to its familiar points of reference and traditional loci.

The ancient, rich, structured topic associated with the term "religion," defines, or rather underpins, a huge corpus of knowledge, which in turn permits the investigation of every domain to which we attach (at times with considerable trouble and uncertainty) the label "religious." This simple operation, the labeling, is usually enough to lock in the terms of the debate, since it defines a priori the nature of the field, the choice of style, and the themes, as well as the range of arguments.

Readers who think that they discern the hint of a tautology here may rest reassured. They are right. The topic and range of fields of knowledge (or disciplines) not only mutually define and constitute one another, they also take reality hostage. First of all, a corpus of knowledge marked religion depends for its global coherence (or, if you wish, its thematic unity), as much as for its means of analysis, on a discursive organization that is itself subject to constraints imposed by the corresponding topic, since it is the latter that definitively regulates the content and form of the various kinds of discourse that will be produced concerning it. In such a process, the real world, the noisy, tumultuous world of life, certainly does not represent as strong a constraint. Why not?

Because the world is mute about itself, something everyone will agree on (although many credulous minds insist on seeking signatures in it and reading symbols that "say something"), and as such it is indescribable. Each of us is confronted with the tangle of events, objects, and beings, with the unspeakable confusion of uncountable life. For there exists no point exterior to the world, no promontory from which it is possible to envision it in its totality. An exhaustive description of the world would, moreover, have to include itself in the undertaking, thus revealing the place and time of its enunciation, and to recognize its own weaknesses (it is not only in literature that the illusion of the omniscient narrator is a practical obligation and a handy convention; to one degree or another, it is needed in every kind of writing).

The project of such a description would in any case be endless (and in any case, too, we cannot wait to finish our description of the world in order to live in it; would we want to?) and would condemn its author to exhausting perplexities: which site should be chosen to begin it? In which order should it be undertaken? Which perspective should be privileged? This is because the real world, as such, is indescribable *and* because we nonetheless need to have a global vision of it in order to live there—or quite simply to think, because our knowledge, created and organized according to the internal necessities of this or that topic, so easily substitutes for it.

The topical inventory provides us with the grid on which we represent reality globally. As Wilhelm Dilthey asserted at the end of the nineteenth century, we live in "the world of representation," not in the "real" world of the physicist or chemist. The confusion that so easily occurs between them is explained by the fact that the first is substituted for the second, given that it alone provides us with global visions, purified and organized, of reality, in which our existences are capable of finding meaning, if not *a* meaning.

In any case, the words "vision" or "representation" create a major difficulty in suggesting that we are dealing with images or panoramas of the world that we somehow view from the exterior. A representation of the world would be a spectacle offered up to our gaze. In reality, these visions of the world rather consist of tight networks made up of loci and discursive themes, which in turn define and organize our own relationship with the world. What we take for a spectacle is in fact the very structure of our own act of observing. How, in the circumstances, could we see anything?

This also signifies that we are probably denied any release from the world of our topics, and that it is difficult to modify them. Just as it would be awkward, not to say impossible, for a Western mind to substitute for one of its topics any that it might borrow from a given era of Chinese or Bantu culture. Each of our worlds in closed in on itself, hermetically.

The sciences, especially the human sciences, probably did no better at first. Their development also passed through a slow elaboration of successively refined topics that shamelessly borrowed from the prescientific traditions in the history of Western thought. As already noted (and we may permit ourselves a brief review), the field of the history of religions is intimately, organically tied to that of the religious history of the West.

In return, these sciences are armed with a double-edged sword, capable of assisting them in cutting through the veils of illusion that enclose them. On the one hand, they have (but should develop even more substantially) the reflective capacity that would allow them to return to the processes that led to their own constitution. In this respect, the history of a science, of any science (especially in the sector of the human sciences) ought to remain a permanent concern. Unfortunately, this is far too infrequent. It alone re-calls to us that concepts, objects, and methods are all—and in the same way—the result of historical formations.[4] On the other hand, the objective of these sciences is to imagine the critical instruments, the only ones they need, that would permit them to analyze these processes. To demonstrate, as we have done, that a specialized poetics and specific topic exist in every field of knowledge, and then to determine what characterizes them, are two tasks that certainly cannot claim to give form on their own to the absolute goal of epistemological thought. But do they not allow us to glimpse a cer-tain kind of progress based on a critical and systematic reexamination of all the linguistic facts that organize the "poetic structure" of our "scientific world"?[5]

A Major Paradigm

When we attempt to draw up an inventory of the topic around which the field of the history of religions has been organized (itself returned to the larger context of Western intellectual history), it soon becomes evident that this catalog ought to be headed by a certain number of exemplary or paradigmatic oppositions.[6] Of these, I mention here only those that are very general in scope and whose antithetical terms are widely known:

— Theists versus materialists and atheists
— Providentialists versus antiprovidentialists (variant: skeptics)
— Religion versus reason (variant: religion versus science)
— True religion versus false religions (or primitive religions)
— Revealed religion versus natural religion

To begin, let us note that these pairs of opposing terms have all had a very long life. Some of them (such as the first two) have even traversed the entire intellectual history of the West from its distant pre-Socratic origins. The arguments of a Xenophon have retained all their flavor, while losing none of their pertinence: they remain, today, fully usable in philosophical debate, and it would probably be impossible to draw up a list of all the vari-ants to which they have given rise.[7] The great paradigmatic models sym-bolized in our eyes by the canonical oppositions—Plato versus Aristotle, Plotinus versus Lucretius—have, as well, remained exemplary to the degree that in many instances they have dominated Western thought by forcing all general opinion concerning the ultimate nature of the world or of mankind to define itself as a function of themselves (or of one of their similarly oriented heirs).

This long duration, even greater than those studied by Fernand Braudel, calls for no other explanation than that offered by the persistent presence of a learned tradition that, through the schools of antiquity and then the medieval and modern universities, has continuously favored a certain conception of intellectual labor founded, above all, on the transmission of the most learned and most venerable writings, the composition of academic and often stereotyped commentaries, the compilation of collections of maxims and *exempla,* and the authoring of paraphrases and more or less explicit borrowings. Here living thought has been smothered under a mass of studies that repeat and gloss one another ad infinitum.

For more than two millennia, Aristotle and Plato have been the object of commentary (on the original texts or on translations); for more than twenty centuries as well, the partisans of Plotinus and Lucretius (or their heirs) have opposed each other by invoking *grosso modo* the same types of opinions and ideas. And are we capable today, respecting these same themes, of discovering other, as yet unheard-of arguments or a more essential, more central paradigm than that symbolized in our eyes by these familiar oppositions? We should add that a comparable conservatism, just as stubborn, is observable elsewhere, for example, in the intellectual traditions of India, China, and the Muslim world. In this respect, the situation of the West, Greek then Christian, offers no particular originality.

The longevity of these paradigms through centuries of troubled history and complex evolution gives our intellectual history an undeniable overall coherence. The persistence of comparable structures, the recurrence of the same general opinions and the same interpretive positions, the revival of the same controversies, the interlacing of contradictory arguments concerning the same debates, the recourse to the same examples—all have contributed to seize and hold the space reserved for the exercise of thought. Epicurus's atom is not that of modern physics, but both are in opposition to theses arguing for the intervention of some form of providence (Platonist, Plotinian, Christian, or other) in the world. On this grid, each square has been localized, sometimes from a very early date, with considerable precision. We know those adjacent to it as well as those at the other end of the continuum.

The principal reason for this general coherence lies in the fundamental and undebatable character of these pairs of antithetical terms. Each of them presents a polemical structure: to the partisans of unchanging transcendence just mentioned (Plato, Plotinus, the Christian thinkers) are opposed those who accept no other influences than those, material and historical, that are immanent in this world. At the same time, the former see a benevolent divine providence intervening in the universe, a providence that the latter reject with arguments symmetrical and inverse to those of their opponents: so injustice, evil, and suffering are everywhere triumphant.

This radical, definitive opposition (providentialists versus antiprovidentialists or theists versus materialists and atheists) on the other hand provides Western thought with what we may here agree to call its major paradigm, one that in all eras seems to have divided and distributed opinions into two adversarial camps.[8] It has served as a model for some other patterns that have followed and that not only reproduce the sense of its general orientation but on occasion borrow their polemical themes and arguments from it. If we first off think of the well-known modern oppositions—religion versus reason or religion versus science—there are also others, more specialized, some of which developed inside the very field of study that here concerns us.

Thus, at the beginning of the nineteenth century, to the symbolism of Frédéric Creuzer—in which Ernest Renan was probably not wrong to see a revival of "the Neoplatonic spirit of Plotinus, Porphyrus, and Proclus"[9]—was opposed as an antithesis the historicist criticism of Karl O. Müller. But beyond their particular characteristics, is not Creuzer's thesis, no less than Müller's, inscribed in a repetitive dialectic movement, whose orientation and general philosophy were born of the first and fundamental confrontation (theism versus materialism)?[10] Similarly, is it not significant that a few years after Renan made the observation quoted above, Émile Burnouf noted that the "materialist systems [of his era] renew[ed], under more specious forms, the Epicurean doctrines of Lucretius"? Yet we are in the year 1872. Similarly, a bit later, at the beginning of the twentieth century and in the still circumscribed domain of depth psychology, the opposition summarized in the names of Freud and Jung—put otherwise, the materialism of the one and the spiritualism of the other—does it not "in the final instance" reproduce the major terms of this very old quarrel?

We rediscover the spirit of this absolute opposition (absolute in any case for our Western minds) like a faithful echo in the major dislocation (soul versus body) that establishes most of the representations that are regrouped under the two great adversarial theses of our traditional anthropology (which has continued to inform theories that are infinitely more learned but, in the final analysis, scarcely more original). This proves that in passing from the most general philosophy to religion, from religion to history and from history to anthropology, we see no true breaks, as if, once it set itself to conceiving large-scale explanations, Western thought in fact disposed of only a small number of theses and models.[11]

The overall coherence of the topic associated with the field of history of religions clearly depends on the polemical structure of this major paradigm, and, as we have seen, it is capable in turn of generating more local and modest paradigms, more specific ones too, but ones that, in the manner of fractals, conserve the general shape and disposition of their larger-scale antecedents. It is likely that such polemical structures organize other fields of knowledge by giving them just that coherence and permanence that the simple juxtaposition of a few great themes (always under threat of losing their substance, of splintering or being transformed) do not offer them. On the contrary, those that we have identified all display the same global organization, capable of reproducing and transmitting itself infinitely, down to the smallest details.

The domain of our opinions, be they scientific or not, is perhaps nothing but a huge system of fractal shapes itself dominated by the incessant activity of polemic and controversy. In this case, this immemorial movement, inscribed in our oldest intellectual tradition, would offer our fields of knowledge the system of references and coordinates in which they inscribe themselves. Every new idea or hypothesis immediately generates its antithesis, whose position is a priori predictable.[12]

On a different scale, one that allows the observation of all these entities, what do we observe? The jumble and diversity of facts seems very great at first view; but, far from generating a tangled disorder, they make it possible to link more solidly those elements that would otherwise risk being dislocated or distanced from one another. The possible confusion that would result from this generalized intertwining is compensated for by the presence of these huge polemical structures that keep intellectual matter captive and ceaselessly reorganize it.

When it's a question of the existence of gods, the soul, providence, the general conception of the world, and the origin of beliefs, the resources of our conceptual and argumentative apparatus seem rather poor and limited. And, from the double point of view of the value of the corresponding arguments and of the structure that supports them, it has evolved, has grown, only very slowly since Plato or Lucretius. What could a fiercely antiprovidentialist materialist add to Lucretius that would be completely original? What new "psychological" arguments would one be able to bring to an explanation of human credulity? What that is really significant or really novel could today be added to the "spirit" of this prestigious ancestor? For in this regard, what we call the "spirit" of a thesis, an idea, or a work is something quite essential, for this spirit, this general orientation, this particular way of expressing or strongly influencing a way of being in the world, is capable of surviving for a very long time, of transmitting itself from generation to generation with great faithfulness—a bit like proverbs and old saws that also seem untouched by time and forgetfulness.

Similarly, has not the subversive spirit of a Critias or a Xenophon survived intact to our own days, as if they had traced an eternal pathway that never closed behind them? The cynicism of the former, which inspired Machiavelli in his *Discourses on Livy* (the gods are human creations intended to inspire a salutary fear in men as political subjects), and the skeptical irony of the latter (men have created the gods in their own image) will always be in opposition to the arguments of Plotinus or Bossuet.

A cursory but nonetheless interrogative survey of the few hundred works from Critias to Jacques Derrida that have questioned the origin of mankind's belief in invisible, immaterial gods quickly reveals that we are advancing in a familiar, well-mapped universe, in which the same ideas never cease to be revived and recombined with one another. On other questions, too (the origin of evil in the world or of moral ideas in human beings; the relations between body and soul, language and reality, etc.), comparable repetitive arguments, identical controversies have similarly never ceased to be repeated, developed, and commented on in the same fashion.

This is due to the convergence of several influences, whose effects are combinatory. On the one hand, there are what we might call currents (first among which are theism, skepticism, materialism, and idealism), in that each of them has for centuries preserved a small number of simple ideas possessed of a general explicative value. In these currents, we find commonplaces, stereotyped opinions, maxims attached to a few great questions, a few recurrent themes. In the constitution of these vulgate forms, this simplicity, this paucity, and this repetition (to which the learned tradition has never ceased to lend the support of its erudition) must be seen as particularly effective factors.

Thus, the answers to questions as traditional as the origin of the belief in gods were subdivided from early on into two groups, in conformity with the grand paradigm outlined above: materialist explanations (that bring, for example, only immanent political or psychological causes into play) versus theist explanations (in which, on the contrary, one or other form of transcendence is a priori evoked). The materialist theses, to take them as an example, would in turn become differentiated as a function of the chosen instance (the Machiavellianism of princes, human psychology, the sociology of human groups, etc.) into more specialized explanations, comprising notions, themes, and arguments perhaps found (if only in spirit) in other debates. For transgenerity, that is, the faculty or aptitude for being present in different genres or fields, is probably one of the most common properties of these general explanations. Theology, literature, and philosophy have continuously exchanged and borrowed arguments. And over more than a century, the human sciences have more than once signed on to the list of the most deeply indebted.

We can see that from the most general explanatory option (one concerning the world or humanity) to a circumscribed detail (the interpretation of one myth or another), there is no true loss of continuity. The spirituality inspired by a given vision of the world is necessarily replicated in the premises that are at the base of a given, isolated interpretive effort. Nor are there any insurmountable obstacles or unbridged gaps between all the global options (skepticism, materialism, theism, and so on), for together they form a kind of system made up of transcendental alternatives that we might be tempted to compare to a vast combinatorics (when and only when p or q, if p then p', p'', p''', etc.).

Each option excludes those on the same level and opens a new (limited) series of options. And this repertory, too, remains limited, because it is closely dependent on a watchful tradition that supplies it with the rules of the game—in addition to most of its arguments. Also the interpretation (Freudian, Marxist, Dumézilian, Lévi-Straussian, and so on) of a myth in a learned journal conforms to a very precise set of editorial constraints and conventional rhetorical procedures. Academic activity is never more than the discursive transcription of a certain ethos shaped by centuries and centuries of tradition. The economy of intellectual production is one of the most regulated and monitored that there is. This "logical conformism" has as its corollary the existence of an institutional rule, imposed and accepted. The corpus of the scholar or academic is a disciplined corpus.

The idea of a combinatoric also naturally appears when, faced with a general problem to which it is possible to give a neat intellectual formulation, we review and list all the possible solutions. Thus, in our culture, as in that of India, the logical relations that people imagine in order to account for the links between the world and the superior entity that gives it a meaning amount to—and can only amount to—a short series of competing options. Between strict dualism and integral pantheism, originality can never address more than the details, the shadings that mask the skeleton of the logically possible. This admitted, it is just as important to add that the logical frameworks never become objects of belief. What has counted in this case has not been the logical nature of any one existing relationship between the beyond and the world, but rather the types of bonds (affective, ritual, ethical, etc.) and situations that have prevailed in the relationship uniting mankind with this absolute entity. In this sphere, if the combinatoric still exists, we would have to count on the degree of complexity that it could achieve making the task of description even more delicate, so numberless are the individual nuances and detailed influences.

The formal constraints associated with the existence of vast paradigms, the multiple resources bequeathed by tradition, the persistence of the same interrogations, the transmission and repetition of the same ideas, the weight and vigilance of learned institutions, all this has entered into a magnificent collaboration in order to create an original topic at the heart of our intellectual history. Moreover, from where would those who would deny its existence draw their arguments and the manner of organizing them, if not from a neighboring topic?

Despite the advantages that they seem to offer, the ideas of topic and paradigm leave themselves open to a radical objection, all the more so when, as here, one has recourse to them within the framework of a reflection that has as its parameters nothing less than the history of Western thought. For the one as much as the other seems fundamentally indifferent to history, that is, to change and evolution. Still, we have too frequently recalled the ephemeral, relative, or instable nature of so many cultural phenomena not to be sensitive to this crucial objection, which is quite solidly founded. Let us try then not to decide a priori in favor of one of these two theses (continuities versus discontinuities), which are too formal and too schematic to be worthy of confidence, but rather to relativize the scope of this opposition by attempting to inventory the subtle shadings with which, on the scale of a multisecular history, the permanence of a general topic or dominant paradigm is colored. At the same time, we shall discover their stunning capacity for adaptation.

Let us first recall that we never deal with other than general arguments as elements of a topic, capable of serving in numerous applications and occurring in different contexts. Such arguments enjoy a certain flexibility, since they are the result of patient screening and long polishing. They have been the object of a careful formulation, not least verbal; this has given them an admirable capacity for adaptation. These are, despite their apparent superficial simplicity, evolved organisms that have shown themselves able to adapt to diverse conditions and environments.

We should not then situate this datum (or a fortiori that explanation) that is valid on the scale of a specific microhistory on the same level as another datum that has been able to resist the erosion of time only because time carefully shaped its particular form, making it able to tolerate the damage done by history.

If Melchior de Polignac took the trouble to write a work intended to refute the theses of Lucretius in the eighteenth century, it was because their "spirit" (if not the precise letter) had preserved great topicality, despite changes and, doubtless, despite some misunderstandings. To assert, in lyrical but somber style, that providence and the interventions attributed to the gods do not exist, and to furnish arguments drawn from ordinary psychological experience in support of this proposition, was a simple thesis (which is not to say "naïve," but rather "perfect"). In this respect, it always had a chance of being understood (and thus feared) in a society dominated by the Roman Catholic Church—even if between Lucretius and the eighteenth century conceptions relative to the gods had been profoundly modified. But conversely and at the same time, institutions and specialists in thought had transmitted the text of Lucretius from one generation to the next, had ceaselessly reread, commented on, and discussed it. That is to say, it was constantly (re)actualized.

Even though it is unquestionable that Marx did not say word for word what Critias said (whose lesson had in the interval been taken up by Machiavelli, Hobbes, Spinoza, and Rousseau), it is, however, undeniable that both, on the scale of Western history, belong to the same intellectual current, that which recognizes in the gods only artificial creations intended to deceive and subjugate a credulous people. In our eyes, this opinion is at once opposed (since it is useless for us to reflect on it at any great length) by the adverse thesis, which is theist and providentialist. And this sacrilegious thesis will probably survive for an even longer time, as long as there are people who try to associate, in the consciousness of their fellows, the idea of unfailing obedience and belief in imaginary beings.

In the same way, the providentialist and antiprovidentialist theses have had recourse since antiquity, since the age of the *Timaeus,* to similar arguments and—what is striking and thus instructive—the "revolutionary" discoveries of modern physics have not appreciably modified the metaphysical terms of the debate. Having arrived at the thesis of the initial Big Bang, having encapsulated all the matter of the universe in a minuscule thimble, some physicists now return spontaneously to an old, very old cosmogonic hypothesis. "The envelopment of the universe took place in this single point. We then conceive of the universe as having been led out of this single point," said Nicholas of Cusa in his *Complementary Theological Considerations* as early as the mid fifteenth century. And we might conclude by asking whether the thesis of the Big Bang is not itself a new variant on the model of Genesis. In our own culture, which, however, flatters itself on having endlessly innovated and discovered, cosmographical models are few in number, and at bottom are summarized in a few simple prototypes.

We can also distinguish the details, infinite in variety, of complexes that are assured of greater longevity. The history of a culture does not unfold at the same rhythm for each of its elements: the history of Christianity is not comparable to that of one of its medieval heresies. The detail, free and original, evolves more easily than the whole from which it issues. The structure, complex and rich, resists change better than the individual contribution. The opposition that exists between Plotinus and Lucretius "resembles" that which we could establish between Jung and Freud, for each occupies a homologous place in comparable paradigms. But in so doing we would not confuse Plotinus's philosophy with Jung's. This does not preclude us from seeking influences or reminiscences in the work of the latter not only of Neoplatonism but also of gnosticism and the alchemical tradition. If it did not limit its investigations to the immediate surroundings, if it took into account the totality of the intellectual history of the West, and if it did not hesitate to reason in terms of macrostructures (paradigms or general topics), *Quellenforschungen,* research into sources, would no doubt obtain additional, perhaps even surprising, results.

In a straight line from the preceding distinction (details versus the whole), we can make a similar observation on the fate of specific works. None exists in absolute, unique fashion, enjoying a kind of perfect, definitive integrity. Every work, Plato's just as much as Sartre's, simultaneously exists in several forms. Let us consider two of them: the first, utopian and inaccessible, aims at exhaustiveness by respecting each nuance, each detail of the thought. According to the other, on the contrary, this same work exists only in the form of schematic summaries, exemplary theses, or partial (and at times erroneous) quotations. Now, who is to tell us that it is not this second form of existence that has played the greatest role in intellectual history? Summary Platonisms have perhaps multiplied the effects of their influence, more decisive than the thousand nuances of the integral work of Plato. Similarly, which Christianity would we say lies at the origin of our idea of religion? The thousands of learned articles on Roman Catholic theology probably do not play much part in it, but rather some very general, simplified ideas that the centuries have carefully polished.

Nor let us forget that at every instant, these works exist in (at least) two distinct universes. First in the historical universe, the one that is most familiar to us: no one is unaware that x follows y, which has itself been influenced by z; thus it is impossible that x should have had any influence on z. On the other hand, in the hypertext that ideally gathers in all the texts of our culture, things are different: it is possible that our reading of z is today influenced by what we know of x. Furthermore, x, y, and z here form a set (or one of the sets) that stands in opposition to the one that groups a, b, and c, independently of any chronological consideration.

In search of providentialist arguments, we can borrow from Plotinus just as well as from Bossuet, from Plato as well as from Saint Augustine, without taking into account the differences (pagans versus Christians) that, elsewhere, would be significant. Saussure lived almost two thousand five hundred years after Plato. But at the same time, Saussure and Plato, the *Course in General Linguistics* and the *Cratylus,* become contemporaries in a certain fashion when we examine fundamental opinions relative to the motivation of the linguistic sign. Thus, in a philosophical dissertation, for example, one could discuss the arguments of the one or the other without taking account of the temporal gap—but one would, on the contrary, do this when writing a history of linguistic ideas. Both procedures are legitimate, since they are equally instructive, as is a comparative approach that would not a priori give a determining importance to the respective position of the objects in history.

As concerns the comparative method in particular, it is indispensable that we add the following detail. Today there is no satisfactory protocol that, on its own and with its own means, could claim to overcome the inherent difficulties of either the continualist or the contrary point of view. To compare (and just what is being compared?) Lucretius to Feuerbach, or Critias to Machiavelli, in order to say, case by case, that they are incomparable, so plentiful and divergent is the information to be drawn from their respective microhistories, or that, on the contrary, they are indeed comparable—now privileging the general orientation of their principal theses— these are intellectual activities that will remain sterile as long as they do not differentiate in their operation the various planes and levels of complexity that we are here trying to distinguish.

Last, it will be recalled that, in the course of the history of intellectual processes, many have obviously been added to all those that have been reviewed, making the ultimate panorama doubtless less harmonious and less intelligible. But the conceptual reelaborations (profound or more superficial), the recycling of ideas and arguments, the migrations or transpositions of notions (metaphorical or literal), the syncretisms and diffuse influences, the more significative innovations—all are nonetheless inscribed in the same history.

As a consequence, to oppose continuity/ies and discontinuity/ies, according to what after all is only one locus among others in the vast topic devoted to ways of thinking and writing history, is a lazy attitude. That the respective significations of these two concepts are opposed in absolute fashion, according to a perfectly symmetrical arrangement, clearly does not imply in any way at all that historical things and events are essentially subject to this bipolarity. Intellectual history, seen within a sufficiently homogeneous framework (itself driven by a living tradition) is made up of continuities and of innovations. It is simply that they are not all situated at the same levels (of generality, abstraction, complexity). Similarly, this history is in the same sense made up of innumerable nuances, sometimes ephemeral, and of solid paradigms, much less numerous but infinitely more stable. This is what permits each culture to evolve, to adapt while conserving in human memory the meaning (a certain meaning) of its inalienable identity. To posit a brutal opposition between continuity and rupture does not offer much sense or interest beyond the kind of artificial exercise that in the Middle Ages was called a *disputatio.* Only the fabrication of finer instruments, capable of registering and storing the least nuance or intonation, would make obsolete that kind of metaphysical debate between theses that are all the more schematic in that they are intended to be as completely antithetical as possible.

This is why, as concerns religion (a theme so central that it has not ceased to occupy Western consciousness for two thousand years, and in that capacity has mobilized the intellectual resources of scores of generations of scholars, theologians, and artists), it seems to me not only legitimate but even indispensable to admit that on a certain scale, on the level of certain structures and certain forms of recurrence (provided we do not neglect the complex processes that underlie them and the thousand nuances that embellish them), there survive or are perpetuated manners of thinking, of choosing arguments and organizing them that, apart from the tumult of history, have constructed indelible points of reference. These familiar loci that our thought inhabits are also the only ones that our memory recognizes.

Exemplary Theses

The progressive construction, around the idea of religion, of a general topic that is more and more ample, and the deployment of vast paradigmatic oppositions orient most of the great intellectual controversies that Western culture has inspired. The exemplary opinions, objects, and theses that were associated with them display a comparable resistance to erosion. Despite the evolutionary currents that have intervened in the world of scientific and intellectual theories (the very ones that were perhaps a bit too quickly celebrated as "changes" or "paradigm shifts"), these elements as well seem to preserve a remarkably stable form and spirit.

In the perception of these permanencies, there doubtless intervenes the deceptive effect that comes from any retrospective reading that reinterprets the past in the light of current knowledge and impressions. But should we, for that reason, deny that something essential has each time remained? Reading Lucian and Sextus Empiricus is always just as enjoyable, and it is difficult to see how the biting irony of the former or the troubling paradoxes of the latter could lack in topicality or, more seriously, could no longer be understood today. Their intentions and spirit have survived, and they have survived because these two authors had heirs who knew how to maintain this multiform intellectual current, whose physiognomy is, however, quite distinctive—and it is true that it brought the West, stuck between materialist and idealist orthodoxies, a little of the oxygen necessary for it to breathe.[13]

Although irony, pragmatism, and skepticism may have experienced many rearrangements since the end of antiquity, it does not follow that the forms they have taken today should have become unrecognizable. Or that they would have been misunderstood two thousand years or more ago. We would surely say as much of many philosophical attitudes, such as incredulity, nominalism, or relativism. Protagoras, Gorgias, Sextus Empiricus, and Lucian (or those who have been confused with them) created types (or rather archetypes) of attitudes that have become emblematic for our intellectual tradition. And it is this ideal character, which only time can create, that has made them apparently unchangeable reference points.

Still today, it is common to hear the opinion that belief in gods is a universal phenomenon, common to all humanity, that these gods are obviously heavenly and immortal, and so on. But these common notions (*koinai ennoiai*) were not born yesterday, or even the day before.[14] Beyond Cicero, Plutarch, the Stoics, Aristotle, and even Plato, do they not go back to the dawn of our culture? Do they not flow together to the point of appearing to be one of our culture's favorite theses? This is why Christian thinkers (Origen, Clement of Alexandria, Saint Augustine, Lactantius, Ficino, and so many others in the course of the past twenty centuries)—the successors of the Greeks in so many respects—did not have the least difficulty in introducing their own conceptions into this enduring mold, making central Christian theses such as monotheism, moral ideas, and the divine creation of the world innate, universal "common notions" in their turn.[15]

Nor should we be surprised to find that the question of "original monotheism" gave the history of religions one of its liveliest controversies right in the middle of the twentieth century.[16] And one of its most anachronistic at the same time, if we care to remember the evolutionist prejudice that rather too quickly confuses science with irreversible progress. In this case, the history of religions was simply reactualizing, with the aid of new information and new instrumentalities, a banal thesis that was nothing other than the resumption of a very old theological quarrel (Christian monotheism versus pagan polytheism). As a consequence, what had fundamentally changed? Was not "scientific" thought once more the rather unimaginative heir of theologico-philosophical tradition?

Similarly, the cosmological arguments still cited today, in order to justify the idea that the universe forms a harmonious, intelligible whole, conceived by a superior being, have been trotted out with admirable consistency for the past twenty-five centuries, that is, since Anaxagorus, Aristotle, Plato, Hippocratus, the Stoics, Cicero, Plotinus, and so on gave them a "classic" form that has somehow become immutable.[17] And the antiprovidentialist countertheses of Democritus, Epicurus, Lucretius, Sextus Empiricus, and so on just as quickly became conventional and stereotyped.

Here, too, we note to what extent good ideas are incredibly resistant, like certain primary organisms that in order to survive at any cost go through an encysted phase, often very a long one, and are then reborn once better climatic conditions reappear. At the same time, these conventional ideas make up more than a simple, easily accessible repertory. Do they not, as if working from within, organize our own ways of thinking of the world? It is equally true that in this last sphere, so specific, it is difficult to conceive of and voice a new and original opinion. The combinatoric seems so well defined, the interplay of positions so long established, that it seems impossible to find a way out, to locate oneself "outside" or speak of these matters in a different way, as if there were no other possibilities, even if they had only a phantom logical existence. This last impression (everything that can be said has been said in one way or another) is, however, only the fruit of an illusion—let's call it "transcendental"—comparable to those on which all cultures are necessarily based. And elsewhere, other worlds, equally locked into their certainties, exist in the same fashion.

Beside these exemplary, matrical opinions are objects and theses that are no less exemplary and have lain in wait for us for centuries. Like knick-knacks that time has made familiar and covered with its patina, we cannot for an instant imagine that they could disappear from our mental landscape.

It is probable that myth does not exist, if by this we understand a single object endowed with a kind of permanence or unchanging ontological identity. And on this point, the metaphysical one, we can only agree with the radical historicism of Paul Veyne and the consistent nominalism of Marcel Detienne.[18] On the other hand, if we consider that the Greeks, then nineteenth-century science, and now ours of the twentieth and twenty-first centuries have never ceased interrogating something that we call myths, we must at a minimum suspect that the question is perhaps poorly put when it is limited to the single choice of being versus nonbeing.

Myth does not exist. So be it. But what does exist is the field of controversy and the system of interpretations that have grown up around it (even if it were only the pretext for these). So that in this capacity it does exist, just as justice, love, and art exist, that is, as objects of discourse. This is why I wrote some years ago:

> [E]ven if the inanity of myth as object were surely established, it would not entail the correlative impossibility and unintelligibility of modern systems of thought that are consecrated to its study, a fortiori, when, as we are trying to do here, we show that the global coherence of these various hypotheses is explained by the existence of a remarkable configuration bound to our own intellectual history. Denying the existence of the object never obliges us to deny that of the discourse, quite real in its own right, that deals with it. A

nonexistent object is capable of stimulating sensible theories, which have a history worthy of study. Paradoxically, nothing authorizes us to assert that hypotheses relative to improbable objects are less indispensable than those voiced concerning verified, undeniable facts. Moreover, do not the fertility and solidity of the nominalist hypothesis need, for their very existence, to prove the nonexistence of that on which they are based?[19]

Let us consider the euhemerist and historicist interpretations of myths, for they, too, deserve to be called exemplary. The euhemerism of Euhemerus and of Léon de Pella, that of their immediate successors (e.g., Diodorus, Cicero, Persaios, Polybius, and Strabo), the euhemerism of Christian thinkers (e.g., Lactantius, Tertullian, Saint Augustine, and Eusebius of Caesaria), and that of certain authors of the eighteenth and nineteenth centuries (Antoine Banier and Herbert Spencer, for example) do not appear to be, cannot be, identical. Different, even very different, intellectual circumstances and issues must, at each period, for each thinker, have in some way or other modified or directed the use of this manner of interpreting mythic narrative. But for all that, would we deny that the object "myth," as unstable as we may conceive it, plus a certain kind of "euhemerist" interpretation, have together formed an exemplary topos since antiquity, then in the era of the first Christian thinkers, and still again in the eighteenth and nineteenth centuries?[20] As much could be said of the historicist theses that have succeeded one another since Palaiphatos, that is, since the fourth century B.C.E.

Would we deny that Myth (the uppercase M is required this time) has been able to impose itself as the religious object par excellence, despite it often having very little of the religious to it? In the nineteenth century, the history of religions, then taking shape, accorded myth a quite exceptional status, one that ritual, for example, would never receive. Andrew Lang, E. B. Tylor, Max Müller, Michel Bréal, Abel Bergaigne, and others reserved first place for it in their studies. Would they have chosen to do so had they not been preceded by that long tradition of which they were to some extent the heirs and continuers (and which supplied them with a complete "turnkey" system of preestablished interpretations)?

It is revealing, moreover, that in line with a conventional genealogy that had become another exemplary topos at that time, Andrew Lang's classic studies start by reviewing our great Greek ancestors (e.g., Theagenes, Metrodorus, Euhemerus, and Porphyry) and then pass, after a brief pause over the Christian euhemerists, to the eighteenth and nineteenth centuries (e.g., Antoine Banier, Charles de Brosses, J.-F. Lafiteau, and Friedrich Creuzer), before addressing the theses that were being discussed in Lang's own day.[21] Among these theses, the naturalist interpretation of myths that prevailed for some few decades was just as venerable, since it was already to be found among the first Greek interpreters of Homer.[22]

And would so many twentieth-century historians of religion, like their predecessors a century earlier, have chosen to put myth at the center of their works and thought if they had not profited from the advantageous dispositions of that tacit contract that a priori binds every Western thinker to the vast complex formed by its interpretive grids?[23] These were indeed very advantageous arrangements, since they permitted historians to erect the most elaborate theories imaginable concerning an ill-defined object whose very existence is today challenged. These theories, even in the twentieth century, often served as models or references for a great number of interpretive ventures or explanations that at times wandered very far from their original site. The works of Lévi-Strauss or Dumézil bear witness to this. Indo-European and Amerindian "myths" provided consistent, indispensable reference points for the development of Lévi-Straussian and Dumézilian structuralism. This is also why, starting with myth, starting with the adversarial interpretations and analyses that it has stimulated for fifty or a hundred years, it would be a simple matter to reconstitute the majority of the great theses that today share the field of the history of religions.

Such convergence, such permanence, and such tacit agreement prove that throughout the centuries and despite the tribulations of history, vast domains of knowledge were organized and perpetuated, endowed with their topoi, their typical objects, interpretive traditions, and indispensable organs of reproduction (schools or currents of thought, academic institutions, editorial norms, learned practices, etc). This evidence no doubt justifies us in applying the term "myth" to something that perhaps does not actually exist, that has never existed, but about which we have heard so much that it has become indispensable—at least, to scholarly discourse.

III | The Genealogy of a Western Science

The consequence that we might draw from this is that Christianity is in its whole an Aryan doctrine and that as a religion has almost nothing to do with Judaism. It was even established despite the Jews and against them: it is thus that the first Christians understood it and defended it at the cost of their peace and at times even their lives.

—Émile Burnouf, *The Science of Religions* (1872)

Max Müller has asked (when speaking of the mental condition of men when myths were developed), "was there a period of temporary madness through which the human mind had to pass, and was it a madness identically the same in the south of India and the north of Iceland?" To this we may answer that the human mind had to pass through the savage state of thought, that this stage was for all practical purposes "identically the same" everywhere, and that to civilized observers it does resemble "a temporary madness."

—Andrew Lang, 1878

6 | The History of Religions in the Nineteenth Century

Ubiquitous Prejudices

If some historians of religion willingly cite unchanging attitudes, experiences or feelings that condense around the eminently mythical figure of a timeless *homo religiosus,* if religion, the principle of religion, is raised by these same thinkers to the supreme dignity of an absolute category, this is, however (and essentially), the twofold result of a very unoriginal thought that was able to exploit the most idealist tendencies and features of a topic whose major orientations have been reviewed here. We have seen from the first part of this work that such conclusions appear convincing only on the double condition of accepting the exemplarity, that is, the universality, of the Western model and of not establishing any excessively serious theoretical requirements, especially in the sphere of anthropological thought. Let us now add a third condition: that we not recall too openly the extent to which the history of religions, in the same capacity as its "object," was itself a unique historical construction, intimately tied to the ideas of its time, on which it was dependent at every stage of development. No more so than the other sciences perhaps, but certainly no less. The study of its first syntheses, drawn up in the second half of the nineteenth century, reveals, among the intellectual factors that surrounded its birth, the constant presence of the most ordinary prejudices of that period.

Paradoxically, certain thinkers persist in seeing in the history of religions—in reality, a discipline shaped by the ideology of its time and devoted to the most ideological of Western creations, religion—a means of better understanding "the religious man of all times and all civilizations," since "religion is the bond that unites man to the sacred."[1] But the ethereal universalism that the historian of religions invokes in this case does *not* have to be accepted without prior examination, as if self-evident, simply because it finds a favorable (ideological) echo in our minds. The corresponding pretension and assertion must be subjected to a rigorous analysis, since it is as historical developments—and uniquely as such—that they exist.

The constant and insidious confusion that was established between science and ideology rested in fact on a small number of prejudices. The industrial capitalist and the scholar, the missionary, and the journalist shared in their premises and spread their watchwords. This confusion did wonders to facilitate the migration and transfer of concepts. Playing on the word "evolution," for example, it made it possible to pass from biology to society and from there to religions, on a path apparently cleared of all annoying epistemological obstacles. And in return it favored all the ideological uses to which were put the pseudo-results of science, since it always confirmed a posteriori the prejudices of the opinion that was in reality its own. Ideology always being reductive, science invented, with its aid, simplistic keys to understanding based in schematic oppositions (primitive versus civilized, Western versus oriental, Jewish versus Aryan, and so on) that seemed pertinent only because they were applied to a reality that had, in fact, been reduced in advance to a few crude categories.

Conversely, this confusion was facilitated by several factors. Has not the most obvious been that at the time, the West knew no rival, no serious competitor? No country and no culture disposed of a comparable arsenal. Economic and military superiority, the cultural imperialism of Europe, and the power of the Christian churches were then unchallenged and unchallengeable. No power was capable of opposing them or even of resisting them. On this gloomy horizon was imposed the "anthropological" concept (albeit with limited capacities) of religion, which no relativism called into question or even nuanced. The Other—alterity—did not exist at this time, save in inferior forms or figures. The "learned" comments then made to describe "primitive" or "savage" peoples and cultures were shot through with profound contempt and horrified condescension.

The most powerful and simultaneously most diffuse prejudice that thinkers of this period expressed in their conceptions of myth or religion depended on an amorphous, ill-contoured grouping of notions, which had at its privileged center "evolution" and "progress" (the process and its result). Everyone shared in it and employed it in explanations.[2]

We would be wrong to recognize here the simple transposition or simple adaptation of the ideas of Charles Darwin to cultural facts. The ideas of the British scientist were more nuanced and often contradict what a certain brand of sociobiology has subsequently sought to have them to express. In particular, because they were antiprovidentialist, these ideas introduced a clean break between "nature" and "culture"; they defended no form of determinism a priori and, lastly, they did not imply the idea of a homogeneous, exclusive process.[3]

On the contrary, the simple-minded evolutionism promoted by historians of religion in the second half of the nineteenth century was rather the result of an assemblage of simple ideas, from among which emerged the outlines of the tendencies now to be discussed.

Thus conceived of, evolution (notwithstanding the degenerate forms and survivals to be observed here and there) is an implacable, and above all exclusive, universal force, whose mechanical laws alone have determined the history of humanity. This uniform vision of historical movement revived the ancient thesis of the three stages—savagery, barbarism, and civilization—through which humanity has supposedly passed.[4] The privileged part of humanity (our own, undoubtedly) has reached the third stage, while others are stilled mired in savagery.

This concept of evolution is uniform as well in the sense that it addresses indistinctly and simultaneously all aspects of life (biological, psychological, social, intellectual and, obviously, religious).[5] On all these points, the white man possesses an undisputed, evident superiority. Despite the varying talents that the Greeks might have had in oratory, or the Chinese in the delicacy of their goldsmiths' work, or the Australian aborigines in climbing trees, E. B. Tylor's Englishman surpasses them all by virtue of his "general condition above any of these races." The evolutionist thinking of the second half of the nineteenth century made possible the reintroduction of a strict hierarchy among peoples whom universalist prejudice in other respects suggested were generically equal. The best-adapted survived, and the best among them dominated.

The progress onto which this irresistible evolution opened was borne along by an unfailing optimism. In many respects, this progress plays a role comparable to that of divine providence in the majority of earlier cosmogonies. It seems to result from a general plan that leads toward a precise end, where Europe already occupies the privileged place. This teleology and this determinism inserted into progress itself also seemed to be inscribed in a providential plan whose meaning the West had understood, so that it showed itself as an admirable figurehead on the prow of humanity. Implicitly, this theodicy of progress, coming as reward to the hardworking, entrepreneurial West, presupposed a harmonious vision of the world, again in the fashion of traditional cosmogonies, always organized and hierarchized. The positivist history of religions was usually content to substitute lay terms for religious concepts ("providence" and "salvation" being replaced by "evolution" and "progress"), but without touching either the general organization of the explanation or the overall plan in which Christian Europe had always occupied and still held the first place. The examples that are customarily cited in order to illustrate the canonical opposition, religion versus science, are relevant only on the condition of not forgetting that on another, more global level, religious explanation and scientific explanation offer, and have long offered, undeniable affinities and amusing similarities.

The feeling of superiority that the thinkers of the Victorian era had of themselves, their most gifted fellow citizens, their spiritual life, and their moral values is so indisputable, and was experienced in such perfect good conscience, that it could obviously lead the science of the time to nothing but a ridiculous failure. Most often their ideas served less to improve the principles or methods of this science than to try to justify the absolute superiority that Europeans unreservedly ascribed to themselves. Verdun and the other battlefields of World War I dealt these ideas a first fatal blow. Auschwitz made them reprehensible. The twentieth century took consolation in structuralism.

Myths and Science

In the introduction to my book *Mythologies du XXe siècle* (1993), I wrote:

> The theoretical richness of the field of mythological studies has certainly been favored by the paradoxical nature of myth. An uncertain, indefinable object, it allows the widest and most opposing variations, was home to the ultrarationalism of Lévi-Strauss as well as the mystical viewpoint of Eliade, the subtle philological and comparativist analyses of Dumézil, and the nebulous assertions of Jung. On the other hand, this unprecedented situation was favored by the characteristic most frequently ascribed to myth. It was the origin of myth, itself traditionally presented as a narrative of geneses and foundations, that modern theories that studied it sought to discover. Without further ado, it was judged that this coincidence was not actually one, that the study of archaic myth offered an irresistible context for the exposition and description of our principal founding agencies. In this respect, one is tempted to add that the comparative epistemology of modern theories of myth is at bottom nothing more than the mythology of our scientific myths.[6]

The comparative study of the great modern interpretations of myth by Dumézil, Lévi-Strauss, and Eliade has persuaded me that these theories, despite their abundant erudition and, in the case of the two first cited, their intellectual rigor, seem nonetheless to obey a certain logic that is proper to mythographic creation. Are not all three dominated by two complementary choices or attitudes that conventionally characterize this kind of discourse?

For each of them, speaking of myth seems possible only on the condition of naming its origin, which, however, eludes and will always elude every kind of serious investigation. The origin of myth, like that of language or thought, is situated beyond the range of science, and it is in any case scarcely likely that such an origin would effectively be ascribable to a given moment and some Big Bang of the kind that we meet in traditional cosmogonies.[7] It would be more reasonable to admit that we can claim to speak of origins only on the express condition of first accepting the premises and rules of writing that all mythographical creation dictates, and as a consequence disregarding those that science would better define and defend.[8]

The work of these three authors, each in its own way, shows this in striking fashion. For just as they seem incapable of resisting the fatal attraction exercised by the mythical question of the origin of myth, so, in answering it, after all is said and done, they can only cite the synthetic and rather mysterious activity of an originary agency (society for Dumézil, mind for Lévi-Strauss, the sacred for Eliade) from which all else emanates.[9] Certain functional aspects that characterize these founding agencies are for this very reason comparable to those possessed by the One of Plotinus.

If, in the most up-to-date science, the influence of mythographic thinking is still very active (to the point where, in the final analysis, it is often this that directs the most general orientation and form of a demonstration), if true mythopoeic devices even seem to control the production of some scientific theses, we should doubtless expect to find them in the first stammerings of nineteenth-century science.

Like ideological discourse, confident in its own prejudices, the discourse that myth projects is filled with a simplicity of the kind attributed only to first causes or to the perfections of God. In nineteenth-century works, this artificial simplicity, the ontological antithesis of the complexity inherent in the real world, is to be found at every level of reasoning, but even more clearly in the valorization of (1) objects whose obviousness is actually false, or at least problematic, such as myth itself or religion; (2) insoluble but still seductive questions, such as those, cited above, concerning the origins of religions and mythology; (3) homogeneous, uniform explanations, favored by the unceasing, mysterious intervention of "evolution"; and (4) archetypical agencies such as the "primitive" and "progress."

Like myth, religion is indefinable—an excellent reason for exploiting the two, making them the excuse for statements that will be able to say much, if not anything at all, since reality will never be able to raise the barrier of good sense against these unreasonable claims. But these vague objects on the other hand possess a terrible, almost an absolute obviousness, for they belong to the oldest cultural and ideological capital of the West. As a consequence, the most rigorous position does not consist in scrutinizing these objects more and more closely, since such an inquiry could never refer science to anything but the tradition from which its own deeply buried premises have issued, but in stripping this false evidence of all the faded trappings that cover it. For the men of the nineteenth century, religion, like myth, referred to universal, undeniable realities. The absence of all religion (when this hypothesis was admitted or discussed) was never considered except as the sign of a savagery and profound mental retardation that progress ought to have erased or would soon erase. This, for example, is the thesis advanced by Herbert Spencer in his *Principles of Sociology*.[10]

Conventionally, the typical and almost exclusive question posed by myths is that of origins (of a given custom or element of the world, etc.). This is also the question privileged by the "science of religions" in the nineteenth century, whence all those theses—one more far-fetched than another—devoted to the most primeval forms of primitive religions (animism, fetishism, totemism, idolatry, etc.) and to the stages through which these must pass before reaching the ideal form of monotheism. The greatest minds of the period applied themselves to this problem with remarkable consistency and obstinacy.[11]

Often, in these debates, the circularity of the reasoning seems almost perfect. Religions were approached by the myths that they contained (and were, moreover, often reduced to them); these "primitive" myths, filled with absurdities and incoherence, then posed the question of their interpretation; such interpretation in turn sent scholars back to their conceptions of the ideas and mentalities of the primitive people who had conceived of these strange accounts, which then led straight to their archaic origin (for the nineteenth century, contemporary exotic civilizations were assimilable to the state of humanity in its distant prehistoric past). In the circumstances, the study of myths could do no more than admirably confirm the thesis of that progress in the name of which they had a priori been judged "primitive" or "savage."

We have earlier seen that the thesis that combined evolutionism and progress—by its extreme simplicity, by its casual way of addressing and treating the facts, by the repetition of the same summary arguments, in brief, by its refined form—transfigured history, the heavy, tumultuous thickness of history, into an airy, die-straight thread. This transfiguration required the prior "reduction" of the real to a very small number of objects, processes, and goals. The ideal in this sphere consisted in having only one element correspond to each of these categories: religion was the privileged *object,* the laws of evolution the *process,* and progress the exclusive *goal.* Under such circumstances, the jumble of the real, as well as its erratic or divergent movements, was hidden behind a clear, geometrical picture, the mythic reconstruction of history and of reality. Here, too, schematic and absolute oppositions (primitive versus civilized or Western versus eastern, etc.) furnished these homogeneous, uniform explanations with the metaphysical reinforcement of simplicity and illusory transparency.

In the first rank of the archetypical agencies that the history of religions called upon to construct a reassuring vision of things that did not contradict what ideology, its neighbor, was fabricating at the same time, we naturally find progress. It was not and still is not necessary that this term be rigorously defined, that it include or permit the possibility of a conceptual deepening, since in the final analysis, in the role selected for it, it was intended above all to permit the erection around it of a discourse whose substance could be summarized more or less as follows: the West is installed at the prow of the ship of moral and intellectual progress; all other cultures are behind it, at times very far behind. But, provided that they imitate it and absorb its lessons, a comparable if not identical fortune will one day befall them.

In order for this lesson to appear even more convincing, the scientific myth elaborated by historians of religions in the nineteenth century needed another figure that was capable on its own of personifying the European figures of science and religion, as conceived of according to the norms of the Western model (the only ones, moreover, that were conceivable!). That figure would be primitive man, who no longer had anything to do with the "noble savage" of the eighteenth century and rather represented his exact antithesis.[12] For the scholar of the second half of the nineteenth century, this "primitive" is at best a simple, naïve spirit, a big, rather awkward child dumbstruck by the many manifestations of nature, when he is not more prosaically considered an idiot or uncontrolled madman:

> To a race accustomed like ourselves to arrange and classify, to people familiar from childhood and its games with "vegetable, animal, and mineral," a condition of mind in which no such distinctions are drawn, any more than they are drawn in Greek or Brahman myths, must naturally seem like what Mr. Max Müller calls "temporary insanity." The imagination of the savage has been identified by Mr. Tylor as "midway between the conditions of a healthy, prosaic, modern citizen, and of a raving fanatic, or of a patient in a fever-ward." If any relics of such an imagination survive in civilised mythology, they will very closely resemble the productions of a once universal "temporary insanity." [13]

Savage, magical, pre- or irrational, confused, crude, blood-stained, prisoner to the excesses of a poorly governed fantasy and sexuality, the religion of the primitive (when he has one) stands in contrast point for point to ideal, purely moral and spiritual Christianity. A veritable topos of the scholarly literature of the period, the primitive, saddled with all the stereotypes attributed by convention to the uncivilized or mentally backward savage, is clearly the symmetrical reverse of the ideal and just as fantastic image that the European had of himself. This is a recurrent process, in conformity with the hegemonistic cultural discourse of the era. [14]

The Church was hardly more charitable with respect to the "barbarians" who "live in the darkness of superstition," being convinced, for example, that "the Negro, because of climate, ignorance, character, is very indolent." The arguments that it drafted at this time, the ideas that it spread, have haunted and burdened the xenophobic imagination of the West ever since.

This primitive man, a joint creation of the human sciences of the period, the Church, and the dominant ideology, is a pure and necessary mythographical invention intended to exalt the indispensable role of the West at a time when colonialist Europe was launching a pitiless policy of conquest, headed by traders, soldiers, and missionaries. Constant recourse to the category of the primitive allowed Western science and the Western conscience to inscribe the Other, and with him all the others, in a universal "civilizing" project that was never, in many respects, anything but the other face of a very brutal, very lucrative imperialist enterprise:

The missions are the indispensable auxiliary of all fruitful colonial policy. Governments, be they Protestant or Roman Catholic, have always sought to rely on the missionary in their work of colonial expansion. In France, we have seen statesmen who were not the least suspect of tender feelings toward the Church, and even partisans of the *Kulturkampf* within the country, energetically support the priest or monk abroad who devoted himself to the evangelization of savage peoples. . . .

With regard to the colonizing fever that has seized all countries, the work of the missions, to envisage the matter solely from the human point of view, appears first and foremost as a civilizing, European undertaking. Leo XIII understood this and it is for this reason that, from the beginning of his pontificate, he strove to give this great work all the impetus that new necessities dictated. Acting in this way, Leo XIII worked not only for the faith and the Gospel but also for the moral and material interests of the colonizing powers."[15]

A Science of Its Time

Unsurprisingly, the history of religions thus reveals itself to be not only a Western discipline but a science born of the closing decades of the nineteenth century. It indiscriminately blended the most tenacious and caricatural prejudices of sententious, triumphant Victorian Europe with the heritage of a long intellectual history that had gone before. These prejudices, for their part, contributed certain forms and orientations, but such particular ones that they can in no way be confused with those that might be expected of a science that set itself the task of understanding humanity. It is also true that this notion of a timeless and unadulterated Science is pure fantasy, for the word "science" does not merit a capital letter (a typographic convention designating ideal entities). For scientific activity, like the rest, like everything, is the result of countless retellings and modifications (often imperceptible, which forces us to group them in huge, all-encompassing categories). And there is nothing to be gained, on the epistemological level, as on so many others, in opposing what has never been with what ideally ought to have been.

In the same fashion, we must give up measuring the history of science and scientific ideas only with the yardstick of their discoveries, and at the same time surrender the naïve image of an all-conquering science, distributing in its wake the benefits of an invincible progress and clearing the way to human happiness. Why should the world of science be any different from other states of affairs?

The sciences, especially the human sciences, are not the pure offspring of parents selected for their eminent genetic qualities. Contrary creatures, formed of diverse influences and heterogeneous elements, they live, in varying proportions, off survivals and inheritances. And they themselves often cannot see what is newest and most original in what they conceive. The elements that have gone into their development are not only heterogeneous (in the sense that they spring from fields of scholarship and levels of abstraction or conceptualization that are very different one from another). They are also heterogeneous because their respective existences are to a degree incommensurable. The history of Lucretian ideas and, consequently, the historicity (the way a particular culture exists in time) of a corresponding work or text are not comparable to those found, for example, in the mediocre 1876 work by Louis Ménard, *Rêveries d'un païen mystique* [Reveries of a Mystic Pagan]. Nor is the influence exerted by the books of Lucretius and Ménard comparable. The one has obsessed Western consciousness for more than two millennia and will continue to plague it for a long while to come, while the other was only a harmless, obscure, and insipid bit of fantasy.

But ideas, just like scientific theories, are made up of all of this at one and the same time, of diverse currents to which we must add those, not the least powerful, of anachronism and misunderstanding. What, as a common example, is signified by "Darwin's ideas"? Those of which he was fully conscious? But at what date? we could immediately add. Those whose novelty he could accurately measure? Those that he had a premonition of but did not dare publish, or published in a diplomatic form acceptable to and understandable by his contemporaries? Those that in distorted form were reinterpreted in other fields than biology? Those that led to discoveries or revisions that he could not have foreseen? Those that we know today in the form of a simplistic summary, or those that biologists are able to evaluate with considerable precision? Those that science later dramatically confirmed? Or those that were translated into ideological terms?

Aside from these general characteristics (and it matters little whether they are specific or not), the history of religions must also take into account a certain number of contradictory elements that intervened during its founding stage.

The preceding chapters have sought to show that ponderous, distant influences weighed in with all their mass in the establishment of this new field of knowledge. For the idea of such a science to be born, there had to be an object (religion) whose existence seemed undeniable to everyone.

But this proof has nothing scientific about it. It depends above all on the strange fact that the Christian West erected around one of its native notions a general topic and a solid network of paradigms that in turn oriented the greater part of our intellectual choices and controversies, among which we can count certain ways of thinking that have remained in use in the human sciences. The existence and reality of the object religion depend much more on this *poetic* activity, inevitably narcissistic, than on some anthropological evidence or other, which was never proven. (Is it necessary to repeat that we are still unable to list and define the terms of the principle on which this expertise would be founded?)

We have also noted that exemplary theses, opinions, and themes (such as myth and its traditional modes of interpretation as transmitted from ancient Greece) had a surprising renaissance in the eighteenth and above all the nineteenth century among a learned public that was very familiar with the classics, which formed the basis of their education.[16] Why should not the dogmatism and inflexibility of Christian theology have served as a model for the intransigence of Western science? Would the latter, the natural enemy of theology, have been capable of resisting the adoption of the most characteristic position of its rival? And was it not necessary that it display this rigidity in order to conquer its own territory at the expense of the other?

It should be added here that, as is better known, and for that reason conceded, to the point of even seeming the distinctive feature of the nineteenth century, that along with these sometimes ancient legacies, this era amassed a mass of new data that, on many points, contradicted or revised what had been believed true until then. And it is very often to this stereotyped vision of a positivist and rationalist nineteenth century that we refer when asserting that the century saw the establishment of a "new paradigm" in science. To the image of a familiar, unchanging, and relatively simple world, over which a severe divine providence watched, there succeeded the image of a much vaster universe, expanded in both time and space, subject to an implacable evolution and displaying an inexhaustible richness.

The discovery of a distant prehistoric human (reported in 1836 by Jacques Boucher de Perthes), so crude and so different from the man of Genesis; the hundredfold multiplication of the depth of historical time; the more attentive approach to strange, exotic societies (henceforth called, with no recourse to euphemism, "savage" or "primitive"); the direct study of the oldest oriental cultures (Egypt, Mesopotamia, India, etc.), thanks to the decipherment of their languages and writing systems); and the almost

startling arrival on the scene of Indo-European ancestors capable of rival-
ing the Hebrews in ancientness are only a few of the best-known facts that
in less than five or six decades shook the old cultural edifice that had been
handed down since antiquity and the traditional cosmogony derived from
the Bible.

The nineteenth century thus gave itself a contrasting image, one in
many ways of embarrassing contradiction. On the one hand, we have the
continuity, permanence, and quasi-immobility of ideas, notions, and ways
of thinking that seem to have survived indifferent, or nearly so, to development and change. On the other hand, and in contrast, there is the appearance of new knowledge and expanded horizons that led, and could not do
other than lead, to a profound modification of the traditional image of the
world, humanity, and societies. On the one hand (if we this time choose
to look at the epistemological face of this dilemma), there were the claims
of a scientific, rational ideal, capable of discovering logical laws and explanations in all the fields of knowledge, from paleoanthropology to the history of religions, from comparative grammar to social psychology. On the
other, there was the active survival of the most ordinary prejudices of an
era that had known many—and had died of them. If we consider only the
first alternative: on the one hand, there was continuity, on the other, rupture. If we address the second: on the one hand, there was science, on the
other, opinion, the ideology of a bourgeois society, triumphant and full of
itself. Aporia? Epistemological impasse?

In fact, this aporia and impasse arise each time we postulate that the
appearance of a new discipline implies and entails (the two movements
often being confused with one another) the emergence of a "new paradigm" (Thomas Kuhn) or a new *epistēmē* (Michel Foucault). This would
then a priori only be one of the particular expressions of a scientistic ideology that saw in the progress of knowledge a kind of irreversible, homogeneous movement. Instead of straying along that path where so many insoluble problems lie in wait, let us rather seek to show the inconsistency,
at least in the domain under consideration here (and without prejudicing
whatever validity it might elsewhere have) of this admittedly curious notion that ideas advance en bloc and in sudden leaps.[17]

In the nascent history of religions of the years 1870 to 1890, new attitudes and data coexisted with ways of thinking that were often very ancient and contemporary prejudices that sprang directly from civil society.
In this sector of the human sciences, a new kind of scholarship was always
constituted of many different things, especially of knowledge and meth-

ods that were not all new. All this made the history of religions a discipline that was both captive and witness to its time, that is, a discipline incapable of saying, by its own rules, not only what it was worth and what it could claim to assert but even what it ought to consider as improbable. The synthesis of these heterogeneous elements (attitudes, knowledge, prejudices, and the like) nonetheless brought about a partial recomposition and reorganization of the scholarly disciplines of the period, something that the institutions creating and recognizing a new scientific discipline sanctioned in their own way. Put simply, it would be risky to see in these events anything like the sign of a brutal rupture.

And if we viewed matters still more closely, we would see that among the methodological principles, premises, objectives, and tools, there often was no harmony or epistemological concurrence. Between the instrumentalities and the global theories (and this is only the most obvious aspect) enormous disparities appeared and often long survived. The philologists of the late nineteenth and early twentieth centuries were doubtless the greatest of all time and surely the most productive. They edited and translated whole libraries, drew up new grammars, and bequeathed to us invaluable dictionaries. And some of these irreplaceable instruments are still being used with profit today. However, these same scholars were singularly lacking in critical spirit once they launched into the interpretation (naturalist or agrarian, for example) of ancient or "primitive" myths. This means, to put it differently, that the most demanding erudition is capable of cohabiting in the same mind with the greatest naïveté. How can we call "new" the paradigm in which the two met and collaborated?

When we consider the heterogeneous collection of these contradictory sources, movements, and influences, instead of invoking a "new paradigm," would it not be more reasonable to speak at best of a "new spirit," provided above all that we not associate with the adjective "new" the idea of a sudden, brutal shift dragging behind it an entire world or culture?

Let me call attention to two positive aspects of this "new spirit." Even though still encumbered by the ethnocentric prejudices of a society obsessed with itself and with its triumphant imperialism, it was at this time that there appeared the anthropological idea that simultaneously promulgated the unity of all human beings, the unity of man, in the phrasing of the times (Tylor, Morgan), and the universality of religion (Tylor, Renan, and so many others). If the first of these ideas is not new (its first formulation is to be found among the Stoics), and if the second is eminently debatable, it is still certain that they represented the indispensable prerequisite for the vast anthropological enterprise that the twentieth century would take up and amplify. This venture, notwithstanding Stoic ideals, Christian personalism, Montaigne and Rousseau, the declaration of the rights of man, modern individualism, twentieth-century science, European imperialism, contemporary ethnology, and so many other influences, had still taken more than two thousand years to make its voice heard and felt! This broad anthropological design is then the result of a slow, broad-gauge historical process in which innumerable heterogeneous factors have intervened. It would be awkward and naïve to see here no more than the late triumph of an eternal, unchanging idea of humankind.

On the other hand, the birth of the history of religions in the 1870s was also, although on another scale, a locatable event (with the appearance of university chairs, learned societies, publication series, and journals). This event accelerated and brought together research that until then had been erratic and dispersed. Moreover, judging by the immediate effects, the institutional creation and recognition of a new field of knowledge are comparable to what linguists call the "performative." They favor and prepare for a different "spirit" and way of seeing reality and speaking of it. They open a new space for exchange, reflection, and innovation that, even if their first results ought to be viewed only with a great deal of care, contribute to perfecting our battery of concepts by enriching them (can contemporary epistemology claim more?), *despite everything and in a certain way.*[18] To assert "that's a scientific issue" tacitly opens up a space devoted to free discussion and refutation (whatever may otherwise be the value and level of the arguments), while saying "that's something for theology" ipso facto subjects the discussion to the dogmatic regime of possible anathema. In this sense, the achievement that willed us this new scientific "spirit" is irreplaceable and its value inestimable.

In the circumstances, asking whether the history of religions introduces a new paradigm in the field of knowledge of the second half of the nineteenth century is somewhat heavy-handed. The question, posed in these terms and in this abrupt fashion, is in fact inappropriate and faintly ridiculous. For, far from having cleared the deck of the methods of the past and the prejudices of its own time, the history of religions on the contrary revived and adopted most of them. In this sense, few of the human sciences of the second half of the nineteenth century have aged so badly or left so disappointing a heritage. According to a convention borrowed from the canonical schemas of cosmogonic myths, we would not say that over the course of this clouded and troubled period (chaos always preceding cosmos), it established conditions indispensable to the development of a radiant future. For us Westerners, who have a tendency to confuse "evolution" or "change" with "progress," this is a crude trap, into which we must avoid falling. With considerable clumsiness and in the midst of contradictions and diverse influences, the field more modestly tried to set forth a fragile scientific ideal that, even today, has to be constructed and defended.

Thus, far from imagining a science that would advance by leaps and bounds and always in a single direction, I would prefer to offer a critical method that never feels obliged to obey the demand that would make it choose one or the other term of an artificial alternative, artificial since it conceives of history and reality reduced to the terms of an ideal, summary metaphysics.

Reality is muddled, "complex," to pick up the word on everyone's lips today; the threads that compose it are as numberless as the rhythms that interlace them. This means that we ought to conceive for it other models and other instruments of analysis that could be substituted for all those that draw their characteristic and ideal forms (unique explanatory agencies, stark dualisms, canonical oppositions, dogmatic rigidities, brutal revelations, linear movements, simple substances, unchangeable hierarchies, etc.) from myth, metaphysics, or theology. In the human sciences, the reductive ideal of "scientific law" has too often served as a pretext for the introduction of transcendental axioms or principles, whose action is always as opportune as that of the demiurges we meet in all the cosmogonic myths.

7 | Three Twentieth-Century Debates

The Sociological Explanation

The profound divergences displayed by the principal sociological explanations of religion(s), on which scholars customarily expatiate so relentlessly, will not be commented on here.[1] They are widely familiar from course outlines (religion according to Durkheim, prayer in Mauss, the Protestant ethic of Weber) and term papers. The contrary conceptions of this school or that, the arguments that they have shaped, and the ritual controversies that issue from them quickly created an autonomous field of study. The existence of a rational domain of this kind, which could doubtless also be compared to any hypothesis radiating from a central point, nonetheless displays a very serious defect. By concentrating all attention and thought on itself, by mobilizing the greatest part of the analytical capacity of a given period, by orienting debate in a direction conforming to its own presuppositions, and by somehow subjecting itself to a powerful centripetal force, this regulated and reticulated domain made us forget a cruel truth.

If the dynamic generated by these controversies and discussions permits the corresponding explanations to be organized as a specific field of knowledge, it is far from lending the latter any other primary or fundamental evidence, other than that which is drawn from this internalized movement of autoconstruction. This dynamic process, focus of the endless interventions and collaborations of numerous rhetorical and poetic procedures (choice of topoi, notion, arguments; style and spirit of proofs, etc.), simultaneously establishes the field itself *and* its epistemological limits; or, put more bluntly, the ordered world of objects *and* what can be said about them at any given moment.[2] The last resort of all realist illusions is there, in this mutual, reciprocal coincidence of words and things become a conflation of the world and discourse about the world. This principle is made all the more "true" when the objects concerned, such as religion, have themselves issued from our own culture, have been constructed and defined by this universe of discourse, as it in turn is modeled on them. Under these conditions, the process just outlined could not justify—on its own and through the resources generated by its own activity—the relevance of the elements or the principles whose existence the culture in question presupposes. It necessarily presupposes them, since they furnish it with its indispensable fundamental axiomatics. The share of this unsaid, of this tacit agreement that the fiercest opponents share by accepting this or that premise, varies according to the scientific discipline. But it must be a very large share in the present instance, since the central notion on which the structure of reasoning and demonstration rests is no other than the very fragile and very controversial idea of religion.

This is why, instead of seeking to learn what distinguishes Weber from Durkheim or from Bourdieu (something that others, better informed, will in any case do much better than I can), let us proceed from these two trivial statements (but are not premises very often trivial as well?):

— These grand explanations of religion all consider it as self-evident, "going without saying," as a undeniable sociological reality—a kind of pure evidence.
— Religion/s is/are uniformly reduced by these grand theories to a certain fundamental "function." All more or less tacitly suppose that at the base of all religion, and a fortiori all social formation (although the distances between them are incommensurable), there exists some identical principle.

The first assertion calls for some commonsense remarks. The second, on the other hand, raises some thorny questions.

In considering Weber, Durkheim, Mauss, or Bourdieu, is it not surprising to note that these authors all admit the idea of religion without hesitation? None of these important authors has questioned it. They have so fully accepted it that we could doubtless consider that sociological studies have done a great deal for the notion—by lending credence to the idea that it is a distinct mark of humanity. And in one of those curious, ironic detours of which intellectual history is so fond, this sociological validation of the universality of religion allowed the proponents of the divine or sacred character of humanity to find there an unexpected argument in favor of their theological thesis.

On what, that is, on what indisputable proof, does the tacit agreement uniting the most celebrated sociological theses of the past century rest? To tell the truth, on very little. Obviously, for these theses, just as for Marx and the evolutionist historians of the nineteenth century, religion is a primary, unchallengeable, evidentiary fact. Admittedly, some shading was occasionally introduced. Here some preferred to speak of religious phenomena, and there religions are grouped with other phenomena such as art and language among symbolic or ideological systems.[3] But nowhere is the idea of the specificity of the religious domain abandoned. Now this evidence, as I have often repeated, rests on nothing or, rather, it rests only on the propensity of the Western conscience and Western science to conceive simultaneously the Other and the universal in terms of their own indigenous categories.

The unanimity in the opinions of sociologists is nonetheless surprising, considering what separates them. The fact that the Kantian spiritualism of Durkheim and the atheist materialism of Bourdieu could agree on this point, while elsewhere they are so often opposed, shows, somewhat absurdly, that once religion is the issue, a Western mind, however agnostic, easily reaches the Platonic paradise of eternal ideas, no matter that these are often nothing more than old, unprovable notions. On the other hand, in considering what unites them, what is it fundamentally but the weight of a cultural prejudice, so perfectly inscribed in their ways of thinking and so well demonstrated in their bookish references that it comes to possess the incomparable savor of things immutable?

Beyond these general remarks, we must now ask ourselves (but in particular ask sociologists) some crucial questions, questions that are not meant to be or to reflect ineffectual sophistic juggling.

All social formations are in certain respects social in the same way (or to the same degree) and thus are capable of creating religions or something religious. This is the simple, irrefutable deduction drawn from the assertion that, since the process leading to religions is universal, it must follow that societies, all societies, whatever their constituent differences, possess a certain identical capacity. But when we consider the extreme diversity of cultures, the extraordinary disparities of all kinds that exist among them, we are forced to ask where and what the principle is that is at the base of this unvarying aptitude. Far from considering it a fragile seed, we must admit on the contrary that it is as robust as it is prolific, since, indifferent to this formidable diversity, it everywhere produces results sufficiently comparable among themselves to warrant being grouped under the same name.

These difficulties, almost all generated by the universalist prejudice alone, ought to appear obvious, just like the question that they inevitably imply: how, at one and the same time, to recognize the extreme diversity of cultures (from some Amazonian tribe with a few dozen members to the immense civilization of China), all the while admitting that they are fundamentally similar? For once we consider their universal, atemporal aptitude (from Lascaux to New Age California) to generate the religious, it is surely a time to recognize in them the same inherent disposition or aptitude.

But then we cannot avoid asking: what functional or morphological elements, unaffected by history, do these cultures have in common? What recurrent mechanisms can we distinguish both there and here? How can entities so dissimilar in scale and organization nonetheless be able to generate something that in the end is shown to be (but on what level?) identical?

It seems impossible to me to respond to these questions with a simple tautology of the type: societies produce religions because the substance of the latter is of a social nature. But it is precisely this mysterious social power that vanishes once we try to grasp it—precisely because in order to isolate it, we would first have to answer another series of questions, no less troublesome than the preceding ones.

Let us begin with the most unremarkable: why do all cultures produce religions the way cows produce milk or books on theology produce boredom? Or, if you like, why would the corresponding theoretical "universal social function" necessarily take a religious form (a particularly bold and venturesome formula, since no one is capable of describing this archetypical form either)? And what is this specific capacity of societies to produce religions or phenomena with a religious objective? In what capacity is it (only) social? Where is it situated *in nucleo*? Is it diffuse or is it concentrated at certain points in the social organization? Through what developmental phases does it pass? Does it change—in nature? in expression? in content?—when societies are transformed? If this capacity is not modified, how can it still be historical? And if it does not change, would we still say of it that it is social? Or would we have to admit that certain social principles scarcely evolve but simply repeat and perpetuate themselves, when others do in fact change? On what unchanging criteria would we base ourselves in order to distinguish these two categories?

Let us conclude with the question that has dogged this book: what is the ultimate nature of this religion or this fundamental religious principle, of this adamantine core that is mounted at the heart of all social formations?

To adduce neat responses to these questions without falling into the tempting trap of tautological reasoning and without succumbing to a conjurer's illusions (replacing, for example, the word "religion" with "religious phenomena," while preserving for the latter the impenetrable attributes of the former) is, I think, scarcely possible, since these questions in their own way reveal the existence of a basic paradox. Thus I shall be content to follow them with a few complementary remarks.

We have seen here that, from a strictly empirical or descriptive point of view, it was impossible (even if we accepted the principle) to speak of and, a fortiori, to describe what constituted the invariable, the immutable nucleus of religions. When we envisage them according to their social dimension alone and according to the principle that would have it that one who is capable of great things is not necessarily capable of ordinary things, we are still perplexed. Are we to seek this nucleus in the area of function, meaning, or form, taking as guide, for example, the recommendations of the best of contemporary hermeneutics (Marxist, phenomenological, structural, historicist)?

What we note is that the most frequently invoked responses refer back to explanations that are transcendental in nature, as with Durkheim, or openly functional, as with Bourdieu. In the first case, they call on a rather enigmatic disposition, apparently innate, of human thought, such as the celebrated *absolute* distinction between sacred and profane, of which *every* "human mind" conceives.[4] This original disposition is then not in fact social in nature, even if, everywhere, it finds expression only in the eminently social institution that is religion.

In the second case, it is the "political functions that religion fills" that are privileged on the basis of "its properly symbolic efficacy."[5] And here we find Critias's old argument (already revived by Hobbes, Spinoza, Locke, Rousseau, Marx, and others), but enriched with new social harmonics. In any case, is there not some theoretical inconsistency in postulating the universality of the political functions of the religious on the basis of its universality? This when it would be difficult in a multitude of non-negligible cases (shamanism, yoga, Taoism, early Buddhism, voodoo, etc.) to say in what way these practices or these conceptions of the world are religious and in what way they were originally the "transfigured and unrecognizable reflection of real social relationships" (Bourdieu).

For contemporary Western minds, persuaded in advance (since it is the totality of their own cultural tradition that prompts them to it) that religion is a universal phenomenon, it seems obvious that if it is not human beings themselves, it is inevitably societies that must possess in their depths some special aptitude for producing the religious—everywhere and at all periods. But this evidence is only false evidence, for if we admit on the other hand that societies, whichever they may be, are committed to generating religious phenomena, do we not have to consider that such a functional invariant would be more fundamental than the *social* itself? In fact, would not a principle so universal and so diffuse become more important than the social shell that housed it? But how can we be sure that this particular religious fact is only social, that the corresponding anthropological facts would all be, from an ontological point of view, social in nature? In fact, having reached this terminus, faced with all these paradoxes, does the psychological explanation given by Lucretius not seem at least as relevant? Anxiety, the sense of abandonment, fear, are they not factors at least as universal, capable on their own of explaining the appearance of numerous superstitious beliefs and magical practices?

In the circumstances, the validating criteria of the sociological explanation scarcely seem any more easy to define than to justify. Too often, things happen as if we found ourselves definitively confronted with options that seem valid only because they are founded on the same premises as those that serve as the ultimate foundations of our culture. In both cases (scientific explanations or indigenous culture), religion is admitted a priori as an obvious, universal, and timeless category. When they address this problem, the great sociological theses (for all, without exception, direct their attention to it) scarcely do much better than the history of religions. And often they do not proceed differently. Instead of starting out from the things themselves, from their diversity and complexity, they are not even based on ideas that the West has of these things but on ideas that the West has converted into things.

All explanations that claim to be scientific but, in the course of their deployment, reduce the infinite diversity of reality to a principle or to a unique, ontologically homogeneous cause amount to real acts of metaphysical aggression. The fascination that the human sciences have for such simple, "theological" explanations probably represents the greatest obstacle that they have to overturn and overcome.

"Historians" and Phenomenologists

It is possible to see only an amusing coincidence in the nearly simultaneous appearance of Émile Durkheim's *Les Formes élémentaires* and Rudolf Otto's *Das Heilige*.[6] We can also see in it something more than the simple conjunction of the first great sociological treatise devoted to religious life with a work that, coming after decades of stubborn positivism and scientism, tried, on the basis of inner intuition and feeling, of awe and mystery, to construct a religious anthropology and a metaphysics founded on the exaltation of the irrational (the subtitle of Otto's book is, moreover, *An Inquiry into the Non-Rational Factor in the Idea of the Divine and Its Relation to the Rational*). In fact it is perhaps not an exaggeration to grant an inaugural and almost symbolic value to this conjunction, to which World War I would bring a powerful reinforcement of all the significations habitually associated with a brutal change of era. Starting with these two works or, in any case, with the intellectual choices that they incarnate better than others of their time, we see emerging two major currents that would develop in the field of the history of religions in the course of the twentieth century.

For a reason that is only too easy to guess and is almost familiar to our ears, the opposition between these two currents is radical and compromise inconceivable. Can religious facts, whose existence we all agree to admit, be explained by a series of causes that themselves have their original site in this world and uniquely in this world or, on the contrary, do they possess some power or some signification that escapes the immanent order of things?

The "historians" (under this conventional heading, I group the advocates of immanentist explanations: sociologists, psychologists, or historians, strictly speaking) keep to the first of these alternatives. Religious facts are not fundamentally different from other facts that the human and social sciences study, unless it is in their stunning universality. In this respect, they deserve to be submitted to the same kinds of explanation, sociological or psychological, for example, since they are facts, only facts, and their entire course unfolds in this world.

On the contrary, phenomenologists are viscerally "antireductionists," and some would say they are only that. For them, religious facts in the final analysis refer to another order of reality. They are unconditional. Behind these phenomena, and because they are in a way intrinsically religious, is hidden another reality, something inaccessible that confers on them unique, incomparable status. Religious facts are then not facts in the same way as others. They reveal an ontological level other than the one on which they are manifest. The religious fact is superior to all others and is distinguished from them because it is the sign, the more or less explicit manifestation, of this other reality.

This last conception of a universe offering two planes, one phenomenal or sensible and the other ideal or divine, more or less distinct from one another (either radical dualism or the one an imperfect reflection of the other), already found in Plato's *Phaedo* and *Timaeus,* and perpetuated by Sallust, Pseudo-Heraclitus, Plotinus, and Proclus, is perhaps the most traditional and archaic of all the commonplaces preserved by Western culture, the one whose influence has been the most widespread. This cliché has informed an incalculable number of philosophical systems and poetic or artistic theories, right through to the mid twentieth century. Inasmuch as it seems as if our spiritual and esthetic culture has basically never ceased to gloss and repeat Plato, and the Western concept of religion is itself based on the masterful Platonic metaphysical division, with its well-known harmonics (soul/body, here-and-now/beyond; humanity/God, etc.), it is not surprising to find this very ancient reflex here.[7]

The theoretical difficulty that "historians" run into lies in the following contradiction, which is rapidly made into a paradox. Accepting the premise of the universality of religious facts, they have to find historical explanations that are not too much so, in other words, that themselves escape the deleterious effects of history. Otherwise, it is this hypothetical universality that in turn becomes inconceivable and inexplicable. It is the universal character of the explanation that establishes that of the object to be explained. From this comes, as we have seen, the inevitable, consistent recourse to global explanatory instances, to rather mysterious mechanisms located at the heart of societies, history, or human psychology. These mechanisms offer that special structural feature, which recalls Kantian simplification and makes them similarly paradoxical, of being, as principles, both exterior to the influences of history and simultaneously capable of generating forms sufficiently unchanging as to be everywhere recognizable.

The origin of this contradiction is scarcely mysterious. Faithful heirs to their own cultural tradition, the "historians" spontaneously adopted one of its fundamental articles, namely, that religion is inherent in mankind, having long been the sign of its divine election. In other words, in order to justify this premise relative to the universality of religious facts, they must manage the feat of explaining incredibly disparate historical facts by unchanging causes and mechanisms. What is ultimately at stake in this intellectual construction is, perhaps, humanity, the universal and generic human being, what an earlier generation called Man, that is, the anthropological conceptions that the West, in the name of its indigenous categories, sought to impose on the world.

Such diverse contradictions and risk-filled constructions indirectly serve the purposes of the phenomenologists. This universality and the kind of constant that the "historians" recognize a priori in religious facts (in the *religio* of religious facts, if you will) are promptly recognized by their adversaries as the signs of an ineffable transcendence. In fact, to admit the universality of religious facts while denying them the providential tie with the beyond condemns the "historians" to recognize the existence of original instances or dispositions, inscribed a priori in human minds or social formations, which in some way transcend the course of history.

Now, to pass from that transcendental possibility to the Transcendental is with our system of philosophical coordinates fairly easy. What is considered innate and a priori, from a gnosiological point of view, very easily becomes transcendental from an ontological point of view. For this, a light metaphysical nudge is enough for the non-historicity recognized in the primary instances to be elevated a degree, and for this elevated level to be conceived of as radically different and superior. Then, having reached this level or stage, reasoning of this kind finds reinforcement en route from one form or another of Platonism, which for twenty-five centuries has continued to proclaim the existence of two opposed, hierarchized planes (mind/matter, soul/body, idea/thing, etc.). To assert, as, for example, Durkheim does, that every human mind conceives of the absolute distinction between the sphere of the sacred and that of the profane is a metaphysical proposition to which it is very easy to add, just as metaphysically, that this aptitude is explained by the intervention of a special experience or revelation. This, then, is the phenomenologists' thesis.

In the same way, because it is materialist and atheist, the Freudian thesis of the origin of religious behavior could readily generate its spiritualist or mystical antithesis. It is enough to assert that the unconscious benefits from the "influence of an invisible presence." This, we know, was Jung's thesis:

> The spiritual adventure of our time is to abandon human consciousness to the indefinite and indefinable, even though it may seem to us—and not without good reason—that in the limitless there also reign those psychic laws that no human being has invented, awareness of which was given to him as gnosis, as "knowledge," through the symbolism of Christian dogma,

which only rash, demented minds would try to undermine, not searching minds concerned with the life of the soul.[8]

Although they all sanction the presence of this fundamental division (sacred versus profane) and unanimously oppose the reductionist theses of the "historians," it would nevertheless be unjust, and scientifically imprecise, to seek to lump all the phenomenologists together in the same intellectual trend. For even if they all postulated the existence of a *meta*physical level, that is, something to which contemporary anthropology can only respond with a shrug, all do not entertain an identical idea of this transcendence and its manifestations. And even if they share this fundamental prejudice and willingly turn to the same slightly vapid lyricism when called on to evoke "the amazed intuition of the infinite that is present in the soul" (Jacques Vidal),[9] beyond this common culture there appear radical divergences, rarely mentioned or commented on, and these divergences are of interest to the historian of ideas.

Starting with an examination of these differences, it seems possible to separate the phenomenologists into two tendencies. The first groups together pastors, theologians, and even bishops of the Lutheran faith (e.g., Söderblom, Otto, Héring, Heiler, van der Leeuw, Kristensen, Bleeker), who were responsible for, or had the honor of, founding what is customarily called the phenomenological study of religions. Beside several easily distinguishable German intellectual influences (pietism, liberal Protestantism, tolerant, neo-Kantian ecumenism, and Husserlian philosophy), one central idea is affirmed here: that by means of the most profound of its innate traits, the human spirit, in its most mystical interiority, is capable of having direct experience of the sacred—that is, of transcendent reality—independently of time and place.[10]

Far from being conceived of as the expression of a collection of dogmas or rites, the essence of religion manifests itself, in the eyes of these churchmen, in the living, existential experience that every human consciousness has when it enters into contact with that other reality, the sacred. A thesis this spare, indifferent to everything that distances human beings themselves, from their own moral and spiritual lives (and which would on this account be incomprehensible to anyone not shaped in contact with or under the influence of northern European Protestantism), was bound to seduce some historians of religion, always ready to transform their own aspirations into universal categories. Is not the extreme austerity of this thesis an apparent guarantee of its ecumenism? Does the emphasis it puts on the radical interiority of all religious experience not flatter our individualist passions? As for its mysticism, indifferent to ecclesiastical orthodoxies and dogmatic subtleties, does it not appear timeless?

Thus, at the price of a juicy paradox, this conception of religion, which in so many respects simply summarized and idealized the deep tendencies of Lutheran spirituality and individualism, nonetheless aspired to speak of religion. This is why the diverse essences that these phenomenologists discovered never represented much more than the sublimated, disincarnated expressions of an admittedly provincial, northern European spirituality in search of the absolute and the universal. We should not be surprised that the conclusion reached afterward, for example, by Otto (at the close of his analysis) was of the superiority of Christianity over other religions. And we note in passing, unsurprised, that the progress achieved on this point in almost twenty centuries of reflection, ever since Arnobius, Tertullian, Lactantius, and the rest, amounts to exactly zero.

Similarly, the ambitious declarations penned by phenomenologists about turning to the technique of the Husserlian *epochē*, that is, the possibility of liberating conscience of its ordinary prejudices in order to permit it to grasp the essence of religious phenomena, are just as unsatisfying, since the *eidos* that they reveal at the close of this demanding intellectual discipline is never anything but one of the sublimated, idealized versions of a Christianity reduced to the spiritual conditions of a pure phenomenon of consciousness. No doubt some will say that their analyses would have been more surprising if they had concluded that the essence of religion lay in the use of hallucinogens intended to provoke a state of trance.

The ideas that the other phenomenological current promotes are not so clear as those defended by the "Lutheran" current. Beneath their literal expression, it is also often possible to make out an unhealthy background and contaminated premises. Here, lyricism and rhetoric are not content to celebrate the metaphysical marriage of human consciousness and a mysterious supernatural reality. In almost insidious fashion, they commemorate other, shameful and disturbing nuptials.

The uneasiness we experience has an origin and a name: the work and thought of Mircea Eliade, who may be judged the most influential and most celebrated representative of the trend that we may call "pagan phenomenology."[11]

Eliade's life, personality, and work are inseparable, just as inseparable as his conception of religious universes and the ideas he complacently promulgated in the interests of the Iron Guard in his native Romania during the 1930s.[12] They are founded on the same dynamic principles: metaphysical antisemitism, rejection of the legacy of the Enlightenment in the name of the unwritten rights of a putative spiritual aristocracy, an exaltation of irrational forces, celebration of a pre-Christian paganism characterized by its bloody sacrifices and sexual orgies, the denial of all humanist morality, the ultra-authoritarian definition of political power, an organic, corporatist vision of the nation conceived on an exclusively ethnic basis, the metaphysical interpretation of law, and so on.

While the contribution of Lutheran thinkers had consisted of sublimating the profound tendencies of their faith in order to make them, in a humanist and ecumenical perspective, the ideal, timeless model of religious life, Eliade's contribution, while pursuing the same absolute goal, took a darker path. If his evocation of the pair sacred/profane is in principle still close to that of the northern European phenomenologists (Otto's *ganze Andere*), his own notions, on the other hand, owe much more to gnosticism (indifference to morality and anti-Judaism), Neoplatonism (ambivalence of the symbol, an elite of initiates), the Western esoteric tradition (the mystical conception of nature), and the macabre religiosity of the fascist Iron Guard than to Lutheran evangelical tradition. There is no possible confusion. Nothing is more contrary to the spirit of Eliade than a faith that would be open to all and in particular to the weakest, that would imply spiritual and moral improvement, and that would rejoice in the progress of a tolerant, welcoming ecumenism.

Eliade's religious universe would be in general agreement with that revered by all the dictators of the past century, starting with Salazar (to whom Eliade devoted an enthusiastic work in 1942).[13] For, according to Eliade, only a spiritual elite, guiding an ethnically homogeneous, largely peasant nation, is capable of giving metaphysical meaning to politics and to life:

> It is the specialists in ecstasy, the familiars of fantastic universes, who nourish, increase, and elaborate the traditional mythological motifs. . . . The different specialists in the sacred, from shamans to bards, finally succeeded in imposing at least some of their imaginary visions on the respective collectivities. . . . All this is as much as to say that privileged religious experiences, when they are communicated through a sufficiently impressive and fanciful scenario, succeed in imposing models or sources of inspiration on the whole community. In the last analysis, in the archaic communities as everywhere else, culture arises and is renewed through the creative experiences of a few individuals.[14]

Beyond a narrow, constraining social framework, spiritual messages are condemned to degradation, on the model of what, according to Eliade, happened to tantric yoga: "Like every Gnosticism and every mysticism that spread and triumph, tantric Yoga does not succeed in avoiding degradation as it penetrates increasingly broad and eccentric social strata. . . . This is the risk run by every spiritual message that is assimilated and lived by masses lacking in a preliminary initiation."[15]

The confusion that Eliade fosters among social organization, political institution, and religious life allows him to think of the first two in the very particular terms that he has conceived for the third, and thus to give a metaphysical meaning or orientation to antisemitism, social progress, or democracy, the "desperate attempt to find in the mass of ordinary people the qualities of the few."[16]

I take the definitive proof (in corroboration of what is here advanced) from the reactions to my own analyses of Eliade's work. His most fervent defenders make up a rather miscellaneous cohort, where we find proponents of European neopaganism,[17] a militant fascist,[18] the inevitable follower of René Guénon,[19] and oblivious or misguided Catholic theologians.[20]

However distressing it may be to see Catholic thinkers join the extremists of the political right, inveterate esotericists, and notorious anti-Christians in order to defend a man who resolutely placed himself on the side of one of the most obscurantist political movements of the twentieth century,[21] it is more urgent to probe the nature of the intellectual confusion that reigns within the phenomenological movement. Erected on a shaky base, formed exclusively of metaphysical prejudice, and nourished by an admixture of heterogeneous materials drawn from different traditions, exoteric and esoteric, phenomenology in its own way and on its own scale reproduces the contradictions and conflicts that have disturbed Christian thought since its origins.

Despite that, despite its incoherences and its obscurity, phenomenology represents such a powerful current within the contemporary history of religions that it can lay claim on its own to be the only party opposing the "historians." Unfortunately, the latter, scattered and divided, tend to avoid overly generalized debate on the very nature of religions, whose existence, however, they recognize or assume. (Can they be aware that this contradiction—accepting the idea of religion without being capable of saying what it is—puts them in an awkward position with respect to their opponents?) This is why, rather surprisingly, the discipline presents an extraordinary appearance, with genuine scholars principally occupied with subordinate questions, while the big questions are left to those who assert a priori that a "science of religions" must necessarily end in a superior hermeneutics, one capable of finally unveiling the ultimate meaning (and necessarily the religious meaning) of religious facts.

This is so much the case that a falsely ingenious solution was proposed by the phenomenologists, taking the current situation into account while seeking to make official a curious division of intellectual labor. The description of the facts would fall to "historians" (or research of the historico-sociological kind) and their interpretation to phenomenologists.[22] It is understood that the latter activity, the more prestigious, alone is capable of restoring the incomparable value of religious facts. Here we find, once again, an old prejudice of the Platonic kind. This division, which subordinates an immanent level to a transcendental level (that of Being, the sacred, or God), faithfully reproduces what Western metaphysics and theology judged fundamental.

Admitting a priori that the intelligible transcends the sensible—and that the latter will never reveal its fullness and completeness except with the support of the former—is an attitude incompatible with the aims of an authentic, well-founded scientific undertaking. For such a venture, the intelligible no less than the perceptible belongs to this world, and both are the issue of comparable historical processes. The meaning of a fact, religious or otherwise, is as historical, as conditioned as the fact itself. The one is no more mysterious and no less immanent than the other. Both are exactly situated on the same level, the human level.[23]

This tricky division of labor and the hierarchy that it implies run into several other objections that reveal its artificial character.

To claim that cultural facts (religious facts or others) can be disassociated from their interpretation is useless and ignores that these facts are no less constructed than is their interpretation. Unlike the natural sciences, the various human sciences never have to deal with raw data. Today, outside of naïve epistemologies, we no longer think that there are "objective" facts on one side and their interpretation on the other. (Where would the elusive boundary be located?) In both cases, it is discourse that has the primary role. Now, discourse describing facts or objects and discourse producing interpretations are based on the same principles. It would then be much more judicious to shift our attention toward the analysis of the poetic and rhetorical procedures that intervene simultaneously in the discursive construction of objects *and* in the similar construction of their interpretation.

This strange dissociation (facts/meaning) in any case ignores another very clear distinction, a capital one proposed in the seventeenth century by Spinoza, between meaning and truth. Meaning belongs to the discursive order of the interpretation, and to it alone, and can then never be other than the meaning of this or that text. The universe of interpretation is closed, turned back onto the text. On the other hand, "in order to avoid confusion between true meaning and truth of fact," it is important to reserve for scientific explanation, which is indifferent to ultimate meaning, the task of understanding this "truth of fact."[24]

To presume that an interpretation is capable of discovering THE meaning of religious facts (while hermeneutical activity can never lead to anything but partial, provisional, and often contradictory significations) ultimately appears as the consummate expression of an idealism and ethnocentrism closely united for the occasion. THE meaning that the phenomenologists disclose is always a meaning that flatters our Western ego, while being presented (but could they do any less?) as an absolute meaning, exterior and irrelevant to history. But, to tell the truth, the hermeneutics of the phenomenologists, like that of Eliade, most often comes down to a much more banal truism: the meaning of a religious fact addressed in a religious spirit is deemed religious.

The originality of the terms of the controversy that opposes "historians" and phenomenologists, like the controversy itself, is weak. The distinction established between them only reproduces more or less faithfully the fundamental opposition found at the heart of the great Western paradigm, itself symbolized by the names of Epicurus and Plato, Lucretius and Plotinus. This paradigm, after having dominated the course of European intellectual life for more than twenty centuries, continues to organize (and this is serious) the contemporary field of the history of religions. It is always this paradigm that introduces the major orientations in the field and that stimulates the spirit of the most meaningful discussions that unfold there. The controversies that oppose "historians" and phenomenologists are thus to a great extent biased and sterile: biased, because at bottom they rest on a debatable notion that presents no valid criterion of universality; sterile, because each too often reproduces old metaphysical and theological debates that have never succeeded in advancing scientific knowledge one iota. Scientific progress occurs only on the condition that the prejudices of an era are overcome and the walls of a tradition breached. In this case, it is highly unlikely, since the liveliest debates are still content to repeat the terms of an immemorial controversy.

The Invention of *Homo religiosus*

Every culture possesses its own conception of humanity (thus we employ phrases like the Greek people, Roman man, and so on) that represents the quintessential values (spiritual, political, ethical) associated with its own vision of the world. Humanity, in the highest signification of the word, is always made specific to the culture in question, which places its representatives at the summit of its own hierarchy: the Greek citizen-aristocrat, the Indian Brahman, the Christian knight, the middle-class Frenchman of the Second Empire. But is it really only a conception? Is it not rather, for every culture, absolute, intrinsic, total, unassailable evidence, since, in the contrary case, it would be its very self that it annihilated by calling the evidence into question?

Let us go even farther. A culture does not have an abstract conception or idea of what a human being is, in the fashion of a belief or superstition that could be isolated from others. Such a conception rather appears as inseparable from a set of socialized practices (educational, institutional, ideological), intended to "fabricate" human beings who incarnate it, more or less successfully, after having incorporated it in what we call, not without reason, their "way of life." This conception of humanity then exists only as realized, incarnated, *lived* in individual destinies, as much as in the collective undertaking. And this undertaking is itself nothing more than the cosmographical projection or transposition of the reality that each culture constructs in order to establish title to the world in which it lives. Each culture realizes, in a manner immanent to itself, its own conception of humanity by deploying the only being that it possesses, that of its own existence, legitimized in its singular form by the culture itself and by itself alone. We should not balk at saying and reiterating that every culture is always just such a collective, constituent closing in on itself. Some will say, perhaps rightly, that a culture is nothing but this tautology.

We then come to the realization that if a conception of humanity does not preexist the polymorphous human activity that seems to make it manifest, while such activity, symmetrically, seems to be informed by that conception at the same time as it in turn defines it, we are confronted with a troubling, irritating paradox. But why should we turn away in advance from the idea that the human condition and its creations might be paradoxical, that is, included among other things contrary to the summary rules of our logic (law of the excluded middle, syllogism, causal relationships in particular)? Once again, as Marx advises, let us not confuse the things of logic with the logic of things. Let us then accept, at least as a heuristic or exploratory hypothesis, the principle of this paradox and consider that praxis only *appears* to reference ideal or transcendental models, since these do not in fact exist outside or anterior to them. This observation reminds us that we must not think that the results of our analyses, carried out a posteriori, could be displaced and relocated, after the fact, to the origin of things: this would amount to saying that various cultures each conform to a conception of humanity that preexists them, in which case we would have to ask where these transhistorical conceptions come from. No matter that the absurdity of such a proposition is obvious, the Platonism that inspires it is no less frequently present in a number of general hypotheses.

But cultures are Platonic only in appearance. In fact, theirs is a mixed being, simultaneously conceived and lived. And we cannot simply add, in a well-known dodge that explains nothing, conceived because lived and vice versa. The case is rather that the reality in which every human being lives (which is certainly not the reality of the physicist or biologist) is a construction of a particular kind, essentially ambivalent, since it is simultaneously interiorized as thought and lived as universe and world.

In particular, a given person's reality and representations (contrary to a stubborn prejudice) are not two distinct entities. The representation is situated in reality, on the same level as it—to such a degree that it is indissociable from it. We do not live in reality with our conceptions of it as some kind of intellectual baggage, but in the lived representation of reality or, if you like, in the living reality of representation. In this respect, the most troubling or awkward example seems to be that which we are presently addressing: how could we objectify the representation of our human "self," of our concrete humanity, or detach it from this humanity, since this representation is constituent with regard to this "self," this humanity? Our individuality is at once, that is, synchronically, the thing and the image of the thing. There is not an empirical "self," on the one hand, and a representation of it, on the other, since we are simultaneously both the one and the other, that is, living individuals and the representation that animates them as beings capable of representing themselves. This aporia makes relative the pretension to objectivity that any kind of knowledge about humanity might advance.

Independently of this little problem where, nonetheless, a good share of our metaphysical destiny is at stake, we could still say that no idea preexists human cultures, not even our own (generic) notion of the human being, still considered as one of the most universal, since this idea is itself the result of an unpredictable historical process that unfolded at the same time in the mode of thinking and in the mode of practical experience. Reality and the world of human beings, the world of a given human being, are never there, as prior givens. Individuals construct them within themselves and beyond themselves, trying to make them coincide (which cannot always be done without creating certain problems).

Let us also recognize that, no more than it is capable of capturing time-space or physical phenomena that unfold at the speed of light, our natural, ordinary, everyday language is not capable of satisfactorily describing such complex, ambiguous realities—mutually constituent and each reversible on the other—in which, to revive (regretfully) the words of the old metaphysicians, substance and form, the word and the thing cease to be primary, indispensable categories of our understanding and only represent one local configuration among all the others.

Despite their diversity, that is, the points of view (psychological, sociological, historical, etc.) from which they address the question of humankind, and despite, as well, the symbolic wounds inflicted on them by the writers and the approaches that have been accused of having contributed to the "death of man" (psychoanalysis, the social sciences, structuralism), one nonetheless has the feeling that the human sciences, even if unconsciously, have often sought to preserve at whatever cost the reassuring image that the West, since the Renaissance through the Age of Enlightenment and up to the scientific optimism of the nineteenth century, has relentlessly, patiently constructed and reconstructed. Unless these sciences have deliberately kept to one side everything that could seriously vitiate this image, which is perhaps at bottom just an indispensable myth.

In this human being, progressively conceived of as a free, tolerant, reasonable subject, committed to happiness, attached to human rights and to democracy, we discover with no difficulty the obvious traces of the sense of superiority and the optimism that Westerners scarcely ever abandon when they compare themselves to others.

The human sciences are an exclusive creation of western Europe, contemporary with the period when Europe unquestioningly dominated the entire world, and they have been built up in the cultural framework of a relatively homogeneous whole, dominated and unified by its Graeco-Roman heritage. Can one imagine for a moment that the conception of humanity that was constituted within these sciences could have brutally contradicted the principles that, on a level that can be designated (for want of a better word) as ideological, justified this success and this superiority? In other terms, would not the human sciences (contrary to contemporary literature or painting, whose pessimistic and even on occasion despairing accents are known to all) be more tributary than they are willing to admit to this optimistic vision, and have they moreover not contributed to its success?

It is indispensable to bear in mind these first remarks, because the premises to which I should now like to call attention are situated on a neighboring level, which means that the intellectual forces, reflexes, and practices that are associated with them are so implicit, so carefully buried in our spontaneous ways of thinking and speaking, that it is at times difficult to extract them from their matrix in order to expose them to the light.

Anyone who is slightly familiar with Buddhist thought, in particular with its conception of human beings perceived as transitory aggregates of heterogeneous elements (corporeal, mental, intellectual, etc.) can probably see that, in this other, Western view, the contemporary human sciences consider the unity of the person or the self as a undeniable datum, that is, as one of those givens that it is not necessary to prove, and on which they consequently do not hesitate to boldly base the most diverse hypotheses.

Admittedly, they recognize the possibility of stratification within human persons (especially under the influence of Freud) or of historical variations in human beings' perceptions, but these concessions never allow the appearance of theses that would demonstrate the futility of the self or the volatility of the psychosomatic aggregate. The human sciences poorly disguise their nostalgia for Man, that is, for a human being who would never be haunted by emptiness or by the threat of perpetual dissolution. To the question "What is this being who speaks?" they almost always respond in a trivial and tautological manner: "Man," as if this answer dispensed them from any further examination.

It would be futile to seek to know whether this massive prejudice owes more to the Cartesian *cogito* than to Kant's reflections, given that it is just a prejudice, however diffuse and global. It is rather a question of one of those charter ideas that (on a level that it is again convenient to call "ideological") organize in common with others a global vision of humanity and the world that is shared by a whole culture. These ideas, which have only scant heuristic value and no scientific status, could be called "cosmographic," since it is so obviously true that a collective belief or illusion becomes, by that very token, constituent of reality itself. From this perspective, we see as well that the "scientific" vision of humanity is not always as removed as one might imagine from the ordinary, naïve or traditional vision. On this level, the distinction drawn between scientific knowledge and common knowledge, still thought to be a defining one, is perhaps not as clear-cut as we might perhaps wish either.

Once this reassuring idea of mankind has been posited, several subsequent conceptions derive from it that are just as implicit and just as arbitrary. But they are all characterized by the same fundamental optimism.

Whatever one might say, the human being of the human sciences is a basically reasonable, rationally motivated creature, who lives in a rather hospitable world, which it is his duty in any case to make better. If you open a current dictionary of scientific anthropology (let's not even mention the history of religions), you are immediately struck by the absence of a certain number of headings. As if it were reluctant to seize humanity live, anthropology keeps a good distance. In fact, in these dictionaries, we find no article devoted to humanity's anxiety, distress, irony, mediocrity, hopeless dreams, anguish, crime, ignorance, vice, and barbarity.[25] Yet do we not see the advantage the human sciences would gain if they put cruelty or vice at the center of their approach to humankind? What could be more concrete and tangible? Or if, like Machiavelli, they admitted that men are "ungrateful, fickle, liars and deceivers, fearful of danger and greedy for gain" (*The Prince*, ch. 17), which no politician is unaware of. But who studies, or, rather, who would dare to study, human cruelty or cowardice? Who, in a word, would dare to propose the creation of the *inhuman sciences,* which, at least as scientific as their congeners, would be to the inhuman what the human sciences are to a humanity too often abstracted and disincarnated?

The human sciences, it is true, dispose of an infallible means to block the study of such facts. They make of them categories that pertain exclusively to individual subjectivity (or pathology); and they are not interested in individuals, in capricious, unforeseeable idiosyncrasies. But, we must then ask, in some perplexity, what is the nature of the humanity of the human beings that the human sciences study if it does not equally and properly pertain to the *individuals* who are these same human beings? Could there be several types of humanity? Or must we consider humans without the aid of this notion of humanity? In the face of this assessment, how can we not see that the darker aspects of the human condition are scrupulously ignored by the human sciences, as if they were fundamentally afraid of the ordinary, fleshy density of human beings? For these human sciences, the inhuman remains an accident, even if it leads to monstrous consequences.

This naïve optimism is maintained intact in a certain number of negative choices made by these same sciences. Excluded, then, from the customary perspective of the human sciences are all misanthropic, pessimistic, nominalist, and relativist conceptions (as in radical historicism or the absolute arbitrariness of human creations). Moreover, when such conceptions are entertained, it is always in selective fashion and under the heading of personal (idiosyncratic) philosophical hypotheses. For its part, skepticism is always perceived in an esthetic mode in order to make it inoffensive.

Advancing in tandem with this soothing optimism is the belief in progress (the progress of humanity, societies, sciences), which, in the finest rhetorical flights of the eighteenth and nineteenth centuries, illuminates the future path of humanity. Yet the humanistic optimism of the human sciences appears just as banal as the theme of decadence in certain thinkers on the extreme right, such as René Guénon and Julius Evola. Perhaps they owe this to the fact that their researchers are still in many respects the heirs of nineteenth-century science, in which case this doxa functions like a true institutional censorship, which would prefer to ignore everything in mankind that threatens its own reassuring vision.

The fact remains that such optimism constitutes a real handicap, and that it is, for example, somewhat troubling to note that the human sciences have still not integrated the drama of the Holocaust into their general anthropology and, even less, all the modifications that such an integration would entail for their conception of mankind. A historical event with "historical" causes, the Holocaust risks remaining only that for a long time to come, since the common anthropology of the human sciences is incapable of analyzing and assimilating such a drama. For them, it remains a monstrous, unique, intolerable event—in a word, inhuman. But to refer it back to this radical singularity and to its historicity alone will never permit it to be given its full and total human dimension. With this remark, I advance the following: why not put the Holocaust at the center of the human imperium, at the heart of every anthropological hypothesis of any scope, instead of making it an isolated phenomenon and thereby leaving it as unthinkable as it is incomprehensible? Does this example not show the conceptual limits that thinking emerging from the human sciences runs up against? What is monstrous, violent, coarse, and obscene in human beings escapes them, along, logically, with everything that devolves from it. They find themselves confronted with something that they absolutely cannot think, as if this "something" did not belong to mankind, was not human.

Here we see the appearance of an idea that it would be interesting to pursue. Proper to the human sciences is what they, by virtue of their own history and above all of the prejudices associated with it, have admitted as being par excellence human. But it is quite obvious that this human/inhuman division is drawn from within, or rather at the limit of our fields of knowledge concerning humanity. Now this limit or these limits are coextensive with the ideal definition of the human being in the name of which these inquiries are undertaken and these boundaries drawn. Judged "human" by the human sciences are the activities, creations, and attitudes that are considered by us Westerners as the unchanging, ideal characteristics of the consummate human being (art, social life, religion, symbolic productions), whence our propensity to so easily award the credentials of humanity to anyone who fits this ideal. Conversely, in order to be fully "human," our human sciences would have to abandon everything that the West (Stoic, Christian, scientific, democratic) has patiently screened out so as to grace itself with an idealized image. But it is precisely this radical experiment that is inconceivable, since it would bring down at a blow the whole edifice (already shaky) on which our civilization is founded.

Even though an optimistic and, in brief, reassuring conception of humanity is widely diffused in the human sciences, we should not forget that in the domains of literature and art, the twentieth century has meditated, ruminated on a vision of humanity that is at the antipodes of the soothing vision implicitly contained in these sciences.

If we consider the major works of contemporary literature, we are immediately struck by the fact that they have emphasized the mediocrity of individual destinies, the absurdity of the social world, the uncertainties born of the too keen and too painful existential contradictions of humankind, all things that are absent from and apparently ignored by the domain of the human sciences. It is as if, fundamentally, these sciences were indifferent to everything that closely touches human reality, subject to its inexorable fate. Would they show more interest in another humanity, one ideal and abstract, one is tempted to asked in perplexity? Similarly, it is obvious that literature has multiplied experiments, at times laughable, at times audacious, intended to break the humanistic, optimistic conspiracy hatched in the aseptic discourse of academic dissertations. Is their emasculated, neutered, uniformly flat language truly adapted to the description of that living object, the human being prey to obsessions, interrogations, and dramas? All these are things equally disregarded by the all too human sciences. Apparently, the human person that they study is an amnesiac who has retained nothing of an original anxious condition.

Against these two antithetical visions of mankind, the rather calming, optimistic one of the human sciences and the other, often dark and desperate, of contemporary literature and art, rises the mystical conception of the phenomenologists.[26] If, for a moment, we disregard the notable differences that separate the "Lutheran" and "Eliadian" currents, we must, in order to understand the genesis and ambition of this figure, bear the following facts in mind.

The idea of a universal, timeless *Homo religiosus* is a creation that has meaning only in the eyes of the West; it would have been inconceivable elsewhere, in any other culture. This figure summarizes most of the elevated conceptions that are found at the base of Christian and European anthropologies. This *Homo religiosus* is simultaneously a synthesis of the most idealist Western metaphysical points of view and a collocation of our keenest ethnocentric prejudices.

The system of intellectual coordinates on which this complex figures rests can be reduced to four principal themes: metaphysical, mystical, anthropological, and epistemological.

On the metaphysical level, the central idea, although common enough, is Platonic in principle and has been seen here many times: another reality ("other" from the perspective of its ontological qualities) looking down on the world of human beings. In this framework, the proper domain of religion appears to be par excellence mediation. It favors communication and arranges contacts between this world and the other. A purely contemplative or ascetic attitude would not easily win its approval, since such a stance amounts to denying its objective and necessity. Irony and critical skepticism are foreign to it.

The influence and contribution of Lutheran thinkers is perhaps more explicit when we address the second theme, mystic experience, although Eliade also frequently mentions it. What establishes the discrete presence of *Homo religiosus* is the direct, lived experience of the individual confronted with the dazzling revelation of a superior reality. This experience is made possible by manifestations, hierophanies, emanating from that enigmatic power that is the sacred. Let us listen to Julien Ries, a great specialist in these fantastic scenarios and these disincarnated contacts with supernatural powers:

> Archaic man discovers a power that has been called *mana* but which is neither anonymous nor impersonal nor collective. Man perceives this power as a spiritual force whose dynamism is reflected in his conduct. In

discovering this power, primitive man acquires the sense of a reality that transcends this world. In him is born the sense of the divine. We are not in the presence of an original monotheism. Archaic man does not discover a first cause, but a unique reality; he is aware of being in the presence of supernatural Beings endowed with will. Man experiences a sense of the sacred that leads him toward a consciousness of the existence of God.

It is then in this contact with the sacred, conceived as a spiritual force in nature, that man experiences the sense of the divine. . . .

It is in man's encounter with the power, with the "astonishing alterity," that the salvation promoted by religions resides: the sense of life, the growth of life, the acquisition of a new life. Man determines his conduct or modifies it according to the experience he has in face of this mysterious power. Between man and this power are formed relations that condition behavior. The historian of religions establishes the facts and the documents. He describes them and classifies them in the cultural inventory of humanity. The phenomenologist conducts an exegesis of this documentation in order to understand it and to state its meaning as a function of religious man who is at the center of his concerns.[27]

The idea that human nature is everywhere the same, that it disposes in this regard of general aptitudes that are also similar and in conformity with a certain universal reason, is widely recognized to be one of the most original concepts of ancient Stoic thought. The fact that Christian thinkers took up this argument while orienting it toward a meaning that conformed to their own theological preferences, adapting it (without too much difficulty) to the argument for a primary or original revelation, proves only one thing: the aptitude and skill that these thinkers displayed in the reinterpretation of certain pagan ideas. In the circumstances, we may ask whether the assertion that there are innate tendencies that in some way endow the human mind with an inalienable religious calling, currently put forward by the phenomenologists,[28] should not prosaically be interpreted as the predictable result of a centuries-old evolution that, in the West and in the eyes of many thinkers, ended up making the religious a distinctive feature of humankind.[29] In the course of this evolution, the ambition of a general anthropology has gone astray, however, it having metamorphosed into an anthropology of religion, since this was supposed to represent the most distinguished and prestigious part of humanity.

Asserting that all human, lived, religious experience refers back to the existence of a transcendental level brings in its wake the indispensable but inadmissible epistemological corollary that the substratum of this experience escapes history, that it cannot be assigned to any of the domains (sociological, psychological, etc.) among which are distributed our knowledge and our explanations of human facts:

> Indeed, if the religious phenomenon cannot be understood outside of its cultural and socioeconomic context, we must recognize that religious experiences are not reducible to nonreligious forms of behavior. Each religious phenomenon must be grasped in its own modality. It can be understood in its totality only if we move past the historical aspects under their various conditioning. Each religious fact constitutes an experience sui generis stimulated by man's encounter with the sacred. At this point, we must illuminate the symbolic face, the spiritual face, and the internal coherence of religious phenomena. The phenomenological modus is an effort to comprehend the essence and structures of religious phenomena, perceived both in their historical conditioning and in the optics of the conduct of *Homo religiosus*. It is a matter of exploring the articulations and significations of this conduct by deciphering religious facts as the experience of man in his effort to transcend the temporal and to make contact with ultimate Reality."[30]

Like every generic, ideal image of the human being (the communist, the fascist, the Christian), *Homo religiosus* is a creation that derives from the mythic imagination—even doubly mythic, given that the elements that comprise it are themselves the result of an ideological development influenced by numerous mythographical representations (mankind, consciousness, the world, supernatural beings, etc.). Its interest, which is rather limited when all is said and done, lies uniquely in the fact that this creation was conceived with materials that interest the historian of ideas. This synthesis is in fact inspired by metaphysics of the Platonic type, by a rather Lutheran conception of religion and religious experience, by a mystical anthropology, and by the naïve epistemological trend that buttresses itself with the idea that history encloses a kernel whose nature escapes it.

IV | From Religions to Cosmographic Formations

Not only by theologians at large but also by some who have treated
religion rationalistically, it is held that man is by constitution
a religious being.

—Herbert Spencer, *Principles of Sociology*

Once a theory is well entrenched, it will survive many assaults of
empirical evidence that purports to refute it unless an alternative
theory, consistent with the evidence, stands ready to replace it.

—Hubert A. Simon, Nobel Memorial Lecture, 1977

8 | The West, Religion, and Science

From the outset, the accumulation of evidence in this book has established a hypothesis that religion is not a simple, obvious phenomenon of which it suffices to say that it exists sui generis as one of the fundamental characteristics of humanity.

It was fairly simple to show that this idea, although thought indisputable, being so omnipresent in our culture and in most of our ways of thinking, faded away or became clouded as soon as we tried to define its conceptual content, to enumerate the formal criteria or objective expressions that distinguished it from other cultural formations or even to draw its boundaries, real as well as theoretical. With each effort, the investigation encountered a pair of alternatives that blocked the forward view of the inquiry and seemed to dash every hope of reaching a satisfactory solution: one either chooses a comparative anthropological perspective, quickly discovering that it is impossible to locate anything that faithfully resembles our native conception, along with the corresponding idea and reality, or one starts with our native conception, raised a priori to the dignity of intangible model or reference, but is then condemned to wander from paradoxes to absurdities, so risky is it to attempt to generalize in the Western case.[1] In a word, the exemplary value of the Western evidence quickly becomes uncertain.

Nowhere else does religion exist as a distinct domain, autonomous and separated from others, as an original structure offering a unique set of stable elements and relations. For it is on this last count, and on it alone, that one would be justified in raising this notion to the dignity of a universal anthropological constant. Without the presence of this structural organization, both idea and the thing slip away, melting into a continuum of divergent beliefs and practices that almost indiscriminately encompass all human activities.

As we have seen, the difference, or rather the opposition, between the sacred and the profane, which so many fine minds have considered deci-

189

sive and so many conventional minds today still stubbornly put at the origin of the religious, scarcely represents a more useful criterion. It is also in the name of an opposition no less irreducible (religious versus nonreligious) that the West excludes from the putative religious field magic, divination, hero cults, popular superstitions, alchemy, and astrology, and it remains quite uncomfortable when it meets them among others, at the heart of what it, despite everything, calls religions. For it must be one way or the other: either it accepts them as authentic religious facts but then finds its own conception of religion and, inevitably, the conception of its *own* religion called into question; or it persists in excluding them from this sphere but then seems to found its analytical categories on arbitrary distinctions. It is no less true that to get out of this difficulty, scientific casuistry, the faithful heir of nineteenth-century ethnocentrism, has an unbeatable trump card that consists of creating, within the religious domain, other subdivisions of lower rank. So it subordinates "primitive" or "popular" religions, with which superstitions and magical practices are lumped together, to spiritually and morally superior religions, shorn of all these unworthy trappings.

In response to this paradoxical situation, there is a global, unique explanation that is now familiar to us. Religion, that is, the word, the idea, and above all the particular domain that they all designate represents an entirely original creation that the West alone conceived and developed after having converted to Christianity. Along with them, in the course of their long anguished history, other concepts were specified, subtle semantic networks and vast intellectual constructions were put in place. Humanity, the world, nature, history, society, power, and existence not only received precise definitions, but were immediately organized into cosmographical systems (or fragments of systems) dominated by the same premises and, it must be said, by a certain common way of perceiving the world; but it was also then that these very notions were fashioned.[2] In this way, in the course of this long development, religion became a complex intellectual construction, a polygon of controversies, and a network where a great number of ideas and arguments meet, without relinquishing its decisive role in the constitution of Western culture, that is, in the formation of its identity. In this respect, religion is at the heart of our "world," the place that we recognize as our own simply because people there speak our language, the only one we know.

After all, such a situation offers nothing that should trouble us in advance. Can we not consider the concept of religion as we would other intellectual or artistic creations of the West, such as pre-Socratic philosophy or cubist painting, which have no exact equivalents in other cultures? We could study it as we study Japanese haiku or certain exotic institutions, that is, as human creations that may legitimately be considered in their original context but without trying to make them the basis of a universal anthropological paradigm (something that no culture beside our own has ever sought to do with its own creations).

In any case, two paired phenomena occurred at the end of the nineteenth century that made it impossible to see things in this benevolent, tolerant fashion. This is what I have sought to show in the third part of this book. After becoming the unquestioned hegemonic power—master of this world—at the end of a process that had begun with the great discoveries and the birth of capitalism, and by defining a triumphant scientific program devoted to the study of human phenomena and inevitably founded on its own system of values and representations, the West had to inscribe religion (if not its own religion) in this ambitious program.[3]

From then on and caused by this inscription, contradictions and difficulties quickly multiplied. Here are the most obvious ones. The history of religions should not have exported this singular notion, found nowhere else, and issuing from a history that took its own unique course, without having subjected it beforehand to a rigorous critical examination. But it did not do so. Instead, it exported it, along with the West's doxa, without the least doubt or scruple, as if it were inconceivable that other cultures should not possess, if only in some primitive, incomplete or aberrant, monstrous form, what seemed to every Western mind the very sign of humanity and civilization.

In addition to this massive prejudice in favor of the idea that religious facts were consubstantial with the human phenomenon, the nascent history of religions adopted, with no particular qualms, all those notions of its era (the inferiority of "primitive" societies, the idea of progress leading to the middle-class nineteenth century, the superiority of white, Christian, European civilization, racist and eventually antisemitic prejudices, a narrow, limited positivism, a fascination with origins, and so on), which very often gave anthropological thought the features of narcissistic special pleading. The European case was tacitly raised by Western science to the dignity of the norm, model, and reference point by which all other cultures were to be measured and evaluated.

The disastrous consequences of these ethnocentric attitudes on the scientific level were aggravated by a supplementary fact. To the extent that "religious questions" have for many centuries nourished and oriented the essential part of European intellectual life, the history of religions, when it came to consider the very nature of its object, remained and still remains largely tributary to the past of the West, to its intellectual choices, its metaphysical controversies, and its system of values. From all of them, for example, it borrows the terminology that serves to describe the facts it studies ("faith," "sin," "priest," "soul," "spirit," "immortality," "church," "theology," "magic," etc.) and to them are referred the kind of questions or facts it considers religious, and to them as well it owes the orientations of its own field of controversy. Lastly, what is fully religious (in the eyes of the history of religions) is what the Christian West has always considered as such, to the extent that it seems superfluous to say much more in order to escape this tautology, which, in its eyes, is not a tautology at all.

How could it leave this magic circle when the object that it is supposed to study is supplied by its own cultural tradition, which also surreptitiously imposes on it the means and frameworks for its inquiry?—thereby condemning it to take up the same prejudices, to ask the same questions, to endlessly redeploy the same arguments, and to leave itself locked in the same paradoxes. The monotony produced by reading most textbooks on the history of religions, with their unchanging tables of contents, as unchanging as the canons of Christian theology, has no other origin than this.

This is why, as we have noted, the modern history of religions remains to a great extent dominated by polemics originating in the West's theological past. The opposition between phenomenologists and historians around which the major (and utterly sterile) debates of the history of religions crystallized for more than sixty years, replicates quite precisely what for centuries defined the meaning of the great metaphysical controversy that passes diachronically through Western history. In opposition to all those who believed in the existence of gods, transcendence, or a superior providence were the various approaches that refused to recognize anything but human causes in the origin of religious facts, be they social, psychological, or political. From Critias to Bourdieu and from Plato to Eliade, there has been no pause in the confrontation between materialist thinkers, for whom there exists only a single world, subject to laws immanent in it, and all those (Platonists, Christians, esoterics, mystics) who subordinate the existence of this human world to principles that transcend it and to which "religious facts" testify.

Against the multiple difficulties issuing from this onerous heritage, the most rigorous and most learned inquiries cannot do very much. Thus the detailed, impeccable philological study of a religious text never allows us to say (other than with recourse to conventional, tautological arguments) just why the text is recognized and said to be religious, or what the *religio* of this religious quality is.

The absence of any epistemological break contemporary with the birth and development of the history of religions is, in the last analysis, explained by this troubling and constant feature. Divided as to the attitude to be adopted toward documents and facts considered religious, Western scholars have on the other hand accepted as obvious and indispensable the idea that religion is a constituent given in the human condition. Controversies of a metaphysical nature almost always avoid the very idea of religion, which is never questioned by writers who might be thought the most hostile to any form of transcendence, such as Marx, Nietzsche, Freud, Bourdieu, and Lévi-Strauss. After all, didn't it give them an unexpected opportunity to castigate human credulousness? Paradoxically, these attacks even did a great deal for the idea by granting it a kind of intellectual legitimacy. Instead of believing in God, Western science and philosophy believed and still believes in religion. Even though drawn from a cultural capital that had never sought its arguments elsewhere than in its own theological and philosophical tradition, the history of religions has somehow conferred on religion an undeniable objectivity and a certain scientific dignity.[4]

In the circumstances, we cannot separate religion, the West, and its science, for example, by assigning them different economies or jurisdictions, separated by insurmountable epistemological barriers. If the fate of the West is intimately tied to a history that it alone calls religious, the history of religions is implicated. Together, the members of this strange trio form a remarkable association that has no equivalent in any other civilization. And if the multiple illusions generated by this tripartite entity seem so obvious, is it not simply because the common anthropology circulated in our culture (in its ideology, textbooks, newspapers) is nourished by the same prejudices and convictions?

In this sphere, the passage from general opinion to scientific thought is accomplished without any theoretical obstacles intervening (those that characterize the regime of the exact sciences: the matter of physicists and chemists is only very partially that of ordinary experience). In fact, only the value and volume of erudition invested in them distinguish them; but we have already seen that the resources and capacities proper to this erudition authorize it neither to justify ordinary presuppositions nor to substitute other, more relevant ones for them.

This situation is very troubling. It makes difficult, if not impossible, any correction, all the more so while scholars persisted in preserving, along with the idea of religion, all the representations and notions that it has carted along with it for more than two thousand years—and that were certainly not conceived with a view to aiding or illuminating contemporary scientific thought. The latter, in any case, does not have to obey a logic constructed as a function of the hegemonic designs of Western anthropology. This anthropology will never, except with great reluctance, think of humanity in other terms than its own, whatever the defects and gaps this terminology presents. What is ultimately at stake in this case is obviously not scientific in nature, since, more prosaically, it targets the ideological control and mastery of discourse relative to humankind. In imposing its vision of humanity, our culture not only exports a corpus of general ideas intended to supply fascinating topics for philosophical dissertations, it also integrates individuals into its world, into its norms; it subjects them to its rules, its values, and its interests. Discourse of this kind does not speak of the world; it invents the world in which people must live.

The fact that in the field of the history of religions, the academic point of view, dominant ideology, and Western doxa are often joined proves by contradiction that the distance that separates them is not so great as one would wish—or that, in any case, a demanding epistemology might wish—and, above all, that unreflected, ongoing, spontaneous recourse to the idea of religion definitively leads to a dead end.[5] Studying it now reveals in exemplary fashion the breadth and influence of premises that were at the base of the discipline, premises consecrated to examining the putative forms or manifestations of religion.

These various remarks bring us back to the general hypothesis proposed in the first pages of this book. Substituted for our old notion of religion, does the concept of cosmographic formations, the category most relevant from an epistemological point of view and most comprehensive from an anthropological point of view, not offer us a more judicious, more efficient conceptual instrument, and thereby prepare a (provisionally) more satisfactory solution to the innumerable difficulties that traditional religious anthropology has proven incapable of resolving?

9 | Prolegomena

For man does not dominate his fundamental conception of the world; on the contrary, it is it that dominates him, animates him, determines, and governs him.

—Ludwig Feuerbach

The prestige and influence attributed for centuries to this idea [of religion] have never ceased to limit and lead astray Western anthropological thought (both scientific and prescientific), by keeping it within certain limits and in the midst of controversies and ways of thinking that had no significance, or that were relevant only for the corresponding intellectual tradition, itself dominated by constant, absolute reference to the Christian model. Imagine what zoology or medicine would look like today if they persisted in classifying their subject matter and forming their key hypotheses entirely on the basis of the essentially unmodified ideas of the Greeks.

How can some historians of religion claim the extravagant privilege of refusing all evolution in and any radical reassessment of their discipline by entrenching themselves behind the unjustifiable argument that, corresponding to their preferred objects of study, there are certain very specific dispositions, religious dispositions as they put it, of the human spirit? For we would then have a right to ask them: where do these come from? Who established them? When? What is their ultimate nature?[1] In what forms and according to what modalities do they appear in history? How (helped by what intrinsic aptitudes) do they adjust to material transformations and changes in mentality? How does it happen that Western speculation, and it alone, arrogates to itself the exclusive privilege of being able to speak of them?[2]

It is all too easy to measure the fragility of the axiomatics underlying the reasoning of these theologians disguised as scholars and the consequences that it implies: if the ultimate objective of the discipline is to discover the "religious invariables" of humanity, seen as manifestations of, or testimony to, some mysterious, transcendental beyond, it ought to claim and preserve this artificial distinction throughout its own inquiry. And it should act as if there were a double rationality, one for each of these two levels of reality: the purely historical, erudite or scientific side of this research should remain subordinate to the interpretation of facts, chosen

195

with care, needless to say, with a view to making them adhere to the unique significance expected of them. Founded neither on close observation nor on the development of a critical method, such studies are condemned tirelessly to repeat the terms of their initial postulates. The epistemological frailty of such an arrangement comes from the fact that it represents only the displacement and transposition of theological and metaphysical premises, themselves drawn from the oldest Western tradition, into the framework of a hermeneutical program with perfectly predictable results.

Other causes have *in nucleo* subverted the ambition of the history of religions to give rise to a true anthropological enterprise. Often reduced to simple projection and simple idealization of our Western categories, this was from the outset embarked on exclusively in the context of dogmatic and polemical traditions entirely derived from Christian civilization: the God/humanity relationship, the triad of body, soul, and spirit, the role of theology and faith, the pairs sacred/profane, religious/nonreligious, exoteric/esoteric, religion/magic, and revelation/reason, the emphasis on personal spiritual experience—all of these directed learned thought, reinforced a complacent ethnocentrism, and nourished a network of stereotyped controversies. With the aid of these unique elements (for the most part, as we have seen, not to be found in any other culture) the history of religions wove the vast conceptual fabric associated with the word "religion," as well as with the principles of a *ratio religiosa* that saw and proclaimed itself as universal. As I have emphasized here, the principles of this "religious reason" are obvious only because they previously shaped an important part of our own intellectual instrumentation and our most intimate ways of thinking. The notions that we so willingly see as transcendental, aprioristic, or original are almost always those that are most deeply buried in our own cultural memory. How many historians of religion navigate and orient themselves with the use of obsolete geographical maps?

How did a discourse constructed on such ethnocentric themes succeed in creating the illusion that, despite everything, it was proclaiming the universal and even in certain cases, yielding to its own impulse, an ineffable transcendence? It is, no doubt, we who were the most active accomplices in this intellectual fraud. Did it not permit us to speak of ourselves and of mankind in the same breath and phrase? (And without our having to surrender our serene, tranquil assurance.) Ethnocentric discourse, which as hegemonic discourse sees itself as uniquely capable of expressing the universal, communicates, to those who speak the language and who profess it, the incomparable sensation that *the* world is everywhere *their* world.

A fortiori, the field of religious anthropology is even more subject to this system of local coordinates, to the point of occasionally verging on the ridiculous: how, for example, can one speak of shamanistic trance and ecstasy with the aid of a religious vocabulary that ignores (and not so long ago arrogantly scorned) the singular nature of this kind of "savage" experience and relegated it firmly to the lowest rank or to the periphery of authentic spiritual life? Would it not be wiser to study such phenomena by first and explicitly abandoning these outdated references, which match only our conception of cultural facts?

As far as anthropology in general is concerned, it has almost always used broad religious, political, magical, social, juridical, and other categories conceived and assembled in that form in only one culture, our own. A division of this kind implies not only a space devoted to religion, but also that all other elements be in one way or another subordinated to it, since they could lay claim only to that which it left them or had marked with its own seal. In the West, the idea of religion is not and never has been an idea like other ideas, but the one that conditioned the form and content of the others, as well as the general tenor of the debates or controversies in which it found itself enmeshed.

The incoherence of this division appears as soon as we leave the shelter of Christian Europe's venerable battlements. We then must have recourse to artificial expressions such as "politico-religious" and "magico- and juridico-religious" (terms we find, for example, in the definition of the Dumézilian first function) to qualify realities and events that obviously do not result from a simple mixture of pure substances borrowed respectively from the "magical," the "juridical," and the "religious." These exotic or archaic singularities are, like the Western "political" or "religious," remarkable historical configurations that are not immediately paraphrasable in our language—in other words, in our world. Although it is fortunate that cultures mutually translate themselves and try in this fashion to understand one another somewhat better, we should not conclude that what we translate into our European languages, and because we translate it without any too great difficulty, refers back to universals to which we have the key. All scientific study today ought to have as its sine qua non the critical, uncompromising study of its own language.

Religion in its Western sense is but one of the possible expressions of an anthropological function that dominates it and entirely encompasses it, in which ideas and behaviors we call religious have to be seen in the light of other principles and other ends. It is the original complexes that correspond to this universal function that I propose to call cosmographic formations.

The elaboration of an anthropological enterprise inspired by this notion imposes a first constraint: that we initially have recourse only to very general, comprehensive notions, capable of subsuming the totality of these particular cultural and historical configurations under designations that are directly drawn from none of them.[3]

Similarly, in order to give some force to such an undertaking, I propose that we substitute for the nebulous semantics deriving from the Western paradigm—everywhere it is used with a clear anthropological orientation—notions more universal because less "marked" (or less ethnocentric, if you will), capable of encompassing this semantics without being dependent on it or on the implicit categories and sterile debates that it entertains. For, like every cardinal cultural notion, religion remains captive to the network of controversies and opinions that were progressively constructed around it, becoming that pretension to which an unpredictable history subsequently accorded a success that would earlier have seemed inconceivable.

This network was so powerful that it was adopted by the history of religions in the nineteenth century, and even today, it conditions its internal organization (summarized in the opposition of historians and phenomenologists). Unfortunately, the existence of this system paralyses thought, confines it to traditional loci, stuffs it with clichés, and compromises all possibility of meaningful progress. The long-consecrated debate between historians and phenomenologists will never produce anything but the reiteration of metaphysical arguments that at bottom are those exchanged for centuries and centuries between Platonists and Lucretians, believers and rationalists, theologians and atheists. Rather than being universal, the terms of such a debate offer but a single advantage, that of being ancient and familiar. And it is because they surprise us so little that we believe them universal. As if we could consider universal only that which was most intimately associated with ourselves!

This book concludes, then, by focusing exclusively on the concept of cosmographic formation, pointing out both some of its likely heuristic advantages and the direction it should take. These propositions are intended only for reflection and rumination. Incitements rather than peremptory assertions, they in any case suggest that the religious in no way constitutes an absolute limit beyond which our mental space is necessarily empty—an argument often advanced as a kind of ultimate proof in favor of the afore-said religious.[4] Stretching beyond it lie no barren steppes of the unthink-able or conceptual vacuousness. Like everything that is thought and that history has thought, the religious is surrounded by other thoughts, not by a void.

In substituting the concept of cosmographic formations for that of religion everywhere its defenders propose to speak of a certain "universal religious," I have a triple objective:

— To determine a general concept capable of encompassing the het-erogeneous totality of facts and notions that, for lack of a better name, we habitually call religious, and to collect all those (ideo-logical, ritual, symbolic, etc.) that are excluded from it on the basis of Christian theological criteria, inasmuch as these perform the same anthropological functions. This functional similarity is more essential than the distinctions or secondary divisions that Western thought, obsessed with its own native categories, claims to introduce among them. We have here a secondary predicate whose significance is circumscribed by a single culture, our own, and a religious symbol is above all a symbol—that, if you will, is its essential or intrinsic character.

— To stimulate contemporary anthropological thought to concern itself with the human condition such as it is, and not only such as it represents itself to be here and there, or as it is represented in a certain kind of science aimed at formulating only congruent hypotheses (remote as the good Platonic notions that they often are) from a too fleshly, even trivial human reality. In this human condition, in its fragile but constant presence in the world, there is something fundamental that does not vary, that is everywhere identical with itself. Everything, absolutely everything, that be-longs to the human world, but uniquely that: this should be the program for this anthropology of living human beings. Why is our discipline so often content to see and invoke only conceptual systems, transcendental categories, unconscious processes, logi-cal mechanisms? The key to so many phenomena is to be found in something much less mysterious, which is easily observable: life, that is, human existence in its most tangible and most banal form. This return to the explicit universe of individuals should above all *not* consist of pulverizing their lives into ethnographical microstudies but of deliberately inscribing them at the heart of all anthropological hypotheses.

— To make obsolete the majority of the debates and categorizations that the history of religions conserves and defends only because it has inherited them from a long tradition, from a culture that continues to be dominated by so many notions and ways of thinking that are relevant only within the points of reference that delimit the space of this culture.

All anthropological reflection undertaken with the aid of these cosmographic formations will initially occasion some eminently symbolic loss. This is why it will be difficult to impose the new ways of thinking that its adoption would entail. To abandon the idea of religion as a general concept, universal in scope, means that the notion of *Homo religiosus* will also have to be relegated to the past. This notion, under one form or another, is frequently inherent in our conception of humanity. In this conception, religion is particular to humankind (or to human societies), whatever the attitude otherwise adopted toward it, whether it be ironic or enthusiastic, skeptical or frankly incredulous.

Must we or must we not replace the idea of religion with an expression that would no longer be defined on the basis of Western experience alone? Behind this question rises a challenge: will Western science be capable of adopting an anthropological concept that is not expressly located in the direct line of its own cultural tradition?

Lastly, aware that this older idea is often only a slightly disguised way of allowing many historians of religion to make an apology for the kind of transcendence in which they believe (God, Being, the sacred, tradition, etc.), we can predict that the feverish resistance that will oppose the concept of cosmographic formations will be dictated by considerations and ulterior motives unhindered by any scientific concern. Let us go even farther. The tenacity with which some will continue to defend the use of the word "religion," perhaps for a long time, betrays a superstitious fear that with the word might disappear the idea, too, that is, the very thing that it claims to designate.

Every cosmographical formation is a world, its own world.

To this axiom,[5] let us immediately add a short series of other aphorisms designed to illuminate its significance, followed by brief commentaries:

(a) All cultures are thereby similar, and likewise, all are different.
(b) The worlds created by human beings are metaphysical worlds.
(c) Each world is a totality, but contingent, unique, and autonomous.
(d) Belonging to a world itself assumes the form of a world.
(e) Every world of this kind is a common world in which people live and age together.
(f) Each world contains our texts, our lives, and our bodies.

(a) All cultures are thereby similar, and likewise, all are different.

This proposition is a means of solving an old problem. The diversity of cultures, which may affect their major aspects and extend to their ultimate elements, is such only because, comparatively, each of them really is, from a functional and structural point of view, identical with the others. An example from a more familiar domain will better show what I mean: Western literary genres such as the novel, the essay, and the short story are not universals, and neither is the notion of literature, unlike the idea of genre, which is.[6] Everywhere, the existence of different discursive genres, themselves comprising an original system, makes it possible to classify particular works. In other words, every discursive production is capable, through its content and its form, of being incomparable (the Indian Brāhmana and Upanishads, for example, resemble nothing else); on the other hand, to the extent that it is defined and determined by a genre illustrating a particular class within a generic whole, its status is similar to that of all the others. In the same way, we can say that no world is, *stricto sensu,* similar to any other, but in their capacity *as worlds* they are structurally and functionally homologous. All worlds are worlds even though none is identical with any one of its congeners.

The relativist point of view, to which one might be tempted to succumb when noting how inexhaustible the capacities of the prodigious diversity of cultures seem, must itself, as a consequence, be relativized.

Considered superficially, from the exterior, as it were, cultures seem to be so many absolute, incomparable creations: how, using what conceptual vehicle and subjecting them to what inconceivable series of transpositions and transformations, can we make the connection between Tungus shamanism and the Roman imperial cult, or between the Christian conscience of a Meister Eckhart and the initiation of a young African hunter? What formidable suspension of judgment and shift in imagery could achieve this? And what conceptual monster would the *eidos* produced in such an experiment resemble? Beyond the attribution of some general references to some equally general themes—which explain and are explained by nothing—these configurations seem irrelevant, each isolated within its own reasoning.

In return, their richness, complexity, the almost infinite number of their rules, their practices, and their beliefs, which are directly responsible for this situation—these possess a remarkable point in common in the sense that they all contribute, in their own place and according to their means, to constructing a particular world. The homology does not concern the level of liaisons and observable elements, their superficial similarities if you like, but that of their function, the ultimate finality.

Here the final cause is more essential than the initial material causes. In order to construct their shelters or houses, humans have used innumerable plans and different materials, but this diversity ought not to make us forget the similarity in the goal pursued. In every human project, we find the same paradox, for every creation presupposes that in its most primitive stage, it had already glimpsed the totality to come and had subsequently ceaselessly pursued the achievement of its realization at each stage of it. This double movement (the step-by-step progression and the anticipation of the end), present at the heart of all activity, of all human production, limits the ambitions of every analytical approach, which often proceeds by acting as if the progressive time of creation were only a cumulative process, incapable of projecting itself into the future in order to preview its own accomplishment. Among all the elements of a finished whole, the most important and the first among them, that which escapes all decomposition is the undertaking itself, its synthetic objective, its global design and final anticipated form, which from the outset have guided the choice of all the others, their disposition, and the numerous modalities of their interaction.[7]

The diversity that anthropological thought seems to run up against represents an insoluble problem as long as we do not admit that it simultaneously shows a remarkable functional homology. It is because each culture resumes a world in itself that they all are globally similar and at the same time different.

That the world is never more than the world according to this or that culture is similarly a proposition that assumes the greatest importance for anthropological thought. If all worlds are different, they are never so to the point where one of them is not THE world in the eyes of those who live there. It is then by putting ourselves in this existential position (what people do in this world, how they have constructed it, and what they expect of it) that the study of cosmographic formations ought to be addressed. Thus it acquires real anthropological weight without being troubled by the diversity of cultural forms. If all cultures are worlds, it is because human beings find such worlds indispensable. This is an undeniable fact; no other human phenomenon is so to the same degree.

(b) The worlds created by human beings are metaphysical worlds.

But for all that, we cannot posit metaphysical worlds on one side and a "real world" on the other. At best, the "real world" is never more than an abstraction, deduced from these metaphysical worlds at the cost of an intellectual effort that strips them of precisely what constitutes their value, namely, their human peculiarities. This "real" world, understood in this sense, can only be that of modern science, positivist and analytical. But would it be capable on its own, on the basis of its own rules and principles, of unifying into the form of a world all the knowledge that claims to be representative of it? Thus breaking with the culture that conceived it, that set the bounds of its provinces, defined the objects, and thematized the procedures. But it matters little in the final analysis, for the world of science cannot be, could never be that in which human beings really live. For this it lacks the ability to become a world for human life, to be capable of responding to humans aspirations and fears, their needs for knowledge and their capacities, which do not have a great deal to do with the respectable objectives of science. Will science ever ask of humans: how and for what do you live? Are your world and mine the same?

Whatever the nature of the conditions and the causes assignable to these human factors (needs, aspirations, capacities, etc., whether they be individual or collective), the fact remains that they are the only stable foundations on which a living anthropology could be constructed, that is, an anthropology that has as its first priority a concern with the real condition of real people. If the life of humanity had no other objective than the manifestation of unconscious structures, of abstract transcendental schemes, and conceptual or symbolic systems (a conception that the procedures of some contemporary science would tend to credit), it would be enough to lock oneself in a library to find them out. On the model of the long philosophical tradition that preceded them, the human sciences display scarcely any interest in real human beings and even less in living individuals, that is, in the central problem represented by the fact of living, and of living in a certain world. This major cosmographical and anthropological question has until now been neglected by scientific thought. The object of the human sciences has never been living human beings, people confronted with the problems of life, the problems of *their* lives. Apparently frightened by this physical, existential density, they have most often preferred to direct their interest to the destiny of disincarnate, anonymous humans (historical, sociological, ethnographical people, but surely not people of flesh and blood).

Contrary to the received opinion implicit in common parlance and embodied in a kind of scientific positivism, people do not live in THE world (that shelters them and would be the same for all), since each human group lives only in *its* world. Each cosmographic formation (re)creates the world and thereby transfigures it. And this world, even if it exists in actuality and is in this capacity observable (facts, beliefs, customs, institutions, etc.), nonetheless exists as, and only as, a unique, exclusive world.

At best (or at worst, as you wish) people are seen as living in a composite or mixed reality. Why?[8] In the final analysis, the great problem posed by reality concerns the presence of human beings at its heart, those talkative creatures who are part of it—while never ceasing to reassert that their world is elsewhere or different. This observation made, another appears at once, with the same evidence. In theory, it perhaps matters little in definitive terms that reality-in-itself, as it really is, remains for the greater part inaccessible to us: the only important things are our own descriptions of situations, of the state of things. However, are we at least capable of distinguishing one of these two types of reality from the other with certainty: the real things on the one hand, the description of them on the other? The world in and of itself on the one hand, our worlds on the other? Probably not.

In truth, the world such as it really is and our own worlds are only abstractions deduced a posteriori; we have to add ourselves to them. We never continuously weave the one into the other in order to slip ourselves into the weave and thus give ourselves the only mode of existence to which we can lay claim. Our representations of the world are a part of this fabric and are inseparable from it, just as our own lives are consubstantial with the successive notions that we have of them. What would these lives become without them? And what would they then be like? The composite, jumbled reality in which we live, the only one in which we can live (since it corresponds to our manner of being in the world) is thus complex, ambiguous, mixed, as real as it is fantastic.

We could complicate at leisure the image of this composite reality that, for us humans, is the only one that counts and that exists. Descriptions that have themselves become fragments of reality are taken over by other, ulterior descriptions whose manner of being implanted in the world is open to infinite variation. And so on, for ever and ever, until this intricacy, become in its turn so dizzying, no longer permits us to escape from it and understand its mechanisms or consider its organization. Our existences unfold neither in cold (or pure) reality nor in our imaginary worlds, but in that intermediary zone, mixed, made up of contacts, interfaces, mixtures, intertwinings. To respond to this situation there ought to be an ontology based on the sacrilegious categories of the mixed and interlaced, themselves returned to the grandiose perspective of perpetual metamorphosis, an interminable gestation. Unfortunately, we are here dealing with notions and perspectives with which Western thought has never formed warm, durable relations. Its preference has rather gone to panoramas in which distinct, pure substances, uniform instances and processes, as well as unchanging oppositions paint their monotonous landscapes.

(c) Each world is a totality, but contingent, unique, and autonomous.

Certain cultures assign greatest value to scars cut into the skin, others to the horsepower of their automobiles, still others to the recitation of incomprehensible formulas. Some sculpt grains of rice, while others erect cathedrals in stone. Some live with the imminence of a final conflagration and others with the certainty of being immortal. Some believe in the virtue of asceticism; others celebrate the occult powers of trance and possession. Some advocate intoxication, others silent withdrawal and the strictest abstention.

From these differences and so many others, each more outlandish and exotic than the preceding one, to which it would be only too easy to add in order to make the picture even more comical and bizarre, how could we possibly not conclude that each culture, each world, is an original creation? And since it is equally the result of an incalculable number of unforeseeable events and sequences, we must at once add that each of these creations is contingent. Nothing, at no time and in no place, either willed or foresaw these complex evolutions, which led to as many unprecedented results.

Unique and contingent, each of these worlds created by human beings is also autonomous, in the sense that even if it needs its neighbors in order to live, it will never see the world through their eyes, since it never succeeds in getting away from itself. At the very most, it can transform itself, modify itself. Similarly, borrowings, cross-fertilizations, or conquests may end, according to the case, in another world or in a mosaic of juxtaposed worlds that all have equal claim to be called worlds.

Let us note the following: speaking of contingency, autonomy, even of isolation or autism, may seem paradoxical when the discussion is focused precisely on the notion of cosmographic formation. Does such a conception tacitly exclude such defects? In reality, we can perhaps already make out what is hidden by the other, more reassuring aspect of this paradox. It is precisely because they are worlds—that is, totalities whose most precious character depends on this capacity, this aptitude to substitute itself for universal, contingent, arbitrary processes—that cosmographic formations rarely appear as what they in fact are, that is, bizarre, unexpected, ephemeral constructions. In Wilhelm Dilthey's words:

> The parts of such an interactive set are then of importance for their relationship to the whole as a support for values and ends. It is above all in their relation to life, to its values and its ends, to the place that something occupies there, that the parts of the course of life have a signification. Historical events then become significant only to the extent that they are elements of an interactive set, by collaborating with other parts in the realization of the values and ends of the totality.
>
> While we remain perplexed in the face of the complexity of history's unfolding and can perceive there neither a structure nor regularity nor evolution, each interactive set where a cultural activity is carried out displays a structure that is proper to it.[9]

(d) Belonging to a world itself assumes the form of a world.

Some of the preceding remarks may perhaps give the idea that by "worlds," I mean closed, homogeneous, simple universes, like monads lined up beside one another on a horizontal plane. This impression—difficult to avoid at first, with attention focused on other questions—needs to be corrected.

In fact, what we observe at first glance is rather successive interlockings of worlds (from local, partial cosmographies, if you will, up to the vastest, most all-encompassing ideological systems), which themselves present, on whatever level they are observed, the form of a world or the capacity to become one. In this ordering of facts, the rules of subsumption and syncretisms will display an exuberant, luxuriant morphology.[10]

The world that an individual conceives of (and lives in!) clearly participates in the worlds of superior groups (family, tribe, ethnicity, social class, nation, and so on), which themselves participate in that or those worlds that dominate his or her culture. For obvious, predictable reasons, I have thus far favored this level, "culture" (e.g., Augustan Rome, the France of Saint Louis, or the India of the Buddha). But this convenient choice, reminiscent of the naïve universe and summary representations of high school history, should neither be allowed to create an illusion nor to make us forget all the other levels. In the same way, it should not lead us to underestimate the incredible complexity at work here. In particular, it should not allow us to be content with a rigidly hierarchical vision, that of a monotonous mass of modules fitting into each other like a set of Russian dolls.

Each individual lives only in a single world, but at the same time, this world (one's own world) is itself a world, that is, a complex machine that, in absolute terms, is capable of providing a response to everything. Each world is sufficient unto itself, and it is normally sufficient for the person who lives there. A world is not a simple superstructure added to reality in order to make it more attractive or more tolerable; it is lived experience.

The "fragile presence" of the self in the world, in Ernesto de Martino's fine phrase,[11] can only take the form of a world. On its own scale, individual life is already necessarily a cosmographic creation, a tireless effort intended to metamorphose contingency and the unforeseen into signs, symbols, beliefs, institutions, rules for living. What we observe in cosmographic formations are the results, whether grandiose or pitiable, of these indispensable metamorphoses. Without them, life would be even more anxiety-ridden. The human condition would crush the individual.

How do these different levels adjust to and harmonize with one another in the minds of individuals? What (morpho)logical principles regulate these subtle processes of inclusion? What types of rationality do they tolerate? What forms of influence do the unpredictable or accidental events that occur have? How are the contradictions that arise in the course of their realization minimized or erased? How, by what paths and in what forms, for a given individual, does the world of level one (the most immediate, most everyday) integrate the elements of levels x, y, or z, which are supposed to surround it? To what end does all this lead?

It is not possible for the moment to answer these delicate questions with complete precision. On the other hand, we can, even at this juncture, add the following complementary reflections.

(e) Every world of this kind is a common world in which people live and age together.

We know that there are psychological explanations, sociological laws, biological processes, historical rhythms, economic movements, and so on. We know, too, that there are interpretations, learned or trivial, of all these phenomena. Should these different rationalities be considered separately and condemned to a splendid isolation, or should they be subordinated to something much vaster, capable of subsuming them and giving them some supplementary being? If we opt for the second choice, in conformity with the hypothesis advanced here, to what must we associate the persistence and omnipresence of this cosmographic function?

Of all human phenomena, the most essential is that of life. Academia therefore takes little interest in it. But nothing gets done without it and nothing is conceived of outside it. Ideas, notions, beliefs are never simple mind games or vain intellectual curiosities. They are at the same time and without any doubt lived conceptions, themselves associated with styles of living, or lived behaviors (Max Weber).[12] I would even volunteer that for me they are intrinsically tied to "existential stances" or to "ways of being in the world." But human life is never reduced to the simple factuality of an immediate, blind "lived." To all forms of life or experience, whatever the crushing role that material constraints at times play there, is added a supplementary orientation that retrospectively gives them a coherence and that in turn becomes an element of life, for life.

Dilthey was correct in writing: "In external nature, coherence is attributed to phenomena through a connection of abstract concepts. In the world of the spirit, coherence is, on the contrary, lived and is understood according to having been so lived. Nature's coherence is abstract, but psychic and historical coherence is living, impregnated with life."[13]

All cosmographic formations are impregnated with life.

A human existence is always a certain "way of being in the world"[14] or, we should perhaps say, a certain "way of being in the world conceived as

THE world." For the limits of this world are at the same time those of THE world. A Hindu ascetic, a Chinese communist, and a Siberian hunter do not live in THE world (that of objective science, ethnography, or history) but in a certain world that is *in their eyes* THE world.

Must we, under these conditions, grant human beings and their coalescence into tribes or societies the favor of a cosmographic instinct that would aid them in transfiguring every event, every object, and every thought into something that would change its simple immediate existence? The word "instinct" is doubtless unsuitable, poorly chosen. But every other term ("tendency," "inclination," "obsession," "reflex," "aptitude," "original disposition," "transcendental faculty," etc.) would be even less so. In any case, it is not a matter of looking for the paleoanthropological origin of this function, but of reasserting: wherever they are, whoever they are, whatever they do, whatever the means they use, the convictions that animate them, human beings, all human beings, continuously resituate their humble condition, their lives, and their bodies in cosmographic constructions in order to suppress discontinuities or incoherences and to forget their pitiless, bitter brevity.

Such worlds do not have an exclusive origin located in a distant abode: they are cosmographic formations. Let us rather say that the question of origin is not a key one or even relevant to them and leave it to the mythographers. Founded in any case on unverifiable conjecture, the answers that we could make would above all betray our secret need to give a definitive (theological?) form to a reflection dealing precisely with our ways of "cosmographing" the world. We would, for example, be obliged to place at the origin of these worlds one or another determining instance (society, the unconscious, this biological instinct or that transcendental category, and so on), for this is what is peculiar to all questions dealing with origins. But how would our comment then be distinguished from the most traditional foundation myths? It is too often our own cosmographic reflexes and traditions that prompt us to give a comparable orientation to our scientific questioning.

The rationality proper to the coherence mentioned above perhaps seems so only a posteriori, to the eyes of the modern observer obsessed with the idea that symbolic systems necessarily rest on impeccable logical structures. We, more prudent and in any case less obsessed by this formalist concern, may be ready to admit that all forms of liaison or connection that are conceivable by the human mind, from the crudest to the most complex, from the most proximate to immediate experience to the most metaphorical, are used, and often used simultaneously. Who could contradict a cosmographic principle or formula and in the name of what? For this coherence is lifelong, and who knows what accommodations it is not capable of finding with rationality when it comes to self-defense. If we withdraw from our existences all the elements that do not display perfect order, that do not rest on impeccable structures, and that are not inspired by ideal rationality, would we be able to bear the weight of life? Certainly not!

This is why these worlds, with their bizarre, unique principles of order, are also strange worlds where imaginary beings, bodily and moral disciplines, schizophrenic tendencies, contagious mythomanias, massacres and murders are all mixed together. Unquantifiable suffering and cruel injustice. Complex structures made of intricacies, repetitions, and transpositions.

Having recourse to a transcendent principle is a logical characteristic, inherent in cosmographic formations, for every construction of this kind is condemned to making its point from outside its immediate environment, putting it outside the course of things, as otherwise this point would seem to share in their fate.[15] To mix this necessary artifice with the existence of a true transcendence is the most visible effect of the power of these cosmographic formations on the minds of human beings.

(f) Each world contains our texts, our lives, and our bodies.

A cosmographic formation is distinguished from an opinion or an intellectual thesis because it forms a functional and nearly harmonious whole with the texts that utter and incarnate it.

It is almost certain that human beings have never experienced their bodies as simple, perishable facts, devoid of meaning.[16] Similarly, they have never seen their lives as chaotic successions of disparate movements and events. In order to resolve the incoherence of this elusive life, people have substituted narratives, histories, descriptions, in a word, texts that have allowed them to grasp life at the center of a global (and often finalized) and thus more reassuring vision. We have done the same with our bodies. Ignorance of physiological mechanisms alone cannot explain the multitude of texts that have been devoted to them. All cultures have composed texts in which we find elaborate descriptions and genuine theories of the body in actuality, theories charged with coordinating, interpreting, explaining the phenomena of death, suffering, sensation, memory, and dreaming.

Here, given that we are dealing with the most perishable and fragile portion of our being, textualization is indispensable. Let us remember that without it we would be reduced to an uninterrupted flow of sensations, joys, fears, sufferings that would continuously disorient us and would scarcely offer us any way out other than self-destruction or madness. In a certain way, and one that is not negligible, our texts (and all our texts display some cosmographic characteristics) preserve us from day to day.

These traditional descriptions and theories of the body in general display a common feature, and it is not for nothing that we have so often, thanks to them, spoken of it as of a microcosm, homologous with the vast macrocosm that contains it. For globally, and if we keep to their most consistent characteristics, we can assert that they all contribute to advancing cosmographies comparable to those that describe the universe. Isn't the universal harmony that issues from them, and that makes it possible to pass gradually (or suddenly) from one to the other, more comforting than the most powerful tranquilizer?

To prove the existence of the soul or of spirits, to imagine explanations relative to the mechanisms that link them to the five senses (or six if, as in India, an "internal" sense is added), to propose a rational conception of desire, memory, dreaming, and so on, are not just so many isolated propositions, indifferent to one another. It is always a matter of assembling disparate elements and facts in order to construct an orderly and thus reassuring textual equivalent. And it is through this that human beings will thenceforth read their own bodies.[17] And this is the essential point. Just as we read the world through the texts that recompose it, so we do not live (in) our bodies except with the aid of those of our texts that offer a synthetic conception of it, one capable of disposing and coordinating all their aspects.

All these descriptions and all these traditional theories of the body lead to its metamorphosis and transfiguration. The translation of the body into texts allows it to become an element of cosmographic formation. At the heart of the latter, our fragile, tired, perishable bodies acquire an enviable status and a new dignity. They are transformed, according to the case in point, into prestigious, heroicized, voluptuous, saintly, immortal bodies, that is, into sublimated and, in short, disincarnate bodies.

This challenging issue is one of the weightiest that any anthropology intent on understanding human beings, simply people, would have to examine. Let us not forget that among those texts that deal with the care of our bodies, we must also count all those that codify and justify bodily disciplines (fasting, penitence, alimentary or sexual regimes, exercises, and so on), tattooing, scarifying and the like (making the body itself a hiero-glyphic symbol), punishments, and rituals.[18] None of these "techniques of the body," in Marcel Mauss's felicitous phrase, could be understood if we did not assign them the unique goal of our well-being or the desire to distinguish ourselves from our fellows. To make of one's body a "Christian body" or a "Brahmanic body" is an operation that day by day engages a whole life, its entire existence. This is consequently a painful task that calls for an incalculable amount of effort, privation, sacrifice, and asceticism, the benefits of which, fortunately, are most of the time intended to accrue to us elsewhere than in this contingent world.

The Brahman in India, who brushes his teeth each morning ritually following the precepts taught in the Sutras—collections of traditional maxims—is not prosaically engaging in a simple exercise of hygiene. Nor do we stand to gain much by calling this a religious ceremony. This modest operation, in its place and according to its importance, participates in a much vaster and more ambitious realization. It is only one of the links in the mesh of an endless discipline intended to preserve the Brahmanic body from all impure contact and thus permit it to escape the infernal cycle of rebirth. Even the Brahman's feces are subjected to equally punctilious treatment and ritual, which is to say that the great cosmographies abandon no part of the human body or cadaver to chance.

If our bodies are disincarnated in our texts by becoming one of the signs recognized in the corresponding cosmographies, this operation, this distillation, we should rather say, in inverse fashion allows these cosmographies to be incarnated in our lives and in our bodies. The rules that govern this fundamental symbolic exchange are at bottom very clear. By agreeing (but do we really have a choice?) to submit our bodies to the prescriptions contained in a given cosmographic description, we metamorphose these bodies into one of its elements. Reciprocally, this cosmography is then incarnated in our own existences, since it is from within it that we thenceforth act. As a consequence it is no longer in our "offensive, pithless" (Maitrāyani Upanishad 1.3) carnal bodies that we live,[19] but in bodies that have acquired reasons for being and for living, which take their place in an immaterial and almost always unchanging totality.

The complicity that links us to cosmographic formations through the intermediary of texts that expound them here finally reveals all its meaning and all its scope. Whatever the degree of duplicity in the powers that turn it to their profit (which may be considerable), whatever the depth of our bad faith, the fact remains that this complicity is rooted in a more pressing and more respectable need, the one we feel each time that we recall that we ourselves, our lives, and the meanings that we had assigned them until now could abandon us for ever and be replaced by nothing.

Notes

1. A Central Concept

1. By the West here I mean Christian Europe (principally France, Great Britain, and Germany, whose contribution to the birth of the human sciences in the nineteenth century was, as we know, decisive). But on numerous, very essential points, it is obvious that we cannot dissociate Christian Europe from its prestigious pagan ancestors, most particularly the Greeks, who transmitted to the Christian West so very many ideas and arguments.

2. Which is not to say the equal, for often the affirmation of the universality of religions has as its corollary the more or less implicit idea that Western forms of religion are the most complete, the most effectively fulfilled—or some would say, the most moral, the most spiritual. Contrary to naïve prejudice, the idea of universality does not preclude the possibility of establishing a hierarchy of institutions, cultures, accomplishments, etc., since on the contrary it makes it possible more easily to evaluate the whole of humanity according to a few criteria that are always flattering to Western conceptions, as is the very idea of universality.

3. Claude Lévi-Strauss, *L'Homme nu,* vol. 4 of *Mythologies* (Paris: Plon, 1971), trans. John and Doreen Weightman as *The Naked Man* (New York: Harper & Row, 1981), pp. 625f.

4. The linguistic process involved is analyzed in detail in Daniel Dubuisson, "Ontogenèse divine et structures énonciatives: La Création illocutoire d'Agni dans le Rigveda," *Revue de l'histoire des religions* 211, 2 (1994): 225–45.

5. Georges Dumézil incessantly repeated that in order to avoid the inherent traps, we should compare only structures, which alone make the inquiry pertinent. Recalling also that human cultures have long worked with only a small number of symbolic modules, borrowed for the most part from agriculture, weaving, hunting, and kinship, he suggested distrust of anecdotal resemblances.

6. Augustine *City of God* 10.1, quoted on p. 23.

7. The "phenomenological" current is represented by, e.g., Nathan Söderblom, Rudolf Otto, Jean Héring, Girardus van der Leeuw, Mircea Eliade, Julien

Ries, and Paul Poupard. Héring, the author of *Phénoménologie et philosophie religieuse: Étude sur la théorie de la connaissance religieuse* (Paris: Félix Alcan, 1926), had been a student of Edmund Husserl's in Göttingen from 1909 to 1912 and was influenced by the Christian phenomenology of Max Scheler's *Von Ewigen im Menschen* (1921), trans. Bernard Noble as *On the Eternal in Man* (New York: Harper, 1961), and Otto Gründler's *Elemente zu einer Religionsphilosophie auf phänomenologischer Grundlage* (Munich: J. Kösel & F. Pustet, 1922). Van der Leeuw's *Phänomenologie der Religion* (Tübingen: J. C. B. Mohr, 1933), was translated by J. E. Turner as *Religion in Essence and Manifestation: A Study in Phenomenology* (New York: Macmillan, 1938).

8. To avoid repetition, I elsewhere speak of cosmological "systems," "productions," or "creations" to designate these universes conceived of by human beings wholly in order to inscribe their persons and existence therein and thereby give them meaning.

9. I am naturally conscious of the fact that this enumeration, here used to suggest the totality of possible philosophical attitudes, is probably meaningful only for the Christian West. But how would one set about drawing up a truly exhaustive list of all the philosophical attitudes conceived by humanity? And in such a context, what would the word "philosophical" signify?

10. As presented in Daniel Dubuisson, *Anthropologie poétique: Esquisses pour une anthropologie du texte* (Louvain: Peeters, 1996), pp. 119–27.

11. Claude Lévi-Strauss, *La Pensée sauvage* (Paris: Plon, 1962), p. 17. [The subtlety and light irony of the author's thought is imperfectly captured in the standard translation of this work: "The thought we call primitive is founded on this demand for order. This is equally true of all thought"; *The Savage Mind*, trans. George Weidenfeld (Chicago: University of Chicago Press, 1966), p. 10.—Trans.] See, too, Baruch Spinoza, *Ethics*, trans. George Eliot, ed. Thomas Deegan (Salzburg: University of Salzburg, 1981), p. 61: "Further, as things which are easily imagined are more pleasing to us, men prefer order to confusion, as though there were any order in nature, except in relation to our imagination."

12. See Marcel Mauss, "La Polarité religieuse et la division du macrocosme," "Les Civilisations, éléments et formes," and "La Cohésion sociale dans les sociétés polysegmentaires," in *Œuvres*, 2: 143–53, 456–79; 3: 11–27 (Paris: Éditions de Minuit, 1968–69). And see also Jean-Pierre Grossein, citing Weber, in *Sociologie des religions par Max Weber* (Paris: Gallimard, 1996), p. 56: "each phenomenon of social reality is a complex phenomenon, that is, it is caught in a network or interlace of 'infinitely intermingled causal connections.'"

13. See the review of the question and conclusions of Émile Benveniste in his *Le Vocabulaire des institutions indo-européens*, 2 vols. (Paris: Éditions de Minuit, 1969), 2: 265–79, trans. Elizabeth Palmer as *Indo-European Language and Society* (Coral Gables, Fla.: University of Miami Press, 1973), pp. 516–28. There is no Indo-European term even tentatively equivalent to our word "religion."

14. See Daniel Dubuisson, "Pourquoi et comment parle-t-on des origines?" *Graphè* (Lille) 4 (1955): 19–31.

15. This Greek word *thrēskeia,* meaning cultural observances and practices, is translated three times by *religio* in the Latin New Testament (James 1:27; Acts 26:5; Col. 2:18). Elsewhere, at the cost of some inexactitude and another anachronism, *religio* translates the Greek *eusebeia,* "piety."

16. Cf. Cicero *Pro Fonteio* 12: "Religione jurisjurandi ac metu deorum in testimonii dicendis commoveri" ("to be inspired in his depositions by the religion of the oath and by the fear of the gods"), cited by Max Müller, *Lectures on the Origin and Growth of Religion* (London: Longmans, Green, 1878).

17. Augustine *City of God* 10.3, trans. Marcus Dods (New York: Modern Library, 1950), pp. 304f.

18. Arnobius *Adversus nationes* 2.71–73.

19. Numerous references in Tertullian, Lactantius, Saint Augustine, etc.

20. *Lactantius' Epitome of the Divine Institutes,* ed. and trans. E. H. Blakeney (London: SPCK, 1950), ch. 69.

21. Augustine *City of God* 10.3.

22. It seems self-evident to us that religious subjects should be addressed with gravity and dealt with in a sober style. But why is this the case? And, in particular, what impact does such poetic treatment have on the formation of the object itself as well as on perceptions of it? Some of the problems of poetics are discussed in *Poétique et rhétorique des savoirs dans les sciences humaines,* ed. Daniel Dubuisson, *Strumenti critici* (Bologna) 85, 3 (1997).

23. The passage that immediately follows draws on Dubuisson, *Anthropologie poétique,* pp. 14ff.

24. Pierre Lévy, *Les Technologies de l'intelligence* (Paris: La Découverte, 1990), p. 209: "The collection of messages and figurations circulating in a society can be viewed as a huge, moving hypertext, labyrinthine, multiform, with thousands of paths and channels. The members of a polis share a number of elements and connections of the common mega-network. However, each of them has only a personal, terribly partial vision of it, deformed by innumerable translations and interpretations. It is precisely these unwarranted associations, these metamorphoses, these torsions effected by local, unique, subjective machines, connected on the exterior, that reinject movement, life, into the great social hypertext, into 'culture.'"

2. A Paradoxical Subject

1. A strict definition of religions inspired by structuralism would doubtless pose thorny and painful metaphysical problems for all those who base the ecumenical idea of religion on the existence of a transcendence, for such a definition excludes every kind of unchanging instance (God, Being, the sacred). From

such a perspective, the essence of religion(s) would actually lie in their immanent logical characteristics alone, that is, in a kind of void or total ontological vacuum.

2. It is not easy, even among Westerners, where the political, the thaumaturgical, and the religious are supposed to be distinct, to say, for example, to which category the coronation of the king of France belongs. And what could we say about the coronation of Indo-European kings, Chinese emperors, or Egyptian pharaohs?

3. *Le Fait religieux,* ed. Jean Delumeau (Paris: Fayard, 1993), offers another variant on this clichéd anthropology's naïve, perfunctory conviction: "[B]ehind each religion, there is the religious man of all times and of all civilizations" (p. 9). The universality of religion is frequently invoked in reference, often implicit, to the old (Aristotle, Plato, the Stoics) commonplace to the effect roughly that error cannot be universal; not all men can be wrong; consequently, the universality of the belief in God or in supernatural beings proves their existence. But what are we to understand by "belief" in this case, if we in fact want to make this position the anthropological nucleus of the religious? Christian theologians have often added the idea of a primitive, original revelation that left traces or memories of it here and there.

4. Michel Duquesnoy, an ethnologist and specialist in shamanism, suggested this example to me.

5. See *Parler aux dieux: Problèmes de pragmatique religieuse,* ed. Daniel Dubuisson, *Revue de l'histoire des religions* 211, 2 (1994): 131–245.

6. See Wiktor Stoczkowski, *Aux origines de l'humanité* (Paris: Pocket, 1996).

7. Marcel Mauss, *Les Fonctions sociales du sacré,* vol. 1 of *Œuvres* (Paris: Éditions de Minuit, 1968), pp. 93f. Eugène Goblet d'Alviella early on regarded religions as "groups of religious phenomena" consisting of beliefs, practices, and institutions, but, like so many others, he saw in every religion "the disposition of the human spirit that generates these phenomena" (*Introduction à l'histoire générale des religions* [Brussels: C. Muquardt, 1887], p. 37).

8. Dario Sabbatucci, *Essai sur le mysticisme grec* (Paris: Flammarion, 1982), p. 23, uses the term *phénomène historico-religieux* ("historico-religious phenomenon"), which is in its own way just as troublesome and as little satisfying. For it explicitly asserts that there are phenomena that are simultaneously "historical," that is, unique, unforeseeable, and subject to a complex of local conditions, and "religious," in other words displaying some invariable disposition of nature or of the human mind. But how are we to imagine the structure and physiognomy of such a phenomenon? How, in other words, are we to justify and logically analyze its strange constituent ambivalence? It is true that when we consider it only in terms of its confrontation with the phenomena it calls religious, we are tempted to recognize in contemporary anthropological thought—so often

torn between a still very Platonic idealism and an earthbound realism—an attitude that is just as problematic. On the one hand, there are the transcendental structures, models, and concepts; on the other, multiform, teeming reality.

Moreover, isn't it disturbing to find once again that what science considers the most immutable, transhistorical anthropological element should be precisely the most typically Western concept, that is, when all is said and done, the most historical? Doesn't the blind naïveté of this fixation make it laughable? By ascribing to itself in systematic fashion the possession, in their most consummate form, of those human characteristics that it itself judges the most undeniable and most prestigious (such as religious and artistic aptitudes), Western thought continues to hold up to itself the flattering mirror of a puerile ethnocentrism.

9. To which should be added the rereading of the always stimulating pp. 21–33 of Paul Veyne's essay, *Comment on écrit l'histoire* (Paris: Éditions du Seuil, 1978).

10. If the most radical historicity were constantly at work everywhere, it would not exclude the existence of broader and slower movements, just as historical as the others. The word "historicity" should not be confused here with radical discontinuities or abrupt modifications. The adjustment of these various rhythms is also part of history.

11. History with an uppercase H, as would have been suggested by Eliade, who attributed an initiatory function and soteriological vocation to the history of religions, which, he wrote, "as I myself understand it, is a 'liberating' discipline. . . . Hermeneutics could become the sole valuable justification of History. A historical event would justify its occurrence when it was understood. This could mean that things happen, that History exists, solely to oblige men to understand them" (*Fragments d'un journal* [Paris: Gallimard, 1973], 1: 537). On this messianic perspective, see further Daniel Dubuisson, "La funzione simbolica in Mircea Eliade," *Prometeo* 58 (1997): 94–100.

12. We might add, a bit maliciously, that the history of religions is a historical science in the sense that history made it such, much more than in the sense of helping us understand anything about history. H. Pinard de la Boullaye's monumental *Étude comparée des religions,* 2 vols (Paris: G. Beauchesne, 1922–25), doubtless remains the last and most brilliant representative of the discipline's infancy.

13. As concerns scientific optimism, whether it is a matter of evaluating every bit of heuristic fallout or, more prosaically, strengthening the morale of researchers, we should never tire of leafing through the few pages of the "Appendix to Transcendental Dialectics" in Kant's *Critique of Pure Reason* (2.3.7).

3. An Uncertain Anthropological Objective

1. Some of these definitions are drawn from the anthology that concludes James Henry Leuba's *A Psychological Study of Religion: Its Origin, Function, and Future* (New York: Macmillan, 1912). [Unless superseded by authoritative modern renderings, the translations of non-English originals found in Leuba have been retained, to give a flavor of the times—Trans.] See, too, the work by Michel Despland, *La Religion en Occident (évolution des idées et du vécu)* (Montréal: Fides, 1979).

2. Karl Rahner and Herbert Vorgrimler, *Kleines theologisches Wörterbuch* (Freiburg im Breisgau: Herder, 1961); for another version, see id., *Dictionary of Theology*, trans. Richard Strachan et al., 2nd ed. (New York: Crossroad, 1981). See also Chapter 2, n. 3, and Chapter 6, n. 1. The fundamental argument of a historian of religions such as Jean Delumeau is literally the same as that of Catholic theologians. In the circumstances, we may ask in some perplexity, of what did the effort of research and scientific conceptualization itself consist?

3. We may note, perhaps with astonishment, that between Littré's *Dictionnaire de la langue française* of 1872 and the *Grand Larousse de la langue française* of 1977, despite more than a century of research into the history of religions, definitions have not appreciably evolved.

4. See Chapter 2, n. 7.

5. On these sacrifices, see Georges Dumézil, *Fêtes romaines d'été et d'automne* (Paris: Gallimard, 1975), pp. 113–38, "Rituels royaux de l'Inde védique."

6. Śruti (revelation) designates the oldest and most venerable parts of the Vedas—Samhitā, Brāhmana, Āranyaka, and Upanishads—whose cosmographical concerns apparently give little place to religious consciousness and feeling as they have been defined in the West since Schleiermacher.

7. This comparison is further developed on pp. 100f.

8. See pp. 13f.

9. From any kind of structural point of view, the Vedic gods, who vary considerably among themselves, cannot be considered the equivalents or homologues of the Christian divinity. Their status, functions, representations, the attitudes and sentiments that they inspire are different, just as the universes of Rudra and Christ are radically dissimilar. In such cases, some more precise term ought to substituted for the word "god" to avoid the misleading illusions generated by this uniform designation.

10. Georges Dumézil, *La Religion romaine archaïque* (Paris: Payot, 1974), p. 145.

11. See Georges Dumézil, *Mythe et épopée*, vol. 1 (Paris: Gallimard, 1968), p. 277.

12. If the struggle against sects is to be effective, it must be situated on a penal or fiscal level, not on a spiritual or religious one, and authorities must

define very precisely on what grounds it is being fought. This means that a sect in which no crimes were committed (such as sexual abuse, extortion of money, etc.) would be practically untouchable.

13. Léon Vandermeersch, "Le Confucianisme," in *Fait religieux,* ed. Delumeau, p. 580.

14. This number conforms to the theory of the three eras (savagery, barbarity, civilization), established in the eighteenth century, although the prototype goes back to Dicaearchos of Messina (fourth century b.c.e.). On the longevity of this Western "tradition," see Wiktor Stoczkowski, "Essai sur la matière première de l'imaginaire anthropologique: Analyse d'un cas," *Revue de synthèse,* 4th ser., nos. 3–4 (1992): 439–57.

15. This opposition goes back, it will be recalled, to the origins of Christianity.

16. Only "historians" of religion who are simultaneously theologians continue, for better or worse (and almost twenty centuries after Tertullian and Lactantius), to claim that the Christian religion is radically different from others, that is, superior to others. See, e.g., Claude Geffré, "Religion et religions," in *Catholicisme: Hier, Aujourd'hui, Demain (Encyclopédie publiée sous le patronage de l'Institut catholique de Lille par G. Mathon et al.),* vol. 57 (Paris: Letouzey & Ané, 1990), p. 802:

> To the extent that it remains faithful to its own genius, Christianity is comparable to no other religion, even if, in the eyes of the historian or sociologist, it displays all the features proper to a great religion. It is in fact essentially defined with reference to the New Testament, that is, the Gospels, good news of a liberation not only with respect to Mosaic law but with respect to every religious code, every set of prescriptive or ritual practices that claims to be agreeable to God through its own offices.

Is there a single philosophical conception of the world that would be artless enough today (that is, after having been under the influence of the Western model) not to claim that it is different from, and on these grounds superior to, every other?

17. What follows has been adapted from Daniel Dubuisson, "Contributions à une poétique de l'oeuvre," in *Poétique et rhétorique des savoirs,* ed. id., pp. 449–66.

18. Creators of general theses include Marx, Freud, Otto, Bourdieu, Eliade, Cassirer, Wittgenstein, Lévi-Strauss, and Dumézil, to cite only the names most familiar from research into the history of religions.

19. Conversely, canonical texts are both read and commented on, which is what distinguishes them from the writings of unknowns.

20. The medieval and even classical traditions of commentary, still very much alive in academia, also contribute to maintaining an exegetical tradi-

tion in these works that supports them and keeps them permanently enshrined among the major contributions that are essential for the comprehension, but above all for the constitution, of disciplinary fields and their corresponding subjects.

21. Moreover, our culture does not propose a synthesis—which is, in fact, inconceivable—of all these opposing theses; rather, it seeks to rationalize and normalize the controversies and debates that stem from them into a fairly coherent whole, itself organized around arguments and familiar loci (the unconscious, language, structure, power, etc.). On its level, it forms an autonomous world, the Western world if you will, alien to the Chinese or Indian worlds.

22. See n. 18 above.

23. That is, basing itself on common opinion, or doxa.

24. This phrasing is borrowed from Marshall Sahlins, "L'Apothéose du capitaine Cook," in *La Fonction symbolique: Essais d'anthropologie,* ed. Michel Izard and Pierre Smith (Paris: Gallimard, 1979), p. 315; trans. John Leavitt as *Between Belief and Transgression: Structuralist Essays in Religion, History, and Myth* (Chicago: University of Chicago Press, 1982).

25. Mondher Kilani, *Introduction à l'anthropologie* (Lausanne: Payot, 1994), p. 157.

26. See Walter Burkert, *Homo necans: The Anthropology of Ancient Greek Sacrificial Ritual and Myth,* trans. Peter Bing (Berkeley: University of California Press, 1983).

27. This analysis is a further development of Dubuisson, "Funzione simbolica in Mircea Eliade."

28. For example, as found in the writings of C. S. Peirce, Gotlobb Frege, Ferdinand de Saussure, Ludwig Wittgenstein, Bertrand Russell, Ernst Cassirer, Roman Jakobson, Claude Lévi-Strauss, A. J. Greimas, Dan Sperber, Émile Benveniste, Tzvetan Todorov, etc.

29. See Tzvetan Todorov, *Théories du symbole* (Paris: Éditions du Seuil, 1977), trans. Catherine Porter as *Theories of the Symbol* (Ithaca, N.Y.: Cornell University Press, 1982).

30. See Henri-Dominique Saffrey, "Les Néoplatoniciens et les mythes grecs," in *Dictionnaire des mythologies,* under the direction of Yves Bonnefoy (Paris: Flammarion, 1994), pp. 771–77 (with a valuable bibliography); Félix Buffière, *Les Mythes d'Homère et la pensée grecque* (Paris: Les Belles Lettres, 1956), pp. 32–44 (on Plotinus, Clement of Alexandria, Sallust, Julian, Iamblichus, Pseudo-Plutarch, Prophyrus, Eusebius of Caesarea, Proclus, etc.). See also, on Proclus, Jean Bouffartigue, "Représentations et évaluations du texte poétique dans le Commentaire sur la République de Proclos," in Michel Costantini et al., *Le Texte et ses représentations,* Études de littérature ancienne, 3 (Paris: Presses de l'École normale supérieure, 1987), p. 132: "Mythical discourse . . . serves as a boundary

between the world of appearances and the world of realities." See, too, the text of Proclus *In Resp.* 1.74.16–30 translated on p. 130 of the same work.

31. With the possible exception of the most barbarous or most primitive peoples, as was thought without the least sense of shame in the nineteenth century.

32. For a critique of the latter, see, for example, J.-L. Le Moigne, *Les Épisté-mologies constructivistes,* Collection "Que sais-je?" (Paris: Presses universitaires de France, 1995).

33. Jean-Pierre Berthon, "Le Shintô," in *Fait religieux,* ed. Delumeau, p. 615.

34. Each of them knows or thinks he knows what a religion is, sick minds always having excelled in ignoring doubt, but above all each one claims to reveal *the* religion that contains the ultimate message, or *the* truth.

35. Still, it is not possible through thought to leave off thinking, in order, from the exterior as it were, to think of thought in the process of thinking. It is not that our thought is the thought of a kind of abstract thinking that is thinking it, but because this thinking is composed of thoughts that assign it certain thinkable objects and certain ways of thinking. On this count, all thinking is a historical phenomenon and exists on this count alone.

4. Christianity and the West

1. The adjective "total" is, of course, in homage to Marcel Mauss, who also drew attention to the significance of the enigmatic paragraph 6.41 of Wittgenstein's *Tractatus Logico-Philosophicus:*

> The sense of the world must lie outside the world. In the world everything is as it is and happens as it does happen. *In* it there is no value—and if there were, it would be of no value. If there is a value which is of value, it must lie outside all happening and being-so. For all happening and being-so is accidental. What makes it non-accidental cannot lie *in* the world, for otherwise this would again be accidental. It must lie outside the world.

In this regard, one cannot but quote Kant: "the concepts of reality, substance, causality, even that of necessity in existence . . . can be employed, therefore, to explain the possibility of things in the world of sense, but not to explain the possibility of the universe itself. Such a ground of explanation would have to be outside the world, and could not therefore be an object of a possible experience" ("Appendix, Regulative Employment of Ideas, Natural Dialectic," in *Critique of Pure Reason,* trans. Norman Kemp Smith, available at www.arts.cuhk.edu.hk/Philosophy/Kant/cpr/. All subsequent are citations from this edition.)

2. *Mahabharata,* quoted by Robert Lingat, *Les Sources du droit dans le système traditionnel de l'Inde,* École pratique des hautes études, Sorbonne, Sciences

économiques et sociales, 1st ser., 32 (Paris: Mouton, 1967), p. 17. Trans. J. Duncan M. Derrett as *The Classical Law of India* (Berkeley: University of California Press, 1973; reprint, Delhi: Oxford University Press, 1998).

3. Conversely, would we dare to suppose and try to demonstrate that the essence of Christianity is dharmic? Who would accept the conclusions of such a hypothesis? And what would they signify for our "anthropology"?

4. Nor can we admit that the universalization of characteristics proper to A could result in their schematization or abstraction for, in that case, we would be accepting their subjection to intellectual operations the criteria of which are in the same way inherent to domain A (this is the very type of eidetic pseudo-reduction mentioned above).

5. Émile Bréhier, in *Les Stoïciens*, texts trans. id., ed. Pierre-Maxime Schuhl, Bibliothèque de la Pléiade, 156 (Paris: Gallimard, 1962), p. lvii.

6. Acts 13:46–48: "Then both Paul and Barnabas spoke out boldly, saying, 'It was necessary that the word of God should be spoken first to you. Since you reject it and judge yourselves to be unworthy of eternal life, we are now turning to the gentiles. For the Lord has commanded us, saying: I have set you to be a light for the gentiles, so that you may bring salvation to the ends of the earth.' When the gentiles heard this they were glad and praised the word of the Lord."

7. With the notable and respectable exception of Buddhism, which also experienced an imperial phase before disappearing, several centuries later, from its native India. But the Buddha never considered that his teaching could apply to all human beings. It was initially intended for a small elite of the "meritorious." Imagine Saint Paul having deliberately chosen to instruct and form only small communities of anchorites.

8. See, too, Hebrews 11, in which Saint Paul purely and simply annexes the Old Testament to his new conception. In the twentieth century, as already noted, this theological exaltation of faith reached its paroxysm or exacerbated form with Karl Barth, who, dusting off the oldest and most naïve Christian prejudices, in particular in his commentary on Romans, contrasted Christian "faith" with various other religions, which he regarded as vain efforts at auto-justification and auto-sanctification. According to Barth, the message of these "religions" bears witness to the "vitality of man the sinner in the presence of grace" (Claude Geffré, *Catholicisme: Hier, Aujourd'hui, Demain*, 57: 799). Note that this inexhaustible vitality is no less a threat to Christianity and Christians, always ready to fall back under the sway of the Law and works.

9. See Marcel Mauss, "Une Catégorie de l'esprit humain: La Notion de personne, celle de 'moi,'" reprinted in id., *Sociologie et anthropologie* (Paris: Presses universitaires de France, 1950), pp. 331–62.

10. See p. 53.

11. Wilhelm Dilthey, *Der Aufbau der geschichtlichen Welt in den Geisteswissenschaften* (1910; Frankfurt a./M.: Suhrkamp, 1970), ed. and trans. into French by

Sylvie Mesure under the title *L'Édification du monde historique dans les sciences de l'esprit* (Paris: Éditions du Cerf, 1988): "The seriousness of northern peoples is here associated with an obsessive need for reflection, which comes from an attention to the interiority of life and which is doubtless associated with their political circumstances" (p. 128).

12. See Grossein, *Sociologie des religions par Max Weber*, pp. 69–71.

13. Auguste Sabatier, *Esquisse d'une philosophie de la religion d'après la psychologie et l'histoire* (Paris: Fischbacher, 1897), p. 284.

14. Benjamin Constant, *De la religion considérée dans sa source, ses formes et ses développements* (1824–31; Lausanne: Bibliothèque romande, 1971), p. 51.

15. See Chapter 1, n. 22, and p. 88.

16. "Seem" because it is simply a matter of poetic effect.

17. Plato *Laws* 10.909d–910d.

18. Is this interiorization and individualization not in the process of leading the great Christian communities (Roman Catholic, Protestant) to fragment into myriad isolated small groups and understandings, united only in a tolerant mutual indifference? If this proved to be the case, if this pulverization continued to its logical end (complete and irreversible disintegration), we would better understand how, on the periphery of this universe, movements are emerging that in symmetrical, inverse fashion exalt vast communal collectivities as bearers of ethnic and cultural identity.

19. Lévi-Strauss, *Naked Man*.

20. What would have happened if Western anthropological thought had chosen this universal, which is dependent on no institution and refers to no particular intrinsic characteristic of our cultural tradition?

21. Cicero *De officiis* [On Duties] 1.50–51.

22. Edward Burnett Tylor, *Primitive Culture*, 2 vols. (1871; New York: Harper & Brothers, 1958–61), 1: 8f.

23. Another way to deny alterity. In addition, on such an axis, it is always easy to move the cursor that serves to mark other cultures, since the selection criteria have no objective value.

5. Continuities

1. See Antoine Arnauld (1612–94), *The Art of Thinking: Port-Royal Logic*, trans. and ed. James Dickoff and Patricia James (Indianapolis: Bobbs-Merrill, 1964), and Daniel Dubuisson, introduction, *Poétique et rhétorique des savoirs*, ed. id.

2. See Dubuisson, *Anthropologie poétique*, esp. pp. 45–100.

3. On the use of this notion intended to reduce "scientific" reasoning to its simple, logical framework, see J.-C. Gardin, *Une Archéologie théorique* (Paris: Hachette, 1979), and Wiktor Stoczkowski, *Anthropologie naïve, anthropologie sa-*

vante: De l'origine de l'homme, de l'imagination et des idées reçues (Paris: Éditions du CNRS, 1994).

4. For a timeless object, a timeless science. We can now better understand why so many historians of religion always seek, in almost caricatural fashion, to dehistoricize the objects of their study or their concepts. Marked inflections such as "religion," "the sacred," and "the symbolic" are among the most visible symptoms. The choice of an ahistorical anthropological perspective is in this case a weak stratagem intended to mask everything that might recall their historical (non)existence. According to the hoariest, most banal of our metaphysical prejudices, it is known that true transcendence escapes time and impermanence.

5. The phrasing is borrowed from Fernand Hallyn, *La Structure poétique du monde: Copernic, Kepler* (Paris: Éditions du Seuil, 1987).

6. Homologous, too, with that which defines the structures of the traditional typologies examined on pp. 70f.

7. "The gods, mortals believe, are born as they are, have their clothes, their voices, and their step. . . . Black skin and snub noses: thus the Ethiopians represent their gods, while the Thracians give them blue-green eyes and hair of fire" (according to Clement of Alexandria *Stromata,* 5.109 and 7.22, quoted in J.-P. Dumont, *Les Présocratiques* [Paris: Gallimard, 1988], p. 118).

8. See pp. 15f.

9. Ernest Renan, *Études d'histoire religieuse* (1857; Paris: Gallimard, 1992), p. 42.

10. It is evident that from another point of view, that of microhistory, it is these nuances or personal contributions that are the most important.

11. The exemplary character and capital importance of this great paradigm did not escape Kant, whose opinion warrants repeating here:

> In respect of the object of all our "knowledge through reason," some have been mere sensualists, others mere intellectualists. Epicurus may be regarded as the outstanding philosopher among the former, and Plato among the latter. The distinction between the two schools, subtle as it is, dates from the earliest times; and the two positions have ever since been maintained in unbroken continuity. Those of the former school maintained that reality is to be found solely in the objects of the senses, and that all else is fiction; those of the latter school, on the other hand, declared that in the senses there is nothing but illusion, and that only the understanding knows what is true. The former did not indeed deny reality to the concepts of the understanding; but this reality was for them merely logical, whereas for the others it was mystical. The former conceded intellectual concepts, but admitted sensible objects only. The latter required that true objects should be purely intelligible, and maintained that by means of the pure understanding we

have an intuition that is unaccompanied by the senses—the senses, in their view, serving only to confuse the understanding.

In respect of the origin of the modes of "knowledge through pure reason," the question is as to whether they are derived from experience, or whether in independence of experience they have their origin in reason. Aristotle may be regarded as the chief of the empiricists, and Plato as the chief of the noologists. Locke, who in modern times followed Aristotle, and Leibnitz, who followed Plato (although in considerable disagreement with his mystical system), have not been able to bring this conflict to any definitive conclusion. However we may regard Epicurus, he is at least much more consistent in this sensual system that Aristotle and Locke, inasmuch as he never sought to pass by inference beyond the limits of experience. This is especially true as regards Locke, who, after having derived all concepts and principles from experience, goes so far in the use of them as to assert that we can prove the existence of God and the immortality of the soul with the same conclusiveness as any mathematical proposition—though both lie entirely outside the limits of possible experience. (Kant, "Transcendental Doctrine of Method, Canon, Architectonics, History" [source cited Chapter 4, n. 1])

12. This way of conceiving of the history of intellectual life is not specific and peculiar to the West. In India, the oppositions between Buddhist and Brahmanic orthodoxies (whether or not partisans of Ātman) and the subsequent oppositions among schools within each have contributed no less powerfully to organizing and structuring the history of intellectual production.

13. On the other hand, Pyrrhonism, the suspension of judgment, never found favor with Western thinkers.

14. See p. 114.

15. "And thus, in all peoples, there shine amidst the most benighted polytheism some gleams of monotheism, to which they have been led, not by reflection and profound speculation, but simply by the natural bent of the common understanding" (Kant, "Ideal of Pure Reason and Critique of Theology," in *Critique of Pure Reason,* trans. Smith, cited in Chapter 4 n. 1). Today, it is religious "feeling" that is the most frequently cited among the common notions.

16. Involving celebrated historians of religion such as Raffaele Pettazzoni, P. W. Schmidt, etc.

17. On the other hand, Kant's objections, better founded this time, are generally less well known:

We should have to demonstrate that the things in the world would not of themselves be capable of such order and harmony, in accordance with universal laws, if they were not in their substance the product of supreme wisdom. But to prove this we should require quite others grounds of proof than those which are derived from the analogy with human art. ("Ideal of Pure Reason and Critique of Theology," in *Critique of Pure Reason,* trans. Smith, cited in Chapter 4 n. 1)

18. See Daniel Dubuisson, *Mythologies du XXe siècle (Dumézil, Lévi-Strauss, Eliade)* (Villeneuve d'Ascq: Presses universitaires de Lille, 1993), pp. 312f.

19. Ibid., p. 314.

20. Conversely, if you wish, the question of demons, which was of such concern to Saint Augustine and his contemporaries, both pagan and Christian, did not become one of these exemplary topoi. It simply fueled a pagan-Christian controversy and only for a rather brief period.

21. Andrew Lang, *La Mythologie,* 1878 *Encyclopaedia Britannica* article, trans. Léon Parmentier (Paris: A. Dupret, 1886); id., *Myth, Ritual and Religion* (London: Longmans, Green, 1887); id., *Modern Mythology* (London: Longmans, Green, 1897).

22. See Buffière, *Mythes d'Homère et la pensée grecque,* pp. 1–4. The interpretation was agrarian, solar, or storm-related, depending on the allegorical intention attributed to the different episodes in the myths. Moreover, for antiquity, as for the nineteenth century, it was people's astonishment at these vegetal and atmospheric phenomena that was at the origin of mythic imagination and creation.

23. E.g., Mauss, Frazer, Dumézil, Lévi-Strauss, Eliade, Cassirer, Freud, Jung, and J.-P. Vernant (it is amusing to note that this interest in myth, often exclusive, was enough to make these scholars into historians of religion). In this sense the notions or ideas that correspond to them behave as true transcendental categories, since they determine a priori the frameworks in which the activity of thought is carried out. That transcendent property, cultural in origin and in nature, for this reason offers an eminent discursive dimension, if only in the form of traditional topoi.

6. The History of Religions in the Nineteenth Century

Epigraphs to Part III: Émile Burnouf, *The Science of Religions,* trans. Julie Liebe (London: S. Sonnenschein, Lowrey, 1888); Andrew Lang in the *Encyclopaedia Britannica,* 1878, s.v. "Mythology."

1. *Fait religieux,* ed. Delumeau, pp. 9, 773; and see also Chapter 2, n. 3, and Chapter 3, n. 2. The terms "man," "religion," and "the sacred" are here clearly to be understood the way we understand locutions in myths and idealist philosophies that designate archetypical figures and essences, even though they possess the faculty of being incarnated or made manifest in this world.

2. Spencer, of course, but also Tylor, Morgan, Gobineau, Lubbock, Leuba, Lang, Burnouf, Reinach, etc.

3. See, e.g., Daniel Becquemont, *Darwin, darwinisme, évolutionnisme* (Paris: Kimé, 1992).

4. E.g., in the writings of E. B. Tylor and in L. H. Morgan. And see also Chapter 3, n. 14.

5. As concerns the latter, we must nonetheless ask what the idea of an evolution of religious facts or sentiments (which a Westerner would accept without too much difficulty) could mean for any mind foreign to our ways of thinking. In what way, for example, would the use of psychotropic drugs when communicating with supernatural beings be inferior to the use of Latin? In the name of what, unless it be the self-satisfaction that possesses it, can monotheism call itself superior to polytheism?

6. Dubuisson, *Mythologies du XXe siècle,* p. 20.

7. See Dubuisson, "Pourquoi et comment parle-t-on des origines?"

8. Such premises and rules include "the use of the simple past tense [in French], which reinforces the illusion of transparency and objectivity; the absence of signs of enunciation, the correlative of the unacknowledged presence of an addressee; the rejection of all form-building that would demand the 'undecidability' of the world; and, lastly, the occlusion of any metalinguistic referent that would suggest that myth is reflexive" (Daniel Dubuisson, "Métaphysique du récit et genèse du mythe," *Homo religiosus* 9 [1983]: 63–78, at p. 72).

9. Forgetting, in passing, the celebrated caution of Wittgenstein's *Tractatus Logico-Philosophicus* 6.41, cited in Chapter 4, n. 1. See, too, pp. 127f., 140.

10. See Herbert Spencer, *Principles of Sociology,* vol. 1 (1876), trans. Émile-Honoré Cazelles as *Principes de sociologie,* vol. 1 (Paris, 1878), pp. 390f.

11. Tylor, Durkheim, Lang, Spencer, Leuba, etc.

12. In the twentieth century, there was a new reversal or inversion in the meaning of this myth, but now in a metaphysical context. In the work of Eliade, for example, the primitive human reacquires an ideal role as exemplary interlocutor of the sacred, that is, of Being. In this capacity, the primitive stands in contrast to the modern human, at the heart of a duality whose nature, too, is eminently mythic. See, e.g., Mircea Eliade, *Le Mythe de l'éternel retour* [trans. Willard R. Trask as *The Myth of the Eternal Return* (New York: Pantheon Books, 1954)] (1949; Paris: Gallimard, 1969), pp. 109f., and *Le Sacré et le profane* [trans. Willard R. Trask as *The Sacred and the Profane: The Nature of Religion* (New York: Harcourt, Brace, 1959)] (Paris: Gallimard, 1965), p. 84.

13. Lang, *Myth, Ritual and Religion,* pp. 55f. This merits qualification, however, because Tylor's views were in reality more original and nuanced, e.g., in his *Primitive Culture,* 1: 22f.:

[N]or, because the religions of savage tribes may be rude and primitive compared with the great Asiatic systems, do they lie too low for interest and even respect. The question really lies between understanding and misunder-

standing them. Few who will give their minds to master the general principles of savage religion will ever again think it ridiculous, or the knowledge
of it superfluous to the rest of mankind. Far from its beliefs and practices
being a rubbish-heap of miscellaneous folly, they are consistent and logical
in so high a degree as to begin, as soon as even roughly classified, to display
the principles of their formation and development; and these principles
prove to be essentially rational, though working in a mental condition of
intense and inveterate ignorance.

14. See, e.g., Raymond Corbey, *Wildheid en beschaving: De Europese verbeeld-
ing van Afrika* (Baarn: Ambo, 1989).

15. Claude Prudhomme, *Stratégie missionaire du Saint-Siège sous Léon XIII
(1878–1903)* (Rome: École française de Rome, 1994), pp. 575, 593, and 600f.,
quoting the *Moniteur de Rome*, July 7, 1887.

16. On this point, my comments complement the argument of Stoczkowski in "Essai sur la matière première de l'imagination anthropologique," p. 454,
who writes:

> In fact, the texts of the naturalists and philosophers of the Enlightenment
> are filled with quotations from classical literature, the profound knowledge
> of which then made up an essential part of intellectual training. This kind
> of erudition, enriched by the mastery of Greek and Latin, was still com-
> mon among the scholars of the nineteenth century. In *Das Mutterrecht [Eine
> Untersuchung über die Gynaikokratie der alten Welt nach ihrer religiösen und
> rechtlichen Natur* (Stuttgart: Krais & Hoffman, 1861)], J. J. Bachofen casually
> disregards information on exotic peoples, preferring to trust in the author-
> ity of the ancients. And what about L. H. Morgan, acclaimed as a precursor
> in this field of research? In the first three chapters of [his] *Ancient Society [or,
> Researches in the Lines of Human Progress from Savagery, through Barbarism to
> Civilization* (New York: Holt, 1877)], dealing with the periodization of uni-
> versal history, economy, and general problems, quotations from the classics
> make up no less than 46 percent of all Morgan's references (most often he
> cites Lucretius and . . . Homer!), while ethnographical references make up
> no more than 20 percent.

When Morgan attempts to set out his hypothesis (but can we in this case
speak of "his" hypothesis?) concerning the origin of language, he quotes Lucretius, who wrote more than one thousand nine hundred years earlier. And he does
so in order to take shelter behind this authority. For the men of the nineteenth
century—and Stoczkowski is right to stress this point vigorously—classical authors remained more than simple learned references; they continued to represent models and sources of inspiration. It would be instructive to know until just

when this influence, diffuse and deep at the same time, exercised its weighty influence and how the modern transformation was effected.

17. It is equally true, mutatis mutandis, in more restricted and more specialized fields. If it is certain that punctual discoveries, bearing on delimited facts and having a specialized methodology, are capable of overturning our knowledge, it is equally true that these unprecedented discoveries are also condemned to borrow some of their explanatory schemas from older transgeneric models. Thus the revelation of Indo-European introduced a new linguistic and grammatical paradigm. Yet as Guy Jucquois and Christophe Vielle have recently recalled in "Illusions, limites et perspectives du comparatisme indo-européen: Pour en finir avec le mythe scientifique des proto-langues/-peuples," in *Festschrift for Eric Hamp,* ed. Douglas Q. Adams, Journal of Indo-European Studies Monograph Series 23 (Washington, D.C.: Institute for the Study of Man, 1997), pp. 162–84, the global conception of Indo-European, in particular that of the mother language and its descendants, long remained captive to genetic models that ill suited the field of comparative grammar.

18. Dilthey, *Aufbau der geschichtlichen Welt,* ed. and trans. Mesure as *L'Édification du monde historique,* p. 123. And see also ch. 9 n. 5 below.

7. Three Twentieth-Century Debates

1. The demonstration that follows could in many respects be broadly reapplied word for word in the context of the "psychological explanation."

2. Although this point of view tends to relativize the importance accorded the sacrosanct objectivity of the object by positivist science, it recognizes the decisive influence of a movement that was a notable aspect of the twentieth century; see, e.g., Alain Deremetz, *Le Miroir des muses: Poétiques de la réflexivité à Rome* (Villeneuve d'Ascq: Presses universitaires du Septentrion, 1995), pp. 21f.

3. We have seen above what is to be said for the rather artificial and not too useful distinction between religion and religious phenomena.

4. Émile Durkheim, *Les Formes élémentaires de la vie religieuse* (1912), 4th ed. (Paris: Presses universitaires de France, 1960), p. 53. By privileging the specificity and autonomy of religious experience and its creations (ibid., pp. 595f., 605), moreover, Durkheim provided future phenomenologists, partisans of a religious irreducible to any historical or social determination, with unexpected arguments .

5. Pierre Bourdieu, "Genèse et structure du champ religieux," *Revue française de sociologie* 12, 3 (1971): 300. In what way is this symbolic efficacy intrinsically social? Are we to consider that "symbolic" and "social" are interchangeable synonyms that are subsumed under the heading of "political functions"? In that case, what is exclusive to this religious, the prerogatives of which are apparently being defended?

6. Durkheim, *Formes élémentaires* (1912); Rudolf Otto, *Das Heilige: Über das Irrationale in der Idee des göttlichen und sein Verhältnis zum Rationalen* (1917), trans. John W. Harvey as *The Idea of the Holy: An Inquiry into the Non-Rational Factor in the Idea of the Divine and Its Relation to the Rational* (London: H. Milford, Oxford University Press, 1923).

7. Cf. Alfred North Whitehead's famous assertion that the European philosophical tradition amounts to "a series of footnotes to Plato" (*Process and Reality: An Essay in Cosmology* [1929; rev. ed. (New York: Free Press, 1978], p. 39). While defending the existence of this rupture, phenomenologists nonetheless very prudently remain favorable to positivist epistemologies. Indeed, by splitting reality in two, making it derive from an exclusive cause and ascribing to it stable significations, they tacitly call attention to their hostility to contemporary constructivist epistemologies. This mixture of a mystical point of view, a traditional or "Platonic" ontology, and realist epistemology is doubtless not unrelated to the success of their theses.

8. Carl Gustav Jung, *Psychologie et religion,* trans. Marthe Bernson and Gilbert Cahen (Paris: Buchet-Chastel-Corrèa, 1958), pp. 199f. This sentence does not appear in the earlier English edition, *Psychology and Religion* (New Haven, Conn.: Yale University Press; London, H. Milford, Oxford University Press, 1938).

9. Jacques Vidal, in *Dictionnaire des religions,* ed. id. et al. (1984; 3d ed., Paris: Presses universitaires de France, 1993).

10. In the sense that the religious capacity and intentionality of human consciousness are considered as a quality sui generis, that is, as a fundamental fact, inscribed a priori in the human mind.

11. See pp. 000f. An extensive bibliography is to be found in Dubuisson, *Mythologies du XXe siècle,* pp. 215–303; id., "Métaphysique et politique: L'Ontologie antisémite de Mircea Eliade," *Le Genre humain* 26 (1992), 103–18; id., "L'Ésotérisme fascisant de Mircea Eliade," *Actes de la recherche en sciences sociales* 106–7 (March 1995): 42–51.

12. See Isac Chiva, "À propos de Mircea Eliade: Un témoinage," *Le Genre humain* 26 (1992), 89–102; Léon Volovici, *Nationalist Ideology and Antisemitism—The Case of Romanian Intellectuals in the 1930s* (Oxford: Pergamon Press, 1991); Mihai Gheorgiu, "Quelques révélations sur Eugène Ionesco," *Liber* (March 1996): 8–10; Adriana Berger, "Fascism and Religion in Romania," *Annals of Scholarship* 6, 4 (1989): 455–65; "Mircea Eliade: Romanian Fascism and the History of Religions in the United States," in *Tainted Greatness: Antisemitism and Cultural Heroes,* ed. Nancy Harrowitz (Philadelphia: Temple University Press, 1994), pp. 51–74; Seymour Cain, "Mircea Eliade, the Iron Guard, and Romanian Antisemitism," *Midstream* 25 (1989): 27–31; Norman Manea, "Mircea Eliade et la garde de fer," *Les Temps modernes* 549 (1992): 89–115; R. Ioanid, "Mircea Eliade e il fascismo,"

La Critica sociologica 84 (1988): 16–29; Russell T. McCutcheon, "The Myth of the Apolitical Scholar: The Life and Works of Mircea Eliade," *Queen's Quarterly* 100, 3 (Fall 1993): 643–63; Ivan Strenski, *Four Theories of Myth in Twentieth-Century History (Cassirer, Eliade, Lévi-Strauss and Malinowski)* (Iowa City: University of Iowa Press, 1987), esp. pp. 102f. Even though written by a fervent disciple, Mac Linscott Ricketts's book, *Mircea Eliade: The Romanian Roots, 1907–1945*, 2 vols., East European Monographs 288 (Boulder, Colo.: EEM, 1988), distributed by Columbia University Press, presents a "selection" of several incriminating documents contemporary with Eliade's fascist commitment.

13. See Volovici, *Nationalist Ideology and Antisemitism*, p. 85.

14. Mircea Eliade, *Aspects du mythe* (Paris Gallimard, 1963), pp. 182f., trans. Willard R. Trask as *Myth and Reality* (New York: Harper & Row, 1963), p. 146f.

15. Mircea Eliade, *Le Yoga: Immortalité et liberté* (Paris: Payot, 1960), p. 294, trans. Willard R. Trask as *Yoga: Immortality and Freedom* (New York: Pantheon Books, 1958), p. 295.

16. Mircea Eliade, *Fragments d'un journal 1 (1945–1969)* (Paris: Gallimard, 1973), p. 394.

17. M. Cels, "Faut-il brûler Eliade?" *Antaios* 5 (1994): 61–65.

18. C. Mutti, *Les Plumes de l'archange* (Chalon-sur-Saône: Hérode, 1993), 10–11.

19. C.-J. Guyonvarc'h, *Connaissance des religions* 43–44 (1995): 207–11.

20. F. Boespflug, "Chronique d'histoire des religions," *Revue des sciences religieuses* 69, 2 (1995): 260–62.

21. Volovici, *Nationalist Ideology and Antisemitism*, 84f.

22. Is it necessary to recall that neither is an interpretation an explanation nor a word, however prestigious, a definition?

23. Adopting this clear position, rid of all ambiguity, still does not mean that we must reduce human and historical reality to its material elements alone. This is just what some scholars rush to do in order to rid themselves at the same time of all the troubling questions that science does not answer or does so only poorly. Metaphysical concerns, even anxiety, as well as everything that derives from them, belong integrally to the history of humanity. This is why, as long as the human sciences persist in excluding from the symbolic productions they chose to study the metaphysical component that they contain—that they contain only because they are fully human creations—just as long, I fear, they will also fail to grasp what is perhaps the essential characteristic of all human activity, no doubt made up of other than simple utilitarian concerns, and they will then cut themselves off from a good portion of their critical objective.

However, it is equally obvious that the attention devoted to these problems ought neither to serve as a guilty or hypocritical pretext to deceptively reintroduce into these same sciences some mystical point of view or other, nor, of course, to lend support to any methodological laxity. Put simply, the metaphysical concerns, aspirations, or even preoccupations that underlie and condition all kinds of symbolic productions ought to be admitted and recognized by the human sciences in order that their influence be precisely measured.

24. Spinoza, *Tractatus Theologico-Politicus,* trans. Samuel Shirley (Leiden: Brill, 1991), p. 143.

25. In the sense in which Simone Weil asserts: "I would propose that we consider barbarity a permanent and universal characteristic of human nature."

26. It would be of interest to juxtapose the three topics that correspond to these three views ("scientific," "literary," and "mystical"), because their influence probably does not stop at the field of anthropological speculation.

27. Julien Ries, in *Dictionnaire des religions,* ed. Vidal et al., 1: 861f. One may ask in amazement how the publishers could have entrusted the task of coming up with a dictionary of religions to Cardinal Paul Poupard, resulting in a work that so noisily vindicates mystical theses and frequently celebrates the highly suspect philosophy of Eliade. If they had asked an astrologer to draw up a *Dictionary of Astronomy,* the effect could not have odder.

28. But coming after the indispensable contributions of Kant, Herder, Schleiermacher, Constant, Söderblom, Otto, etc.

29. See, e.g., Alexandre Men, *Les Sources de la religion* (Paris: Desclée, 1991), cited by Cardinal Poupard in *Dictionnaire des religions,* ed. Vidal et al., 1: v: "The thoughtful observer has difficulty finding in the spiritual life of men anything capable, over the course of centuries, of playing as decisive a role as religion. From the Stone Age to the Atomic Age, undergoing astonishing changes and multiple metamorphoses, religion is indissolubly linked with the human spirit, with world culture."

Does this singular movement not also mark the present point of an evolution whose further stage is not easy to discern? Would it be possible to go farther on the path of interiorization with the assertion that religion is, ultimately, the unutterable but lived quality of a personal, mystical experience?

30. Ries, in *Dictionnaire des religions,* 1: 863.

8. The West, Religion, and Science

1. It should, however, be noted that in these general debates as a whole, the various adverse theses are almost always set forth and commented on without the comparative method being sufficiently exploited. Put differently, very general—most often too general—theses dealing with the existence of *religious facts* have been advanced without detailed comparative studies having been previously conducted—even, in fact, without an effort to define and perfect the comparative approach. On this point, Dumézil's work remains a rare exception and magnificent example. It would thus be unwise to assert today that wider

use of the method and the correlative improvement of its instruments will not someday upset our old habits of thinking by opening new perspectives. For Dumézil was doubtless right when he asserted that the comparative method represented, for the human sciences, the equivalent of the experimental method in the natural sciences. Only systematic, methodical recourse to an exact, inventive comparative methodology will authorize modern anthropological and historical thought to escape the dusty dead ends in which it is still too often blocked. The use, as well as the soporific tradition, of commentaries will have to be reconsidered as a consequence, for by favoring a kind of sedimentary, vertical accumulation, they smother original points of view that arise from "horizontal" comparative studies. See J. Scheid, "Georges Dumézil et la méthode expérimentale," *Opus* 2, 2 (1983): 343–51. In thus mentioning this esteemed mentor, I cannot resist the pleasure of quoting one of his finest pages, written more than half a century ago and opportunely recalled by Scheid in his article (p. 351):

> Unfortunately, there is still more: the most noble instances of fidelity have their petty sides. The prestigious past of classical humanism has bequeathed to its current representatives corporate statuses, traditions of imperious caste or clique, and also a code, a jurisprudence that interested parties take very seriously. This ritualism has advantages and disadvantages. It is permitted, for example, that any far-fetched thesis at all, on whatever subject, can be ventured (and philologists have no qualms about this) provided that all the traditional forms are respected, all the bibliography is cited, all the literary, epigraphical, and archeological documents utilized: this is called "renewing the subject"; it seems that a grand indulgence, a kind of tasteful skepticism concerning the use to which the material is put, is paired with a no less great susceptibility concerning the orthodoxy, the quality of the material itself. On the contrary, were a book to advance a well-constructed thesis, based on the essentials but neglecting more or less intentionally the "standard bibliography" or committing an error in the translation of a minor text, the learned assembly, according to circumstances or to the mood of its dignitaries, would immediately veil its face or raise an uproar and refuse to hear so obviously profane an innovator. (Georges Dumézil, *L'Héritage indo-européen à Rome* [Paris: Gallimard, 1949], pp. 250f.)

2. What languages have words for "nature," "history," "person," and "humanity" as we, *grosso modo,* understand them? The meanings that we attribute to them (like the corresponding domains), we consider to be objective. Are we to conclude that we alone have succeeded in seeing reality as it is or should we not admit that our most rigorous definitions, those most obvious to us, are also the product of a very particular conceptual tradition? Scientific thought is a cultural fact before being an objective procedure; nothing is a priori.

3. "Inevitably," since this scientific program, shorn of its confused style and

its Enlightenment mythology, always appears in the service of this intellectual, economic, and military hegemony by furnishing it with a kind of intellectual legitimacy. No historian of religions of the period challenged the dogma of Western superiority. In this sense, the "science of religions" took up, without a hitch, the torch that the Church had been carrying for centuries.

4. As observed in Chapter 2, n. 3, this strict positivism, deflected from its purpose, furnished phenomenologists with an unexpected argument: if the religious fact is objective and universal, then the proper and ultimate object of religions (the sacred) has a good chance of being so as well. This famous argument, that of universal consent, was popularized by the Stoics, but it is already found in Aristotle (*On the Heavens* 1.3.6) and in Plato: "Why, to begin with, think of the earth, and sun, and planets, and everything! And the wonderful, beautiful order of the seasons with its distinctions of years and months! Besides, there is the fact that all mankind, Greeks and non-Greeks alike, believe in the existence of gods" (*Laws,* in *Plato: The Collected Dialogues,* ed. Edith Hamilton and Huntingdon Cairns, Bollingen Series 71 [Princeton, N.J.: Princeton University Press, 1961], 10, 885e–886a).

5. For this demanding epistemology to avoid any deleterious surrender to pessimism, which by defeating science would probably bring other catastrophic consequences in its wake, it is indispensable to make this point. Although it is not possible for scientific thought to do without overall synthetic visions, or, as a consequence, without the "transcendental supposition" that they imply, viz., that between the organization of their worlds and that of the (real) world, there is a certain homology, we must nevertheless take care not to confuse the intelligible qualities of the former with the concrete properties of the latter. On this count, we do well to rehabilitate the Kantian idea that science, a dynamic activity, has never, especially in the human sciences, had anything but a heuristic value and function. No assertion that is advanced there is ever more than provisional, and it is then valid only "to a certain degree," "as much as possible," by saying "as if" or "by analogy" (all these phrases are borrowed from Kant): "The idea is thus really only a heuristic, not an ostensive concept. It does not show us how an object is constituted, but how, under its guidance, we should seek to determine the constitution and connection of the objects of experience" ("Regulative Employment of Ideas, Natural Dialectic" [cited Chapter 4, n. 1]) This is why the ultimate ambition of this study can only be methodological in nature, since it progressively discovers its own systematicity only in rules that the analysis of other systematicities impose. Disregarding all metaphysical demonstration, it takes pleasure in taking apart as correctly as possible all those, complex or fragmentary, that it meets on its path.

9. Prolegomena

1. Images? Symbols? Algorithms? Logico-semantic structures? Transcendental cognitive schemas? Archetypes? Psychic dispositions? Mysteries!

2. It is true that they would answer us, like Heidegger (and in agreement with the now useless conventions of an old topos) that these dispositions cannot be understood "on the level of causes and explanatory grounds [*auf Ursachen und Erklärungsgründe*]" (*Letter on Humanism*, in *Martin Heidegger: Basic Writings*, ed. David Farrell Krell [San Francisco: HarperSanFrancisco, 1993], p. 223).

3. In order to describe human beings and apes in differential fashion, it would doubtless be necessary for science to invent a nomenclature that did not derive from the term that was most familiar to us, that was not, in a word, conceived only according to human beings. Primates are not exclusively defined with reference to the anthropomorphic characteristics of the most prestigious representative of this order.

4. But this argument neglects to say that the limits of the religious are in any case those of a culture that itself drew them on the basis of its own notional resources and system of values.

5. See Dilthey, *Aufbau der geschichtlichen Welt*, ed. and trans. Mesure as *L'Édification du monde historique*, p. 123:

> The question of knowing whether submission to such an absolute, which is a historical fact, should be referred in man, in logically compelling fashion, to a universal, temporally unlimited condition, or whether it should be considered as a product of history, leads to the depths of transcendental philosophy, which go beyond the empirical sphere of history and from which even philosophy can extract no sure response. And even if this question were to be settled in favor of the first view, it would be of no use to the historian in making his choices, in understanding, in discovering its sets, unless the content of that absolute could be determined. Thus the intervention of speculation in the empirical domain of the historian can scarcely expect to be crowned with success. The historian cannot renounce the attempt to understand history from itself, on the basis of the analysis of these various interactive sets.

To counter Dilthey's pessimism and excessive epistemological caution, we may point out that informed, systematic recourse to the comparative method (see Chapter 8, n. 1) will one day make it possible to distinguish the province of general anthropology from what refers only to our own cultural sphere. Only the comparative method will be capable of reformulating and resolving most of the paradoxes of all transcendental philosophy.

6. This distinction is borrowed from J. M. Schaeffer.

7. This paragraph is borrowed from Dubuisson, *Anthropologie poétique*, p. 59.

8. The three following paragraphs are inspired, with some modification, by Dubuisson, *Anthropologie poétique*, pp. 93f.

9. Dilthey, *Aufbau der geschichtlichen Welt*, ed. and trans. Mesure as *L'Édification du monde historique*, p. 119. But to the extent that they are worlds, these structures all display a certain homology.

10. See Chapter 1, n. 9, and the corresponding paragraph.

11. Ernesto de Martino, *Il mondo magico: Prolegomeni a una storia del magismo* (Turin: G. Einaudi, 1948), trans. Marc Baudoux as *Le Monde magique: Parapsychologie, ethnologie et histoire*, Collection Marabout université, 215 (Verviers: Gérard; Paris: l'Inter, 1971), p. 86.

12. "This ethos, far from confining itself to the level of ideas, reflects a system of dispositions that imprint an orientation on action, structuring it into a 'conduct of life' (*Lebensführung*)"; by this term Weber understands a structured complex of behaviors and practices that draw their logic and internal unity from principles of life, that have their "foundation in personal life" (Grossein, *Sociologie des religions par Max Weber*, p. 61).

13. Dilthey, *Aufbau der geschichtlichen Welt*, ed. and trans. Mesure as *L'Édification du monde historique*, p. 73.

14. Clifford Geertz, *Local Knowledge: Further Essays in Interpretive Anthropology* (New York: Basic Books, 1983), trans. Denise Paulme under the title *Savoir local, Savoir global: Les Lieux du savoir* (Paris: Presses universitaires de France, 1986), p. 122.

15. See Chapter 4, n. 1. Dilthey similarly says:

In fact, history has seen more than one absolute arise, whether it refer to a value or a norm or a good. The phenomenon does not cease to occur, the absolute that is advanced being situated now in divine will, now in a rational concept of perfection, in a teleological coherence of the world, in a practical norm with universal scope that would have a philosophico-transcendental foundation. But historical experience knows only processes, so important for it, according to which these determinations of an absolute take place; but in itself it knows nothing of their universality. (*Aufbau der geschichtlichen Welt*, ed. and trans. Mesure as *L'Édification du monde historique*, p. 123)

16. The following paragraphs are borrowed with some slight modification from Dubuisson, *Anthropologie poétique*, pp. 150–53.

17. Or will attempt to do so, for this is an objective that is most often inaccessible in an ideal, consummate form. Our bodies, like our lives, too often remind us that our textual and cosmographic constructions are perhaps only illusions; but at the same time, their weaknesses make these illusions only more indispensable. In the interest of clarity, as much as for other reasons, I have not wished to add to this discussion the analysis of all the modalities, all the nuances,

that humans introduce into the multiform relations that they entertain with their bodies. Such a text would have been unreadable.

18. Is there a single ceremony, profane or solemn, in which bodies are not subject to a canon of very strict rules intended to metamorphose them into signs? But do there exist signs beyond the cosmographic creations of human beings?

19. Maitrāyani Upanishad, trans. Max Müller in vol. 1 of *The Sacred Books of the East:* "What is the use of the enjoyment of pleasures in this offensive, pithless body . . ." (1.3). See http://www.hinduwebsite.com/sacredscripts/maitrayana_max.htm.

Index